Explorations

Explorations
Educational Activities for Young Children

Lucille R. Clayton

1991
TEACHER IDEAS PRESS
A Division of
Libraries Unlimited, Inc.
Englewood, Colorado

TEACHER IDEAS PRESS
A Division of
Libraries Unlimited, Inc.
P.O. Box 3988
Englewood, CO 80155-3988

Library of Congress Cataloging-in-Publication Data

Clayton, Lucille R., 1957-
    Explorations : educational activities for young children / Lucille
R. Clayton.
    xiii, 203p. 22x28cm.
    Includes bibliographical references and index.
    ISBN 0-87287-863-5
    1. Education, Preschool--United States--Activity programs-
-Handbooks, manuals, etc. 2. Activity programs in education--United
States--Handbooks, manuals, etc. 3. Teaching--Aids and devices-
-Handbooks, manuals etc. I. Title
LB1140.35.C74C59 1991
372.13'078--dc20   91-24849
                                                          CIP

To
Irene August, Janet Kellner,
Arleigh Watkins,
and
Dr. Billie Underwood

Very special thanks go to *Elsa Marcano* for her creative ideas,
to *Carol Holland* for her rhyming words,
and to *Andrew Clayton* for his artistic abilities
and unfailing support.

CONTENTS

INTRODUCTION

Explorations: Educational Activities for Young Children is a book for teachers of young children whether they are employed by private or public schools or Head Start programs, whether they volunteer in a cooperative preschool or teach their own children at home. With this book, I hope to introduce the unit plan to teachers unfamiliar with the idea and to provide fresh activities to teachers already organizing their curriculum in this manner. In addition to preschool teachers, parents will find the activities in *Explorations* fun and easy to do, requiring little advance preparation and using inexpensive materials. Many activities may be done on the spur of the moment, allowing odd bits of free time to become learning experiences.

Explorations is divided into eleven chapters or units. Each chapter explores one theme. Teachers often schedule one unit per week, allowing an in-depth look at each topic. Other teachers may wish to organize a theme day, enabling them to draw attention to a local event. For example: a teacher may develop a "Circus Day" in honor of the big top's visit to town.

When using a weekly theme, keep in mind that it is not the task of the unit plan to provide the pupil with a mountain of information about the current topic. The purpose is to introduce language, math, science, and other activities in a way that captures the children's interest and holds their attention.

This book solves the problem of having adequate time to plan a unit, enabling teachers to spend more time with the children than behind desks full of activity books or in libraries searching for appropriate literature. Once a unit is planned, it is tempting to use the same activities over and over again each time a similar theme is used. Unlike many resource books, *Explorations* contains enough information in each chapter to repeat a theme many times, using fresh activities each time. A chapter may also be subdivided into different themes. For instance, a teacher may do a short unit on clowns using ideas from the circus chapter or a unit on camping using lessons from the forest chapter.

Although the learning experiences contained in each chapter can stand on their own or be adapted to fit each teacher's established program, the unit plan offers an exciting alternative to the commonly haphazard preschool curriculum. Using activities such as the ones in this book, the unit plan incorporates both the common and the individual characteristics of any group of two-, three-, four-, and five-year-olds. All of the children would certainly like the exercise and excitement a rousing game of "Duck, Duck, Goose" would provide, but it is often the age of the child that determines what is learned from each activity. For example: during any given art project, two-year-olds may simply enjoy the teacher's hand guiding theirs while attempting to cut construction paper. At three, a child may concentrate on identifying the colors of paper used to construct a project. At four, they may have mastered cutting and gluing, enabling them to complete their projects without help. What a huge boost to self-esteem! Five-year-olds might take the art project past what is planned, nourishing their creative spirit by adding their own embellishments. In this way, each activity in the book is customized to fit the individual child, no matter what the age.

In addition to the sheer entertainment provided by "studying" about the zoo, the Old West, and dinosaurs, the continuity provided by the use of themes also benefits the child. It provides a means by which a child can learn to carry one thought through the day and the repetition needed to help assimilate that thought.

Although there is importance in the way the activities have been organized, the *type* of activities used in this book are equally important. In his famous work, *The Great Didactic*, John Amos Comenius suggested that sensory education formed the foundation for all learning.* Maria Montessori and Jean Piaget later extended and refined this idea. Contemporary educators are still trying to implement programs whose emphasis is on the concrete and sensory. Effective teachers know that if one were to only talk about an object, teaching would be strictly one-dimensional. If one were to use touch, teaching would become multidimensional and multisensory. For this reason, the learning experiences in this book strive to be "actively academic."

The activities and information in each chapter are grouped as follows:

Focus On   An introduction to each chapter, listing possible topics for interesting discussions.

Motor Skills   Games for exercising the whole body and activities designed to develop small motor skills too.

Language   Listening and speaking experiences planned to provide a rich verbal environment, complemented by pre-reading activities.

Math   Hands-on counting, sorting, and shape identification; introduction of sets.

Science   Projects and experiments that explain some of the mysteries of the child's universe.

Art   Projects that delight children and help develop small motor skills.

Class Project   While field trips are often called for in the culmination of a theme week, an alternative plan sometimes is needed. These projects provide an opportunity for the class to work together over several days to achieve a common goal, a fun activity with which to end the week.

Story Time   Includes ways to interest the children in reading as well as extension activities for favorite books.

Poems, Songs, Fingerplays   Use to practice language and memory skills, as well as to entertain and provide a smooth transition from one activity to another.

Music List   Tapes and albums that provide appropriate musical accompaniment and extension activities for each unit.

Book List   A bibliography of popular picture books that pertain to the current topic of study.

---

*John Amos Comenius. *The Great Didactic of John Amos Comenius.* Translated and edited by M. W. Keatinge, 1896 and 1910. New York: Russell and Russell, 1967.

Explorations incorporates a large variety of activities into each chapter. To accommodate a unit plan format, the teacher would simply select various activities from one chapter at a time. While some activities are meant for a large group of children, many of them have been written, for clarity's sake, in a one-on-one style. While parents at home often engage their children singly, most teachers lack the time to do this. It is therefore up to the teacher to judge how many children to gather per session of these learning experiences. Each child's age, attention span, and personality play a large part in making this decision.

Another decision to make involves the activities in the classroom. One to four activities may occupy the classroom at any given time, depending on the number of children and adults present. One table may be set up with a small motor activity which one or two children may work on without super-vision. Another table may be set up with one adult and five children completing an art project. As one or two children finish a project, they may leave the table to engage in free play, inviting another child to take that place. In a quiet area of the classroom, an adult may engage in a math activity with three more children. After activity time, all of the children may come together to hear a story, sing songs, and discuss their ideas concerning the current topic of study.

By incorporating both the idea of the weekly theme and emphasizing hands-on, active learning experiences, I have used concepts conceived of long ago, but that remain basic to any good course of study. I hope that *Explorations* will prove useful to both the experienced and the novice teacher in implementing their own "actively academic" preschool programs.

1
AT HOME
(My Family, Myself)

Focus on My Family, Myself

A unit on members of the class or on the family is especially useful at the beginning of the year. Many of the activities in this chapter will help children become comfortable in the classroom.

Consider discussing these subjects:
Family makeup: traditional, extended, blended
Family trees: relationships of uncles, aunts, cousins
Role of child in the family
Family pets
Special occasions: birthdays, holidays, vacations
Favorite activities
Responsibilities
Chores
Friends
Housing: apartments, condominiums, single family, trailer homes

My Family, Myself Motor Skills

1.   **FINGER PUPPETS**. With a pen or washable marker, paint faces on the children's fingertips. Ask the children to make their puppets run, jump, play, sing, etc.

2.   **GOING HOME**. Make a road on the floor by putting down two parallel pieces of masking tape. At the end of the road, place a play house or cardboard box that has a door and windows drawn on it. Paint a face on a Ping Pong ball and have the children take turns blowing the ball down the road until it reaches home.

3.   **DRESSING DOLLS**. Cut plain doll shapes out of felt. Give the children felt clothes with which to dress their dolls on a flannel board.

4.   **JACK AND JILL**. Choose two children to be Jack and Jill. The rest of the children join hands in a circle around Jack and Jill. Blindfold Jack. His job is to tag Jill. He can ask Jill where she is and she *must answer*. When Jack tags her, he picks a new Jack and then joins the circle. Next, it is Jill's turn to be blindfolded.

5.   **IN AND OUT THE WINDOW**. The children form a circle and hold hands shoulder high. One child is picked to go in the center of the circle. The children sing:

> Go in and out the window,
> Go in and out the window,
> Go in and out the window,
> As fast as you can go!

The child in the center winds his or her way in and out the windows (outstretched arms). The children sing:

> Find in the house a partner,
> Find in the house a partner,
> Find in the house a partner,
> And bow before you go.

The child chooses a partner, bows, and takes his or her partner's place in the circle. Repeat the song with the new child going through the windows.

6. **HAPPY BIRTHDAY.** Have the children wrap pretend birthday presents using newspaper comics or tissue paper decorated with markers to cover small boxes or items found around the classroom. Provide scissors, yarn or curling ribbon, masking tape, or inexpensive stamp-type stickers. Let the children take turns opening the presents.

7. **HOLD ON!** Have all the children but one hold on to each other. Any position is okay, as long as they maintain the connection. The remaining child weaves his or her way in and out among the bodies, over arms, under legs, any way he or she wants. A length of string or yarn may be used to keep track of the pattern as it develops. When the child reaches the end, the child must turn around and return by the same path.

8. **MOTHER, MAY I?** One teacher stands at the front of the play area in the role of mother (or father). The children line up at the other end of the play area. The "mother" commands the other children in various movements, such as "Billy, take five giant steps," or "Debbie, tiptoe ten steps." If the children reply, "Mother, may I?" they may advance toward the mother. If they forget to ask permission, they must stay where they are. When children reach the mother, they win!

9. **KITTY.** One player is the "kitty" and the rest of the children sit in a circle around the kitty. The kitty must crawl around the circle and stop in front of one child. The child must pet the kitty, look the kitty in the eye, and say, "Poor kitty!" three times without laughing or smiling. The kitty, acting like a cat, is of course trying to make the player laugh. (No tickling is allowed!) If the kitty fails with one player, it moves on to another. The first child to laugh becomes the kitty.

10. **SHOE LACING.** Fold a large sheet of paper in half. Place the shoe pattern (see figure 1.1, page 4) on the paper with the pattern's fold line on the fold of the paper. Trace around the pattern and then cut it out. Now transfer the large pattern you have just made onto a piece of thin cardboard or poster board and cut it out. Fold the sides of the shoe up along the dotted lines then fold the back of the shoe together and tape. Punch holes where indicated. Ask the child to step onto the bottom of the shoe. Lace a long shoestring or length of yarn through the first few holes, showing the child how to continue. After practicing several times, graduate to bow-tying.

My Family, Myself Language Skills

1. **KID TALK.** Tape the children's voices using a tape recorder. Have the children try to identify one another's voices. Next, interview the children on tape and let them take turns listening. Older children may interview each other, asking questions such as, "What is your full name? How many people are in your family? What is your favorite television show? Color? Food?"

2. **HAVE YOU SEEN MY FRIEND?** Have the children sit on the floor in a circle. One child is chosen to sit in the center. Have that child shut his or her eyes for one moment while you silently point to another child. The child in the center then asks, "Have you seen my friend?" The other children reply, "Yes, we have seen your friend." The children describe the child who was pointed out earlier, giving clues to the child looking for his or her friend. The clues continue until the child guesses the right "friend" from the clues.

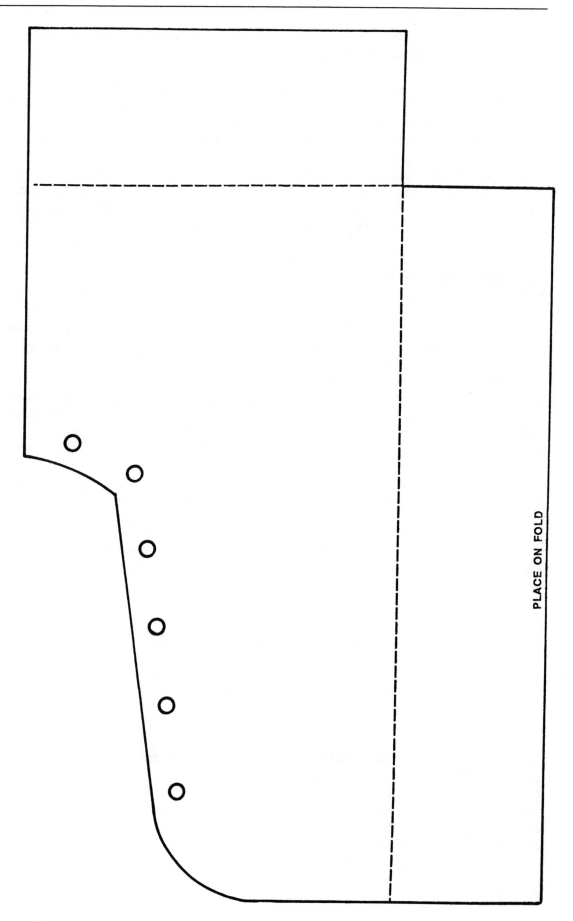

Fig. 1.1.

3.   **GUESS WHO?** Play a game of "Guess Who" by describing one child until the rest of the class guesses who that child is. Once everybody is familiar with each other, play "Who's Missing?" The children close their eyes. The teacher taps one child on the shoulder and that child leaves the room. The other children try to guess who is absent by asking questions of the teacher.

4.   **MAIL A LETTER.** Here is an activity in which children can pretend to mail letters to a friend or family member. Obtain 26 plain envelopes and 26 index cards to fit in the envelopes. With a marker, write one capital letter on each envelope then write the corresponding lowercase letters on the index cards. Mix up the cards and envelopes in a pile on the table. The child will then pick a letter card and put it in the appropriate envelope. The child may then slip it through a slot in a cardboard mailbox. A more advanced activity would include pictures of items representing letters glued to index cards to match the appropriate lettered envelope.

5.   **TRUE OR FALSE.** Hold up a picture of a child, a house, or other items interesting to the children. Make a statement about the picture, such as "The boy in this picture has green hair." The children say if it is a true or a false statement.

6.   **WASH DAY.** Obtain colored plastic clothespins. Using construction paper the same colors as the pins, cut out socks, shirts, dresses, pants, etc. Have children pick a clothespin and identify the color. Ask them to find a piece of "laundry" of the same color and hang it up on a string clothesline. This activity may also be used with the letters of the alphabet. Use a pen to write a letter on each *wooden* clothespin. Have a child hang up laundry which has a corresponding letter on each piece of clothing. Children who know their alphabet may hang up the clothes in alphabetical order.

7.   **WHO'S WHO?** Have the children bring pictures of themselves from home. Working with six or seven photographs at a time, spread them on a table. Hold the pictures up one at a time and see if a child can name all the faces. Next, mix up the photos and call out a name. Ask the child to find the picture of the child that you just named.

8.   **TELEVISION.** Obtain a large cardboard box and cut out an imaginary television screen from one side of it. Provide an array of dress-up clothes. Let the children dress up and get inside the box to put on their own television shows.

9.   **PARROTS.** Sing in varied tones simple statements such as, "I love you," or "I'm glad to see you," or "Hello there." Ask the children to repeat the statement exactly the same way.

10.   **COLORFUL CLOTHES.** Have one child stand up where the others have a good view of him or her. Name a color. Have the rest of the children look carefully at the child and name all of the items of clothing that the child is wearing of the specified color. Can the children say what other colors he or she is wearing? Have the child select someone to be next.

My Family, Myself Math Activities

1.   **FAMILY PHOTOS.** On index cards glue pictures cut from magazines of children and adults. If you can find pictures of family groups, all the better. Start with cards containing pictures of only one person. Next attach pictures of two people to a card, then three, four, five, etc. Make another set of cards with corresponding numbers of people on them so that the children can match the cards. Numeral cards may also be made to match to the picture cards.

2. **PHOTO ALBUM.** In a small photo album, place various numbers of pictures of people. One page may contain five people, the next page only one, the third page ten. Keep the numbers in random order. The child's job will be to write the appropriate numeral on each page with a wax crayon. The crayon can be wiped off the pages at the end of each child's turn. For younger children, simply let them put a mark on each person as they count.

3. **FELT HOUSES.** Make felt houses of various colors, square and some rectangular. Put the houses on a flannel board and have the children take turns coming up to the board. Ask the first child to take down all of the square houses. Put them back and have the next child remove only rectangular houses. Place the houses back on the board and have a child select any one house from the board. What shape is it? What color is it? Have the children remove one, two, or three houses. Next ask them to remove a square or rectangle of a certain color.

4. **SORTING.** Bring household items to class for the children to sort. Examples: a laundry basket filled with different colored socks to sort into pairs, silverware to be sorted and put into appropriate slots in a cutlery tray, or have all the children remove their shoes and put them into a large pile. Have a few children at a time work to find the pairs again.

5. **CLEAN UP.** For this activity you will need 10 small sponges or washcloths numbered 1 through 10, and 10 small soaps numbered likewise. The children's job will be to arrange the sponges or washcloths in numerical order. Next, they visually match the numerals by placing the soaps on the corresponding sponges. Cups and toothbrushes or toy combs and brushes also make good objects to match. For younger children, use only numbers one through five.

6. **COUNTING CLOTHESPINS.** Obtain 10 clothespins and a coffee can. Paint little faces on the clothespins and number them 1 through 10. The child's job will be to clip the clothespins in the correct order along the rim of the can. Younger children may simply clip a specified numeral one at a time to the coffee can rim.

7. **1, 2, 3.** Go to the house or kitchen play area and ask a child to find one of something. Example: one doll. Next ask a child to find two of something. Example: two cups. Next find three of something, etc.

8. **TELEPHONE NUMBERS.** Write telephone numbers on index cards. Have the children select a card and then dial the telephone number on a play telephone. Let them practice dialing their own home number, or their parent's work number. Teach them to dial 911 for an emergency.

9. **LITTLE HOUSE.** Select two boxes of different sizes. With paint and scissors, transform the boxes into houses by adding windows and doors. Ask the children to choose one of the houses. Have them find or tell about something in the classroom that is small enough to fit into the house. Repeat with the different size house.

10. **FIND A FRIEND.** Cut geometric shapes from tagboard, two of each shape. Make enough sets for all of the children. Attach a long piece of yarn to each shape to form a necklace. Let each child wear one necklace. If there is an odd number of children, have an adult play too. Have the children walk or dance around the room to music. When the music stops, the children must scramble to find a friend wearing the same geometric shape. If two children pair up correctly, they sit down together. Put the music back on after a few seconds, and repeat the procedure. Continue several times until all of the children have found their friends.

My Family, Myself Science Activities

1. **FINGERPRINTS.** Place each child's thumb on an ink pad, and then press it onto a clean sheet of paper with the child's name on it. Repeat with each finger. The fingers can be cleaned with rubbing alcohol. Let the children observe their prints with a magnifying glass. Compare the fingerprints. What are their differences and similarities? Point out that no two prints are the same. Discuss the uses of fingerprints. If you wish, the children may decorate their prints with crayons or markers.

2. **PHONE HOME.** Punch a hole in the bottom of two paper cups. Connect the cups with 20 feet of string, using a toothpick to prevent the string from pulling through the holes. Have the children take turns talking and listening to each other. The string must be kept *taut* for the phone to work. The sound vibrates along the tight string, traveling from ear to ear.

3. **MY GREEN HAIR.** Provide each child with a shallow tuna or cat food can. For each can, cut a strip of construction paper the same size as the label on the can. Have the children create a self-portrait on the strip of paper, drawing eyes, ears, nose, and mouth. Help them glue their self-portraits around the outside of the tin cans. While the cans dry, moisten a bag of potting soil in a large bucket. Let the children spoon the potting soil into their cans, filling them half full. Sprinkle about a tablespoon of rye grass or blue grass seed onto the soil, then cover with a ¼-inch more soil. Explain to the children that the seeds need the same things that we do to grow: air, light, water, and food. Explain that the grass gets its food from the soil. Setting the cans on a shelf near the window will provide the air and sunlight. Add water to the soil whenever it dries out. In a few days, grass will start to sprout.

4. **HEART CHECK.** Use a stethoscope for heart checks. Show the children that the heart is located a little bit to the right of the center of their chests and is about the same size as a person's fist. Let the children listen to the thumping of their own heartbeats. Compared to an adult's heartbeat, it beats more quickly. Ask the children to run in place for a moment and then listen again. Does the heart beat faster with exertion? Can it be heard to slowly return to a slower beat? The heart makes a thumping sound. If you listen to the lungs (on the back) the sound is different, more like a swooshing sound.

To actually *see* the heartbeat, do this: Bend a paper clip as illustrated (see figure 1.2) and slip a drinking straw over the bent end. Tape the paper clip to the child's wrist, where the pulse is felt, just under the fat part of the thumb. Ask the child to sit as still as possible with his or her arm resting on the table. Does the straw move? If it does not work, try adjusting the straw. If it still doesn't work, have the child bend his or her hand backward over the edge of a book to bring the artery closer to the surface.

Fig. 1.2.

What causes the pulse in a person's wrist? Each time the heart pumps blood out into the arteries, the walls of the arteries expand. Most of the arteries are buried deep under layers of tissue, although in a few places, such as the wrist, the arteries come close to the surface.

5. **WEIGH AND MEASURE.** Tack a large sheet of butcher paper to the wall. Line the children up along it, shortest to tallest, marking each child's height. Measure and record the heights on a graph, making sure to list the children in the correct order. Now weigh the children and mark their weights on the graph in a different color. Examine the data. Are the taller children heavier for the most part? Make one graph of the girls and one of the boys. Is there a difference in the sizes and weights

of the girls and boys? Weigh and measure again at the end of the school year. Who grew the most? Who stayed the same?

My Family, Myself Art Projects

1. **NAME COLLAGE**. *Materials*: Magazines or advertisements, construction paper, glue, scissors, markers, or crayons. *Directions*: Help the children search through a magazine for the letters in their names. Ask them to cut the letters out and paste them to the construction paper, spelling their names. Markers, crayons, or more pictures cut from the magazine can be used to embellish the collage.

2. **BALLOON FAMILY**. *Materials*: Balloons, markers, glue, yarn or curling ribbon, scissors, and string. *Directions*: Ask the children to draw faces on the balloons with markers. Curl the curling ribbon or let the children cut lengths of yarn for the hair and have children glue the hair on to the top of the balloon. Tie a piece of string to the knot in the balloon. Let children make one balloon for each member of his or her family.

3. **DOUGH FACES**. *Materials*: Each child will need ¼-cup of Play-Doh® or modeling clay, a coffee can lid or similar shallow lid, and collage materials such as buttons, yarn, toothpicks, pieces of ribbon, etc. *Directions*: Ask the children to place their balls of Play-Doh in the bottom of the lid. Ask them to spread it out smooth, covering the surface of the lid. The Play-Doh is the face. They may press in small pieces of yarn along the top edge for the hair, use buttons for the eyes and nose, etc. Toothpicks may be used to poke holes for some of the features, or extra Play-Doh may be used for eyes, nose, and mouth. The children may change the faces over and over again without damaging the materials.

4. **FUNNY FACES**. *Materials*: For each child you will need one paper plate, lots of pictures of eyes, noses, and mouths cut from old magazines, scissors, glue, yarn, and a craft stick. *Directions*: Ask the children to select two eyes, a nose, and a mouth from the ones provided. Have them glue these to the paper plate to make a face. They may add yarn to the top of the plate for hair, and then glue a craft stick to the bottom of the plate to use as a handle. When dry, poke two small holes for the children to see through for a silly mask.

5. **MAN'S BEST FRIEND**. *Materials*: One piece of paper, 7 to 9 inches wide, crayons or markers. *Directions*: Help the children to fold their pieces of paper in half, diagonally. The corners on the right and the left should be folded downward to create the dog's ears. The remaining corners should be folded up inside the puppet (see figure 1.3). Next, poke a hold about 1½ inches up from the bottom of the dog's face. The child's fingertip will be placed through the hole both as a way of holding the puppet and to provide a cute little button nose. Once the children draw the eyes and mouth on the puppet's face, they can name their new friends!

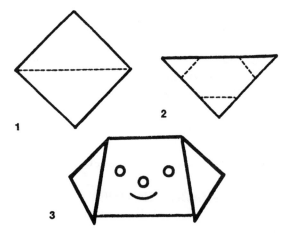

Fig. 1.3.

6. **FRAME UP**. *Materials*: Each child will need one sheet of paper, about 8 inches square, preferably *not* construction paper. *Directions*: Help the children to fold the paper diagonally, then open it up. Fold diagonally in the opposite direction and open it up again. Fold all four corners to the center. Keep folded. Flip the paper over and again fold each corner to the center. Keep folded. You may wish to add a dab of glue to hold these flaps down.

Turn the paper over again, and fold the tips of the paper back to the corners, forming the frame.

The child may insert a photo brought from home, or draw a self-portrait in the center of the frame. For a fancier two-tone frame, use two squares of different colored paper. Fold as one piece.

7. **NIGHT LIGHTS**. *Materials*: Each child will require one glass jelly jar, or another jar roughly that size, several colors of wide gift wrap ribbon (*not* the curling kind), glue, scissors, and one votive candle. *Directions*: If there is still a label on the glass jar, soak it in hot water until it can be removed easily. Help the child measure the ribbon and cut several to fit the circumference of the jar. Have the child smear the glue all over the outside of the jar and then encircle it with the colored ribbons from top to bottom. When dry, set the candle in the bottom of the jar. These night lights will cast a magical glow at lullaby time, but should always be blown out when Mom or Dad leaves the room.

8. **VIP GALLERY**. *Materials*: For each poster you will need one 10- by 13-inch poster board, markers, scissors, yarn, ribbons, and other collage materials. *Directions*: Cut an oval hole in the middle of the poster board the approximate size of a child's face. Let the children decorate the poster. They may wish to cut strips of yarn and glue them to the top of the oval for hair, also gluing a bow in place. Help the children write sayings on each poster such as "I'm a Very Important Person," or "I Am Special," or "Class Clown." They may decorate the posters further with markers, glitter, or collage materials.

To make a gallery of several posters for the class to share, punch two holes in the top of each poster. Thread long pieces of yarn through the holes and tie in place. Hang the posters from the ceiling in a row, the correct height for the children to easily place their faces through the holes. Supply a large hand-held mirror so that the children can go from poster to poster, inspecting themselves.

9. **SPATTER ART**. *Materials*: Thinned tempera paint, an old toothbrush, paper, cutouts, and a paint frame. (To make a paint frame, cut the top and bottom out of a cigar box and staple a rectangle of wire screening to one side.) *Directions*: Make cutouts of shapes such as hearts, flowers, stars, circles, squares, etc. Have the children place one or two cutouts on a sheet of paper. Place the paint frame on top of the paper. Ask the children to dip the toothbrush into the paint. Show them how to rub the toothbrush across the top of the screen, making spatters on the paper below. Rinse the toothbrush between colors, or use a separate brush for each one. After removing the cutouts from the paper, let dry.

Greeting cards can be made from spatters on folded construction paper, or make spatters on shelf paper or tissue paper to make gift wrap. Try using the same method on T-shirts using acrylic paints.

10. **PEEKABOO HOUSE**. *Materials*: Each child will need two pieces of construction paper, one plain and one cut with windows and a door as illustrated (see figure 1.4); markers, crayons or

colored pencils, glue, and magazines are optional. *Directions*: Place the "house" over the plain sheet of paper and trace around the edges of the doors and windows. Remove the "house" and ask the children to draw people, pets, furniture, etc., in the spaces provided. Explain that these items will be seen through a window or door. An alternative would be to cut such items out of an old magazine and glue in place. When the children are ready, have them spread glue all over the empty parts of the paper. Help them press the "house" into place. After drying

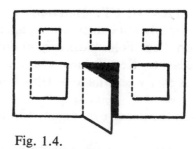

Fig. 1.4.

briefly, let the children decorate the outside of the house. Collage materials may be used, if you wish. After the house is complete and dried, the children can peek inside by folding back the flaps on the doors and windows.

My Family, Myself Class Project

Playhouse Make-Over

Most classrooms already have a playhouse, home area, or dress-up corner. Take a good look at yours. Are the dress-up clothes dirty or in tatters? Should the cardboard playhouse be replaced? Do the dolls look shabby? If so, enlist the help of the children and their parents in making over the role-playing area. First, take an objective look at the area. Decide if anything should be discarded; clean or fix anything that needs it. Ask parents for "new" dress-up clothes. Involve the parents and children in the project by playing scavenger hunt. Help the children make up a wish list of items needed. Divide the list into three or four smaller lists, and make a few copies of each. Send the lists home, along with a roster of parents and their telephone numbers. The parents' and children's task is to first find other team members (those with an identical list), and be the first team to assemble all items on the list. Make award ribbons for everyone so everyone involved will be a winner: the children will have a revived play area and the parents will have some new friends.

My Family, Myself Story Time

1. **BOOKS FROM HOME.** Most children have a favorite book or story. Make a special reading corner in which children display their favorite books, and share them with their friends. For the children who do not wish to bring a book from home, cover some plain white paper with a colorful piece of construction paper and staple together to form a book. Have the child dictate the title of his or her favorite story to you, and print the title on the front cover of the book. The child may then complete the book by drawing pictures about it on the blank pages.

2. **PARENT STORYTELLERS.** Guest storytellers always capture a child's attention. What better guests to visit the classroom than Mom, Dad (or big brother or sister). Arrange ahead of time for family members to read favorite books or tell best-loved stories to the whole class. Encourage them to rehearse at home before coming to the classroom. Their participation could be a secret until story time.

3. **BIRTHDAYS.** Children love birthdays, even if they belong to other people! During family week, give every child a birthday. Stick pretend candles in a pretend cake and sing "Happy Birthday." Let the birthday child choose the book to read at story time.

My Family, Myself Poems, Songs, Fingerplays

1. Two little feet go tap, tap, tap.
    Two little hands go clap, clap, clap.
    A quick little leap up from the chair.
    Two little arms reach high in the air.

    Two little feet go jump, jump, jump.
    Two little hands go thump, thump, thump.
    One little baby turns round and round.
    One little child sits quietly down.

    (*Perform all actions specified.*)

2. *Touch appropriate body parts.*

    I have ten little fingers, ten little toes,
    Two little arms, and one little nose.
    One little mouth, and two little ears,
    Two little eyes for smiles and tears.
    One little head, and two little feet,
    One little chin, and that's me complete.

3. Shake them, shake them
    Put them in your lap.
    Shake them, shake them,
    Tie a little shoe.
    Shake them, shake them,
    And play peekaboo.

    (*Perform specified actions.*)

4. Here are Grandma's spectacles,
    (*Form circles with fingers and place in front of eyes.*)
    And here is Grandma's cap,
    (*Place hands on top of head.*)
    And this is the way she folds her hands,
    And puts them in her lap.
    (*Fold hands and place in lap.*)

5. *Touch appropriate body parts to the tune of "London Bridge."*

    Head and shoulders, knees and toes,
    Knees and toes, knees and toes.
    Head and shoulders, knees and toes,
    Eyes, ears, mouth, and nose.

6. In and out, in and out,
    Now I roll my hands about.
    First up high and then down low,
    This is the way my fingers go.

    (*Perform specified actions.*)

7. Tippy, tippy, tiptoe
   See how we go. (*Hands to eyes.*)
   Tippy, tippy, tiptoe
   To and fro. (*Hands out and then back in.*)
   Tippy, tippy, tiptoe
   Through the house. (*Tiptoe around in a circle.*)
   Tippy, tippy, tiptoe,
   Like a mouse. (*Hunch down.*)

8. Bye, Baby Bunting,
   Father's gone a-hunting,
   Mother's gone a-milking,
   Sister's gone a-silking,
   Brother's gone to buy a skin,
   To wrap the Baby Bunting in.

9. There's something about me
   That I'm knowing.
   There's something about me
   That isn't showing.
   I'm growing!

10. The fish lives in a brook,
    The bird lives in a tree,
    But home's the very nicest place,
    For a little child like me.

11. I have ten little fingers
    And they all belong to me.
    I can make them do things.
    Would you like to see?
    I can shut them up tight
    Or open them wide.
    I can put them together
    Or make them all hide.
    I can make them jump high,
    I can make them jump low,
    I can fold them quietly
    And hold them just so.
    (*Perform specified actions.*)

12. There were five in the bed
    And the little one said,
    "I'm crowded. Roll over."
    So they all rolled over
    And one fell out. (*Pause.*)

There were four in the bed
And the little one said,
"I'm crowded. Roll over."
So they all rolled over
And one fell out. (*Pause*)

There were three in the bed
And the little one said,
"I'm crowded. Roll over."
So they all rolled over
And one fell out. (*Pause*)

There were two in the bed
And the little one said,
"I'm crowded. Roll over."
So they all rolled over
And one fell out. (*Pause*)

There was one in the bed
And the little one said,
"Good night!"

13. Here are Mother's knives and forks,
    (*Palms out, interlock fingers.*)
    Here is Father's table,
    (*Keeping fingers interlocked, face palms down.*)
    Here is Sister's looking glass,
    (*Raise index fingers from the table to form a triangle.*)
    And here is Baby's cradle.
    (*Raise pinkies into a triangle in addition to the index fingers and rock cradle.*)

My Family, Myself Music List

Cassettes

"Brother, Come and Dance With Me." *Disney's Children's Favorites, Vol. 4.* Walt Disney Music Co. 606084, 1990.

"Dry Bones." *Disney's Children's Favorites, Vol. 4.* Walt Disney Music Co. 606084, 1990.

"He's Got the Whole World in His Hands." *Disney's Children's Favorites, Vol. 4.* Walt Disney Music Co. 606084, 1990.

"If You're Happy and You Know It." *Disney's Children's Favorites, Vol. 3.* Walt Disney Music Co. 606074, 1986.

"I'm My Own Grandpa." *Disney's Children's Favorite Silly Songs.* Walt Disney Music Co. 2528B, 1988.

"It's a Small World." *Disney's Children's Favorites, Vol. 4.* Walt Disney Music Co. 606084, 1990.

"Just for You." *Disney's Children's Favorites, Vol. 3*. Walt Disney Music Co. 606064, 1986.

"Reuben and Rachel." *Disney's Children's Favorites, Vol. 4*. Walt Disney Music Co. 606084, 1990.

"Skip Along Tippy Toes." *Disney's Children's Favorite Silly Songs*. Walt Disney Music Co. 2528B, 1988.

"What's Your Name?" *Disney's Children's Favorite Silly Songs*. Walt Disney Music Co. 2528B, 1988.

My Family, Myself Book List

Fiction

Blume, Judy. *The Pain and the Great One*. Illustrated by Irene Trivas. Bradbury Press, 1984.
A brother and sister explain why they don't get along.

Borack, Barbara. *Grandpa*. Illustrated by Ben Schecter. Harper and Row, 1967.
Marylin enjoys a visit with her grandparents and has a special time with her grandfather.

Byars, Betsy. *Go and Hush the Baby*. Illustrated by Emily McCully. Viking, 1971.
A clever young boy tries to quiet the new baby.

Hazen, Barbara Shook. *The Gorilla Did It*. Illustrated by Ray Cruz. Atheneum, 1976.
Did you ever wonder who makes those messes and breaks those valuables? The gorilla did it!

Henkes, Kevin. *Sheila Rae, the Brave*. Greenwillow, 1987.
Engaging characters tell a warm story of sibling sympathy and support.

Hoban, Russell. *Bedtime for Frances*. Illustrated by Garth Williams. Harper and Row, 1960.
Frances tries every excuse to delay bedtime.

Hutchins, Pat. *Titch*. Macmillan, 1971.
Titch was little, Mary was bigger, and Pete was the biggest. Titch has faith that he, like a tiny seed, will someday grow up.

Long, Earlene. *Gone Fishing*. Illustrated by Richard Brown. Houghton Mifflin, 1984.
This is the story of a boy's special fishing trip with his father.

Maschler, Fay. *A Child's Book of Manners*. Illustrated by Helen Oxenbury. Atheneum, 1979.
Hilarious verses remind us how to behave and tell about the consequences if we do not.

Paterson, Diane. *Wretched Rachel*. Dial Press, 1978.
Sometimes Rachel is good and sometimes Rachel is terrible. She knows her parents will always love her, regardless of her behavior.

Rees, Mary. *Ten in a Bed*. Little, Brown, 1988.
    Children will love the antics of the 10 silly friends who illustrate the familiar counting rhyme.

Rice, Eve. *Benny Bakes a Cake*. Greenwillow, 1981.
    Benny's dog eats Benny's birthday cake and goes on to cause even more trouble.

Rockwell, Anne, and Harlowe Rockwell. *Can I Help?* Macmillan, 1982.
    A little girl loves to help with chores around the house.

Viorst, Judith. *Alexander and the Terrible, Horrible, No Good, Very Bad Day*. Illustrated by Ray Cruz. Atheneum, 1972.
    Ever have one of those bad days? Alexander is sure having one.

Waddell, Martin. *Once There Were Giants*. Illustrated by Penny Dale. Delacorte Press, 1989.
    As a baby girl grows up and becomes an adult, the "giants" in her family seem to grow smaller.

Williams, Barbara. *Someday, Said Mitchell*. Illustrated by Kay Chorao. E. P. Dutton, 1976.
    As Mitchell plans how he will help his mother when he grows up, his mother tells Mitchell how he can help now while he is still little.

2
IN THE KITCHEN
(Foods)

Focus on Foods

Healthy eating habits are formed at an early age. Many of the activities in this chapter will help children to recognize nutritious foods.

Consider discussing these subjects:
Food as fuel
Four basic food groups
Nutritious food vs "junk" food
Healthy food that pleases the senses
Cooking
Kitchen safety
Etiquette and table manners

Foods Motor Skills

1. **CEREAL NECKLACES**. Provide each child with a long shoelace and a bowl of O-shaped cereal. Fruit rings work well because they are so colorful. Have the child string the cereal onto the shoelace. When the shoelace is full, help the child tie the ends together to make an edible necklace.

2. **FEELERS**. Sit around the table with several children. Hide an eating or cooking utensil, fruit, vegetable, or other object in your lap. Pass the object from child to child under the table, letting the children feel it all they want, but not letting them look at it. After the object has been passed all the way around the table, each child gets a chance to say what he or she thinks the object is. Reveal the object, and then start over with a new one.

3. **TWISTER**. Spread 12 colored beanbags on the floor, four of each color. Ask all but four children to sit down on the floor. Using a drum or tambourine, sound out a slow beat to which the four selected children walk around the beanbags in a circle. As the children walk, give directions such as, "When the drum stops, place your head on a green beanbag." As the children become adept at following the instructions, make it more difficult by combining two tasks at once such as, "Put your foot on a yellow beanbag and lift up a red beanbag." To take turns playing, all four children can be replaced after a few turns, or the two children who take the longest to perform their task may be replaced by two new children each time.

4. **KNEE RACE**. Have the children stand behind a starting line. Give the children oranges to hold between their knees. At the signal, the children race forward. If the children drop their oranges, they must stand where they dropped them and put them back between their knees before moving forward again. Continue the race until all of the children have crossed the finish line. The children may also divide into relay teams and have a knee race. After the races, the oranges make a refreshing snack.

5. **TOWERS**. Show the children how to make a tower using paper plates and paper cups. A cup is placed on the floor first, with a plate on top of it. Continue the cup-plate pattern until the tower topples. Have a contest to see who can build the highest tower.

6. **PICK A PAIR**. Collect two each of a variety of food-related items. Two forks, two jar lids, two small lemons, etc. Place one of each item in a paper sack, and hand the child the other items one at a time. Ask the child to reach into the bag and try to find the match.

7. **HOT POTATO.** Have the children stand in a circle, passing a real potato or a beanbag around the circle while playing music. When the music stops, the child holding the potato steps out of the circle.

8. **GROCERY RELAY.** Divide the class into two teams and place two hula hoops on the floor. Place three or four items in each hoop, such as empty milk cartons, cereal boxes, or soap bottles. The contents of each hoop should be identical to keep the game fair. Have a relay race. The first player knocks over the items, the second player stands them back up; the first player takes them out of the circle, the second player puts them back in; the first player puts them in a grocery sack, the next player takes them out of the bag and stacks them in the hoop. Whichever task you choose, continue one way until all the children on a team have had a turn.

9. **CHERRY DROP.** One child is chosen to be a cherry tree. The child is blindfolded and stands with arms and fingers outspread. The rest of the players are the "cherries." Each of the cherries holds onto a finger of the tree. The tree asks, "Are you ripe?" When the cherries reply, "Yes," the tree counts to 10 and all the cherries run from the tree. As soon as the tree counts to 10, it shouts, "Cherry drop!" All the cherries must stop and stand still. The tree tries to find all the cherries that have fallen from the tree. The last cherry to be found is the new cherry tree.

10. **A TISKET, A TASKET.** All but one of the children sit on the floor in a circle. The child who remains standing is given a small basket which contains a sandwich (a piece of bread in a sandwich bag or a piece of cardboard cut into the shape of a sandwich). The children all sing:

> A tisket, a tasket
> A pretty picnic basket.
> I made a sandwich for my friend
> And on the way I dropped it.

The child who carries the basket then drops the sandwich into one of the sitting children's laps. This child must then jump up and try to catch the child who carries the basket before that child sits in the empty seat. If the child isn't caught, the other child takes over the basket and the sandwich.

11. **FOLDING NAPKINS.** Provide the children with cloth napkins and teach them to fold the napkins in quarters or into triangles. Experiment with fancy ways to fold them. When a favorite way to fold the napkins is found, have the children place them in the appropriate spot in a place setting.

Foods Language Activities

1. **RESTAURANT.** Have the children cut pictures of food out of magazines or coloring books, or use plastic play food. Arrange the "food" in a place convenient to the "waiter." Have two or three "customers" sit at a table set with paper plates and plastic utensils. Have the customers order lunch from the waiter. The waiter uses a pad and pencil to record the order (probably drawing clues), then brings the food back to the table. The customers tell the waiter if he or she remembered their orders correctly. If the children use paper food, it may then be glued to their paper plates and labeled with their names, Mary's Lunch, Andy's Appetizers, Frank's Food, etc.

2. **FOOD CARDS.** Make food cards by pasting pictures of all kinds of foods onto index cards. In addition to the basic food groups, you may have groups of pictures of beverages, breads, potato dishes, junk food, etc. Pick a category of food, but don't tell the child what it is. Place three cards fitting the category on the table. Add one more that doesn't fit. Ask the child which food card is different. If the child can, have him or her place the different card in its appropriate pile.

3. **SCRAMBLE.** Using alphabet cereal, scatter a handful of the letters on the table in front of three or four children. Call out a letter and let the children scramble to find it. The child finding the correct letter may eat it. For younger children, hold up a picture of the letter to use as a reference.

4. **VEGETABLE STEW.** Sit on the floor in a circle with the children. Hold a mixing bowl or large pot, and stir with a large spoon. Start the game by saying, "I am making vegetable stew. I am putting *peas* in my stew." The next player will say, "I am putting peas and *carrots* in my stew." As the game progresses, the players must repeat the foods previously mentioned and then add one of their own to the stew. Continue until the list gets too long for the children to correctly remember the foods, then start a new game. Perhaps the next cook could make meat or fruit stew.

5. **GROCERY SHOPPING.** Collect labels from cans and boxes of food. Keep matching containers intact so that each box or can has an extra matching label to go with it. Place several boxes or cans on a shelf as in a grocery store. Give the child the set of loose labels and ask him or her to match the labels to the similar ones on the shelf.

6. **RIDDLES.** Have the children bring different foods to school. Place the foods on a table in front of the children, and make up riddles about each food. (For example, what fruit has seeds on the outside rather than inside? Answer: a strawberry.) Keep going until each food has been identified.

7. **BAG IT UP.** Obtain plastic play food representing the basic food groups. Cut pictures of foods in the basic food groups to paste on paper bags. One bag would have pictures of fruits pasted to it, one would have vegetables, one would have milk and cheese products, etc. Have the children identify the play food and place it in the corresponding paper bags.

8. **CARD GAME.** Make playing cards by cutting out pictures of foods and gluing them to index cards. Place the cards face down on the table before three or four children. Have each child draw a card, in turn. The child must identify the food and tell to what food group it belongs. If correct, the child keeps the card. If incorrect, the child places it back in the pile. Keep going until all the cards are gone from the pile, then have the children count to see how many cards they each have. For younger children, have them identify the food and tell what color it is before telling them to what food group it belongs.

9. **LABEL LETTERS.** Collect cans, boxes, and other food containers with their labels intact. Put the food containers on the table and ask the child to look for certain letters on the labels. The child may even be able to discover what certain words are with other clues from the packaging.

Foods Math Activities

1. **FOOD SHAPES.** Obtain one round box (such as an oatmeal box), a square box, and a rectangular box. Cut pictures of similarly shaped foods out of magazines or coloring books, or draw your own pictures. Reinforce the food pictures by gluing them on poster board with rubber cement. After the pictures have been mounted and dried, cut around the edges of the picture to refine the specified shape. The child's task is to place the food shapes into the appropriately shaped box. For example, a picture of an orange that has been glued to poster board and trimmed to a circular shape will be identified and placed in the round box. In addition to sorting the foods in this manner, discuss the names of the foods, their colors, taste, etc.

2. **NUMBERED CUPS**. Turn a paper cup upside down and print a number on the bottom. Place the corresponding number of treats under the cup. Use peanuts, cereal, mints, etc., for treats. Ask the child to lift the cup and count the treats. As the child counts, let him or her eat each treat, eliminating the danger of counting it twice.

3. **KNIVES AND FORKS**. Use plastic knives and forks to make two unequal sets. For instance, place two forks in one set and five knives in the other set. Ask the child to determine which set has more than the other. After the child understands the concept of "more than," use different combinations and ask the child which set has fewer. Demonstrate equal sets. With younger children, use only a few utensils. To make it more difficult, use larger numbers of forks and knives.

4. **UNDER THE CUP**. Place four cups on the table and place a small treat under one of the cups. Ask the child to tell which cup the treat is under, using ordinal terms, first, second, third, or fourth. If correct, give the child the treat to eat.

5. **WHAT DID THE WORM EAT?** Place three to six pieces of fruit on the table. Have the children count the fruits, name them, discuss their colors, textures, shapes, etc. Have a worm puppet "eat" one or more pieces of fruit. Ask the children if they can tell how many pieces the worm ate. If they cannot, have them count how many are left over; produce the missing fruits and count them too.

6. **BEAN TOSS**. Use five to twenty dried beans and a paper sack. Ask the child to toss them into the sack. When they have all been thrown, help the child to count how many went into the sack and help the child to write the number on the outside of the sack.

7. **NUMBER CARDS**. Help each child write his or her favorite number on a large index card or a piece of sturdy paper. Have the child glue that many objects onto the card. The objects to glue may be popcorn, dried peas or beans, pieces of macaroni, etc. Over the course of a couple days, the child can make a complete set of cards, each one with a different type of food glued to it.

8. **PIZZA PIE**. Obtain a pizza wheel and divide it into eight sections (see figure 2.1). Paste a different number of pepperoni made from red construction paper in each section (one through eight

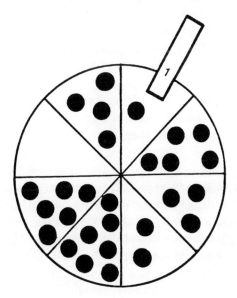

Fig. 2.1.

or zero through seven). With a marking pen, write the matching numerals on spring-type clothes-pins. The child's task will be to clip the clothespins to the appropriate section of the pizza.

9. **FIVE-CUP SNACK**. Have the children help with the following snack recipe. Mix together 1 cup of pretzels, 1 cup of peanuts, 1 cup of dry corn cereal, 1 cup of dry rice cereal, and 1 cup of small cheese crackers. Have the children do the measuring. Once all the ingredients are in the bowl, measure them back out to show that even mixed up, the bowl contains 5 cups of ingredients. For older children, use 1 cup of the pretzels, two ½-cups of the peanuts, three ⅓-cups of the cereal, etc., to demonstrate fractions. After the snack has been mixed by everyone in the class, use a ¼-cup to measure out each child's share of the snack. (For a class of 24, make 6-cup snack, etc.)

Foods Science Activities

1. **BLIND MAN'S LUNCH**. Place several foods in front of a blindfolded child. Ask the child what he or she is eating. There are three basic tastes: salty, sweet, and sour. Have the child tell which taste the foods are.

2. **BUTTER AND NUTTER BUTTER**. Children do not always realize that the foods they eat started out in a different form. For instance, butter is made from cream. Have the children make their own by giving each child a small jar with a tight-fitting lid. Pour whipping cream into the jar until it is half full, then carefully drop two ice cubes in. Screw the lid on tightly. Have the children shake their jars vigorously until butter forms. Eat the fresh butter on crackers.

Most children know that peanut butter is made from peanuts, but they do not know how it is made. Have the children shell a large bag of peanuts. Place two cups of shelled peanuts in a blender, grind for a few seconds, then add a little salt for flavor and a little vegetable oil as an emulsifier. Blend at high speed until smooth. Let the children taste the peanut butter. How does it compare to the product bought in the grocery store?

3. **FRUIT JUICE**. Bring a variety of prewashed fruits and vegetables to class. Separate and identify them; explore their color, smell, shape, and texture. Define fruit as that part of the plant which contains the seeds, and cut open the fruit to show the children the seeds. You may choose to show the children a strawberry, which is odd for having its seeds on the outside. Vegetables are plants that are grown for their edible parts. The parts that we eat may be the stem, root, leaf, or flower of the plant. Identify the vegetables and tell what part of the plant it is.

Discuss different ways of preparing fruits and vegetables. Place some fruit and even some of the vegetables (such as carrots) in a blender. Add ¼-cup of crushed ice and blend using the highest speed to make a refreshing beverage. Experiment with different combinations of fruit and vegetables.

4. **SMELLS WELL**. Explain to the children that our sense of smell is related closely to our sense of taste. Illustrate this by blindfolding a child and having him or her pinch the nose shut. Place a bit of food which we usually associate with a strong smell into the child's mouth. Bananas are a good example. Can the child identify the food without using the sense of smell? Try again without having the child pinch the nose. Does the food taste better?

Have some more fun with smells by placing some "smells" in small glass jars: mint leaves, crushed peppermint candies, orange peels, cinnamon. Make two jars with each scent. Have the children close their eyes and let them smell two of the jars. Can they tell whether the scents are the same or different? Can they identify the scents?

Here's another activity using the scented jars: Have the children close their eyes and let them smell three or four jars, two of which have the same scent. Can the children pick out the two jars that smell the same?

5.   **FLAVORFUL TOOTHPASTE**. It is important to keep teeth clean by brushing them after meals. A good-tasting toothpaste makes it fun to brush. Let each child measure out 1 tablespoon of baking soda, ½-teaspoon of salt, and 1 teaspoon of flavoring such as vanilla, lemon, or peppermint. Mix together. Store in a tightly closed jar to keep fresh.

6.   **ICEBOX**. Refrigerators are an important part of all kitchens in that they prevent perishable foods from spoiling. Make this insulated box to show the basic way a refrigerator works. *Materials*: One large, clean, sturdy cardboard box, newspaper, a smaller clean, sturdy box, aluminum foil, and ice. *Directions*: Crumple up the newspapers and place some of them in the bottom of the large box. Line the smaller box with aluminum foil and put ice in it. Place a food that you would like to refrigerate in the smaller box. Close the smaller box, and place it on top of the newspapers in the large box. Put more newspapers around the small box until the large box is filled. Close the lid. Let the food stand in the icebox for an hour or more, then check it. Is it colder than when it went in? Compare it to a sample of the same food that has been left out. Place the refrigerated food back in the icebox and seal it once more. Can the children predict how long the icebox will continue to work? Record guesses and check the food in the icebox periodically. Each time compare the refrigerated food to the food left out. Keep the experiment overnight and check the food in the morning. Is the food in the icebox still edible? What about the food left out of the icebox?

Foods Art Projects

1.   **POTATO PRINTS**. *Materials*: Potatoes, paring knife, powdered tempera paint, paper, paper towels, and several pie pans. *Directions*: Peel the potatoes and cut them into cubes, cylinders, triangles, or other shapes. Set them on paper towels to let them dry out. Mix the tempera paint a little thicker than normal, and pour onto folded paper toweling placed in a pie pan. Give the children some paper and two or three pie pans with different colored paint in them. Have the children dip the potato shapes into the paint and then make prints on the paper.

2.   **EDIBLE SCULPTURES**. *Materials*: Apples, pears, gumdrops, raisins, marshmallows, and toothpicks. *Directions*: Provide each child with one apple or pear, and several each of the rest of the materials. Encourage the child to put several gumdrops, raisins, marshmallows, etc., on each toothpick before attaching it to the piece of fruit.

3.   **COLORED RICE PICTURES**. *Materials*: White rice, food coloring, several glass jars with lids, paper, glue, and marking pens or crayons. *Directions*: Give each child a jar and have him or her scoop some rice into it. Let the child put a few drops of food coloring on the rice, screw the lid on the jar, and shake it up. Notice how the rice becomes the color of the food dye. The child may now glue the rice to the paper to make a collage, and then finish the design with markers or crayons. If you wish, provide the child with a design already on the paper, and let him or her fill in the design with the rice.

4. **FLAVORED STAMPS.** *Materials*: Magazines with glossy pages, scissors, newspaper, a spoon, a saucepan and source of heat, water, and 1 teaspoon of flavored gelatin per child. *Directions*: Have the children cut interesting pictures (not too large) from magazines. Place 1 teaspoon of flavored gelatin for each child into a sauce pan. Add twice as many teaspoons of water. Bring to a boil over a medium heat and stir until the gelatin dissolves. Take the mixture off the heat and allow to cool. Have the children place their cutouts face down on newspaper. While the gelatin mixture is still warm, ask the children to use their fingers to spread an even coat of the mixture on the back of each cutout. Let the stamps dry for one to two days. (They may curl slightly.) When the stamps are dry, the children can lick them and stick them to a variety of surfaces.

5. **NATURAL DYE.** *Materials*: Cranberry juice, blueberry juice from canned blueberries, grape juice, paper cups, string, yarn, muslin, and scissors. *Directions*: Provide the children with some fruit juice in paper cups. Allow them to use the juice as a dye for muslin, string, etc. The muslin may be cut into large squares for tie-dyeing, or cut into little shapes and dyed for collage material. The yarn and string may also be cut and used for making collages.

6. **PLACEMATS.** *Materials*: One 12-by-18-inch piece of construction paper for each child, smaller pieces of paper, glue, scissors, pencils, small plate, cup, fork, knife, and spoon to trace around. *Directions*: Have the children trace around the plate, cup, fork, knife, and spoon on different colors of construction paper. Ask them to cut them out and glue them onto the large piece of construction paper arranging them as a place setting would be. Print the children's names on them and they have their own placemats for snack time.

7. **FRAGRANT FRUITS.** *Materials*: Gelatin powder in a variety of fruit flavors, paper, glue, and crayons. *Directions*: Provide the children with a picture of a type of fruit for them to color, or ask the children to draw and color their own pictures of fruit. Using glue in squeeze bottles, the children can outline the piece of fruit. The next step is to sprinkle the gelatin over the glue, shake off the excess gelatin, and let dry. The gelatin used should correspond to the type of fruit in the picture. For example, a picture of strawberries would be outlined in strawberry flavored gelatin. Tell the children not to eat the picture.

8. **REFRIGERATOR MAGNETS.** *Materials*: Black construction paper, white construction paper, red markers or paint, white paint, scissors, clear adhesive paper, magnetic tape or small, flat magnets, and the pattern given (see figure 2.2). *Directions*: Make templates from the salt and pepper shaker patterns. Let each child trace around them, one on black paper and one on white paper. Help the children cut out their shakers and ask them to draw dots on the top of the white shakers (where the salt comes out) and then to draw a large red "S" on them. Have them draw white dots on the pepper shakers and then to draw a large "P" on them using the white paint. When dry, have the children place their two shakers face down near the corner of a piece of clear adhesive paper. Cut around the shakers, leaving plenty of room around the edges. Now flip the shakers over and place the raw side down on more adhesive paper. Trim to within ¼-inch of the edges. Cut a small piece of magnetic tape for each shaker and let the children stick it to the back of the magnet. If you are using small, flat magnets, let the children glue them to the back of their shakers. When dry, the salt and pepper shakers may be used to hold memos to the refrigerator or stove.

9. **I'M A COOKIE (decoration).** The following amounts of flour and salt will be enough for about 20 cookie decorations—this recipe is *not* for edible cookies. *Materials*: 2 cups of flour, 1 cup of salt, 1 cup of water, baking sheets, gingerbread boy or plain round cookie cutters, aluminum foil, paper clips, watercolor tube paints and paintbrushes (optional), and clear acrylic spray. *Directions*: Mix the flour, salt, and water, adding more flour or water as needed to make a firm, nonsticky

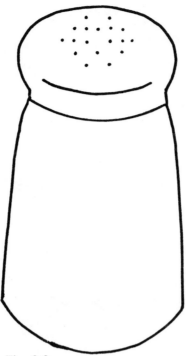

Fig. 2.2.

dough. Knead for five minutes until smooth and pliable. Divide the dough among the children. Have them flatten their dough on individual pieces of aluminum foil. Let the children cut out their cookies with the cookie cutters. If not using paint, a toothpick may be used to poke holes and make facial features. Press a paper clip into the back of the cookie near the top. Bake the cookies at 325 degrees for 30 minutes for each ¼-inch thickness. If cracks appear during baking, fill them in with more dough and continue baking. If the dough gets puffy or if it burns, reduce the heat of the oven by 50 degrees. If painting the cookies, allow them to cool before the children paint them, and then return them to a warm oven for half an hour to dry the paint. When both painted or unpainted cookies are finished, spray with several coats of the clear acrylic varnish. Loop a ribbon through the paper clip along with a name tag. Use the cookies as decorations in the classroom. They also come in handy when taking roll if the children remove their cookies from their resting places and put them into their cubbies upon arrival. A brief glance up will tell the teacher who is missing. If making the gingerbread man shapes, a good extension of the activity would be to read and talk about the story of the little gingerbread boy.

10.   **RECIPE HOLDER**. *Materials*: Each child will need 1½ paper plates, yarn, markers, scissors, and a hole punch. *Directions*: Punch holes at ½-inch intervals around the perimeter of the whole and the half paper plates (see figure 2.3, page 26). Have the children bind the plates together by stringing the yarn through the holes and around the outside edges of the plates. Help them write "Recipes" on the bottom half of the recipe holder and let them decorate. The recipe holder can be hung on the wall or pinned to a bulletin board.

11.   **DRINKING CUP**. Here are directions for folding a plain sheet of paper into a drinking cup that can be folded and carried in a pocket or lunch box. *Materials*: Each child will need one square sheet of smooth paper (*not* construction paper) measuring at least 8 inches wide and a crayon for decorating the outside of the finished cup. *Directions*: Have the children place their sheets of paper

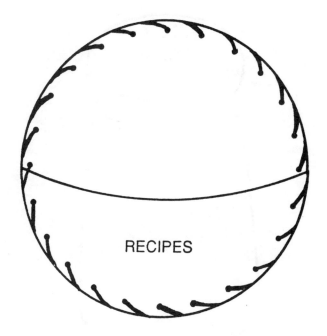

Fig. 2.3.

on a table. Help them fold the bottom point up until it touches the top point making the square into a triangle (see figure 2.4). Next, fold the point on the right over until it touches the middle of the left side of the triangle (A touches B). Repeat with the left point touching the right side of the triangle (C touches D). Ask the children to fold down the top edges. The cup may be decorated on the outside with crayon, and can be used several times if it's allowed to dry between uses.

Foods Class Project

What better way to celebrate good nutrition than to serve a "square" meal. On day one, have the children decide which foods to serve, making sure each food group is represented. Once a simple menu is planned, day two may include a field trip to the market to buy ingredients for the meal. Day three may be devoted to preparing some of the dishes ahead of time if necessary. The last day of the project will be the day of the meal, spent preparing the rest of the food and eating it. To help commemorate the meal, make copies of the recipes used and prepare a recipe book. Give the children construction paper for the cover and help them staple the book together. The recipe book may be decorated with crayons and markers and taken home as a souvenir.

Foods Story Time

1. **GREEN EGGS AND HAM**. Read Dr. Seuss' story, *Green Eggs and Ham*, and as a surprise ending, make the real thing for snack time. Hard boil eggs and use Easter-egg dye to color them green. Dice ham and mix it with some green food coloring. Would the children need to be persuaded to eat it, as in the story? Does the green coloring affect its taste? Read other stories about food such as Eric Carle's *The Very Hungry Caterpillar*, and put the mentioned foods on the menu for a snack after story time.

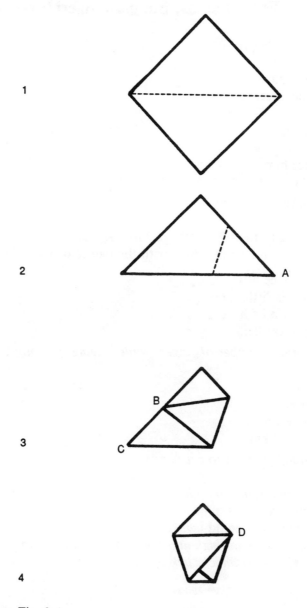

Fig. 2.4.

2.   **COOKBOOKS**. Read recipes from cookbooks and decide on a recipe to prepare at story time. The children may wish to assemble a classroom cookbook by drawing pictures of their favorite foods on construction paper. Have each child dictate simple cooking instructions for the foods drawn, and write the instructions down on more construction paper. Punch holes in the pages and place in a loose-leaf binder for your own classroom cookbook.

3.   **PEANUT BUTTER AND JELLY**. Read the book *Peanut Butter and Jelly* by Nadine Bernard Wescott. Use actions illustrated in the book to make pretend sandwiches, and then use the same actions to make a real sandwich.

Food Poems, Songs, Fingerplays

1. My father owns the butcher shop,
   My mother cuts the meat,
   And I'm the little hot dog
   That runs around the street.

2. Davy, Davy Dumpling,
   Boil him in the pot,
   Sugar him and butter him,
   And eat him while he's hot.

   (*Perform actions stated in poem.*)

3. Sing the following song to the tune of "Ten Little Indians." Let the children choose common vegetables for the song, and supply them with the names of unfamiliar vegetables.

   One little, two little, three little _____,
   Four little, five little, six little _____,
   Seven little, eight little, nine little _____,
   I just picked from my garden.

   (*Hold up the appropriate number of fingers while singing the song.*)

4. I eat my peas with honey,
   I've done it all my life.
   It makes the peas taste funny,
   But it keeps them on my knife.

   (*At the end of the song, pretend to eat peas.*)

5. Way up in the apple tree (*look up high*)
   Two little apples smiled at me (*smile*).
   I shook that tree as hard as I could (*shake tree*)
   Down they came (*hold hands up high and then slowly lower them*).
   Mmm, they were good (*rub stomach, lick lips*).

6. Jump rope jingles:

   Mabel, Mabel, set the table.
   Don't forget the salt and pepper.

   (*When you say "pepper," the rope goes very fast.*)

   Strawberry shortcake
   Cream on top.
   Tell me the name of your sweetheart.
   A, B, C, D, etc.

   (*When the child misses, the letter is the first letter of his or her sweetheart's name.*)

7. One potato, two potato, three potato, four
   Five potato, six potato, seven potato, more.

(The teacher and children stand in a circle with their fists upright in front of them. The jingle is recited by all, and the teacher taps the top of a child's fist each time a number in the jingle is recited. At the word "more," the child whose fist is tapped must leave the circle. The game goes on until only one person is left in the circle. This recitation game is used to determine who is "it" for some subsequent game.)

8. Pease porridge hot,
   Pease porridge cold,
   Pease porridge in the pot,
   Nine days old.

   Some like it hot,
   Some like it cold,
   Some like it in the pot,
   Nine days old.

(Use as a clapping game. Sit in a circle. On "pease" the hands slap the thighs. On "porridge" the hands clap once. On "hot" the hands clap against their neighbor's hands, and then their own again to keep time with the rhythm of the verse. Repeat the same actions to the rhythm of the rest of the verse.)

9. Hot cross buns!
   Hot cross buns!
   One a penny, two a penny,
   Hot cross buns!

10. (*This is the simplified version for younger children.*)

    Pat-a-cake, pat-a-cake, (*clap hands together for the whole verse.*)
    Baker's man!
    Bake me a cake as fast as you can!

    Roll it up and roll it up, (*roll hands around each other.*)
    And toss it in the pan! (*fling arms up.*)

11. To market, to market, to buy a fat pig,
    Home again, home again, jiggety jig.
    To market, to market, to buy a fat hog,
    Home again, home again, jiggety jog.
    To market, to market, to buy a plum bun,
    Home again, home again, market is done.

12. Simple Simon met a pieman,
    Going to the fair.
    Says Simple Simon to the pieman,
    "Let me taste your ware."

    Says the pieman to Simple Simon,
    "Show me first your penny."
    Says Simple Simon to the pieman,
    "Indeed, I have not any."

13. Jack Sprat could eat no fat,
     His wife could eat no lean;
     And so, betwixt them both,
     They licked the platter clean.

14. Handy, Pandy, Jack-a-dandy,
     Loves plum cake and sugar candy.
     He bought some at a grocer's shop,
     And out he came, hop, hop, hop!

     (*Hop three times at the end of the verse.*)

15. Ladies and gentlemen come to supper,
     Hot boiled beans and very good butter.

16. Molly, my sister and I fell out,
     And what do you think it was all about?
     She loved coffee and I loved tea,
     And that was the reason we couldn't agree.

17. There dwelt an old woman at Exeter,
     When visitors came it sore vexed her.
     So for fear they would eat,
     She locked up all her meat,
     This stingy old woman of Exeter.

Foods Music List

Cassettes

Bartels, Joanie. "Animal Crackers." *Sillytime Magic.* Discovery Music Co. ISBN 5-550-31594-7, 1989.

Bartels, Joanie. "I Like Bananas Because They Have No Bones." *Sillytime Magic.* Discovery Music Co. ISBN 5-660-31594-7, 1989.

Bartels, Joanie. "Silly Pie." *Sillytime Magic.* Discovery Music Co. ISBN 5-660-31594-7, 1989.

"Carrot Stew." *Disney's Children's Favorites, Vol. 2.* Walt Disney Music Co. 606064, 1979.

"I'm a Little Teapot." *Disney's Children's Favorites, Vol. 4.* Walt Disney Music Co. 606084, 1990.

"Pizza Pie Song." *Disney's Children's Favorite Silly Songs.* Walt Disney Music Co. 2528B, 1988.

Foods Book List

Fiction

Barrett, Judi. *Cloudy With a Chance of Meatballs*. Illustrated by Ron Barrett. Macmillan, 1978.
The town of Chewandswallow is lucky to have food drop out of the sky, until the "weather" takes a turn for the worse.

Berenstain, Jan, and Stan Berenstain. *The Berenstain Bears and Too Much Junk Food*. Random House, 1985.
Mama Bear starts a campaign to convince her family to cut down on junk food.

Carle, Eric. *The Very Hungry Caterpillar*. Putnam, 1981.
The caterpillar eats and eats until he becomes a butterfly.

Giesel, Theodore. (Dr. Seuss.) *Green Eggs and Ham*. Random House, 1960.
What would it take to make you eat green eggs and ham?

Green, Phyllis. *Bagdad Ate It*. Illustrated by Joel Schick. Franklin Watts, 1980.
A dog on a diet gets into trouble when he tries to eat things that he shouldn't eat.

Marshall, James. *Yummers*. Houghton Mifflin, 1973.
Emily the pig sets off on a walk in order to exercise and lose weight. However, along the way she really "pigs out!"

Root, Phyllis. *Soup for Supper*. Illustrated by Sue Truesdell. Harper and Row, 1986.
A small woman catches a giant stealing vegetables from her garden, but decides that they can both benefit if she shares them.

Sendak, Maurice. *In the Night Kitchen*. Harper and Row, 1970.
Mikey helps the bakers make cake in the night kitchen.

Sharmat, Mitchell. *Gregory the Terrible Eater*. Illustrated by José Aruego and Ariane Dewey. Macmillan, 1980.
Gregory the Goat's parents wish that Gregory would eat a proper billy goat diet.

Wescott, Nadine Bernard. *Peanut Butter and Jelly—A Play Rhyme*. E. P. Dutton, 1987.
Wescott illustrates the traditional play rhyme in which the reader is invited to take part in the construction of a delicious sandwich.

Cookbooks for Children

Barrett-Dragon, Patricia, and Rosemary Dalton. *The Kid's Cookbook*. Original artwork by children. Bristol Publishing Enterprises, 1982.
This is a wonderful cookbook designed expressly for children by two teachers who often use cooking as a teaching tool.

Klutz Press. *Kid's Cooking: A Very Slightly Messy Manual*. Klutz Press, 1987.
This children's book contains kitchen crafts and cuisine.

3
AROUND THE TOWN
(Transportation)

Focus on Transportation

Transportation is the act of moving people or their goods from one place to another. Activities in this chapter will show children many ways to move across land, over water, and through the air.

Consider discussing these subjects:
    Modes of transportation
    Vehicle names
    Traffic safety
    Traffic signs and signals
    Recreational vehicles
    Work vehicles
    Types of propulsion

Transportation Motor Skills

1. **SPARE PARTS.** Have the children stand in a circle. Give simple commands, such as "Pinch your nose," "Touch your toes," etc. Work up to using "right" and "left" in your commands: "Lift your left foot," or "Touch your right ear." (A ribbon may be tied to each child's right wrist.) Older children may wish to play "Simon Says."

2. **REPRODUCTIONS.** Prepare as many 9-by-11-inch reproduction cards as you wish, using poster board or sturdy construction paper. For each card, draw a simple shape on the left side, leaving the right half of the paper blank. Draw wheels, traffic sign shapes, or arrows pointing different directions on each card. Cover the surface of the card with clear adhesive paper. Have the children use crayons to try to reproduce on the right side of the card what they see on the left side. Erase the crayon marks with a tissue when it is time for the next child to play.

3. **FOLLOW THE LEADER.** Lead the children around the classroom or playground. Skip, hop, walk backwards, etc., giving "left" and "right" instructions when possible. Any child who does something different than the leader must go to the end of the line. Have the children run "home" when the leader claps and yells, "Go home!" The child to reach "home" first becomes the new leader.

4. **RED LIGHT, GREEN LIGHT.** Stand at the head of the class and have the children stand several yards away and face you. When you call "green light!" the children walk toward you quickly. When you call "yellow light!" the children walk toward you slowly. When you call "red light!" the children must stop in their tracks. Children not responding to the command correctly must go back to where they started. When a child reaches the head of the class, he or she becomes the new commander and a new round of play starts.

5. **MOUNTAIN ROADS.** Using your crayon as a car, make a straight line. Then make curves, switchbacks, and zigzags. Can the children do the same?

6. **PATHWAYS.** Draw two straight lines parallel to each other and about 1 inch apart. Ask the children to "drive" down the middle with their crayons. Change the lines to a curving river

that the children float their boats down. To increase the difficulty of this exercise, make the lines narrower. A house, an ice cream shop, or a toy store may be drawn at the end of the road to encourage the children to reach the end.

7.   **TRAIN GAME.** Have all the children make a train by standing in line and holding on to each other. The leader must lead the train around and through any obstacles he or she encounters. When it is time for a new leader, the former leader goes to the end of the line.

8.   **COLOR RACE.** Name a color and let the children run to touch something that color. The children can pretend to fly, float, drive, or skate to the object.

9.   **STOP AND GO.** The children walk or pretend to fly, roll, chug like a train, or drive like a car in any direction. When a whistle is blown or the lights are turned off or a stop sign is held up, the children must stop immediately. Those who do not stop must sit down.

10.   **MAGNET MOVERS.** Using a sturdy paper plate and a strong magnet the child must move a small metal object along the top of the paper plate by holding it to the plate's surface with the magnet underneath the plate. Draw a road, a river, or train tracks on the paper plates to make the activity more challenging.

Transportation Language Activities

1.   **TRAFFIC SIGNS.** Make traffic signs out of felt and put them on a flannel board. Give clues to the children about a particular sign. Say, "I'm thinking of a sign that means 'stop'." Have a child come up and take the correct sign off the board. When all the signs have been removed, use different clues. The child holding the sign you are talking about should put it back up on the flannel board.

2.   **DIRECTIONS.** Name a nearby place familiar to the children and ask them to think of different ways to get to that place. For example, ask the children how they would go to the playground.

3.   **FLY, DRIVE, OR FLOAT.** Divide a bulletin board into three sections. Place a picture of the sky in the first section, a picture of a road in the second section, and a picture of a body of water in the third section. Provide pictures of all kinds of vehicles that have been cut out of magazines, ads, or coloring books. Have the children tack the pictures up in the appropriate area.

4.   **SOUNDS LIKE.** In different tones, sing the simple sounds of different vehicles. Imitate a car, a motorcycle, a train, and a boat. Ask the children to repeat the sounds you make and to identify the vehicle.

5.   **CITY STREETS.** Use a large piece of vinyl or cardboard and some marking pens to draw the layout of a city. Put a road around the perimeter of the map and then divide the rest into six to eight blocks. Draw roads between the blocks, and draw in houses and shops, making them all different colors. Allow each child to drive toy cars on the roads. Next, ask the child to pretend to be a taxi driver or delivery person who must drive to specific colored houses, pick up a customer or package, and deliver it elsewhere. See if the child can follow simple requests such as, "Turn left at the corner," or "Stop after going two more blocks."

6. **ACTION**. See how many words the children can think of that "move." Example: hop, run, skip, bounce, roll, etc. Have the children act out the activity named.

7. **DISTANCE WORDS**. Use the following activity to teach these distance words: here, there, near, nearer, nearest, far, farther, and farthest. Select a person to be "it." Ask the child to leave the room while you hide a toy car. When the child comes back in, he or she looks for the car. You and the other children provide clues using distance words. When the child is close say, "There!" and let him or her find the car.

8. **MATCHING LETTERS**. Prepare the manila file folders as shown in figure 3.1. Glue a picture of a vehicle onto the left side of the folder. On the right side, print the name of the vehicle vertically in capital letters. Across from the capitals, put the same letters in mixed up order, using lowercase letters. Use a paper punch to make a small hole next to each letter. String a shoelace through each hole on the left side and secure the shoelaces with masking tape. The child will put the strings through the hole on the right side to the one that matches the capital on the left.

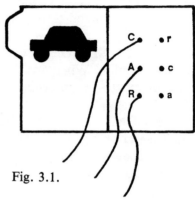

Fig. 3.1.

9. **SELECTIONS**. Spread a small number of vehicle pictures on a table. Name a vehicle and have the child find the picture, then select a picture and have the child name it. If a vehicle can be called by more than one name, be sure to point that out.

10. **MEMORY**. Use as many toy cars, trains, and planes as you can gather. From a pile of colored cards, the child draws one card, looks at it, and places it face down, then tries to select one of the toy vehicles of the same color.

Transportation Math Activities

1. **GADGETS**. Fill a large, widemouthed jar with nuts, bolts, screws, washers, hooks, or any small gadget. Use 12 different types of items for sorting into an empty egg carton. After the children are through sorting, have them count how many items they have placed in each section.

2. **NUTS AND BOLTS**. Gather an assortment of several different-sized nuts and bolts, the larger, the better. Mix them up in a container. The children can then match the ones that fit together. For very young children, use only a few of the largest bolts.

3. **CARGO SHIP**. Float a large plastic boat in a tub of water. Use nuts and bolts or other small, heavy items as cargo. Have the children count how many items the boat can hold. If more than one boat is available, count the cargo on each one to see how they differ.

4. **FREIGHT TRUCK**. Cut truck shapes for use on a flannel board. Make the first one short, the second one longer, and the third one even longer. Use as many trucks as you wish. Ask the children to place them in order by size on the flannel board.

5. **COINS**. For this activity, you will need a penny, a nickel, a dime, a quarter, and a 50-cent piece. Tell the children that they are going to ride an imaginary bus and that the fare requires exact change. Help the children identify each coin. Make rubbings of them with paper and pencil. Place the coins

in order according to value. After the children are familiar with the coins, make up bus fares for them to put together. For instance, tell a child that he or she needs one penny and one dime to go downtown or a quarter and a nickel for a ride to the zoo.

6. **NUMBER TRAIN.** Draw a 10-car train on felt or cardboard. Cut out the cars and number them. The child's job will be to place the train cars in the correct numerical order.

7. **GARAGE.** Using an in-out file with several tiers, have the child drive and park a toy car on the first floor, second floor, etc. Numbers written on the side of the garage may be helpful.

8. **SKYWRITER.** Give the child a toy airplane and have the child "skywrite" the numbers you dictate.

9. **WHEELS.** Cut pictures of various vehicles out of magazines or ads. Have the children count how many wheels there are on each.

10. **MATCHING CUTOUTS.** Cut a 12-by-4-inch piece of tagboard. With a marker, divide the card into three 4-by-4-inch sections. In each section draw a vehicle shape, a geometric shape, or a numeral, and make a cutout to match each shape on the card. The child's task is to match the cutouts to those on the board.

Transportation Science Activities

1. **GEARS.** Use an eggbeater to show children how gears work. Show them the large and small gears that make the blades of the beater rotate. Put a chalk mark on each gear and slowly turn the crank. As the crank turns the large gear once, the smaller gear turns many times. Gears are really wheels and axles that have been modified to either increase force or increase movement.

2. **WHIRLY GIG.** Give each child a 2-by-6-inch piece of sturdy paper or poster board. Help them cut a slit 3 inches into the paper as shown (see figure 3.2). Bend these flaps in opposite directions to form a propeller. Attach a paper clip to the bottom of the whirly gig, and have the children toss their whirly gigs into the air and watch as they slowly make their way back to the ground. Of what vehicle does this remind the children?

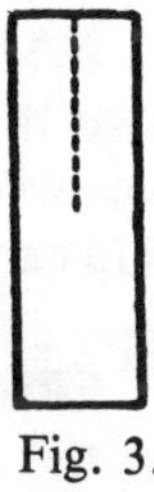

Fig. 3.2.

3. **JET PROPULSION.** For this activity you will need a toy balloon, an eyedropper, and a pan of water. Blow up the balloon and let it fly uncontrollably in all directions. Take the glass tube from the eyedropper and insert it into the neck of the balloon. Blow up the balloon and place it in a pan of water and let go. The escaping air is now controlled.

4. **BALLOON ROCKET.** Tie one end of a long piece of string to a curtain rod, light fixture, or vent. Thread the string through a drinking straw. Blow up a balloon and have one of the children help you tape it to the straw. Hold the balloon while one of the children holds the string and stretches it tight. Let the balloon go for another example of jet propulsion.

Air pressure inside the balloons in these experiments is greater on the inside than on the outside. As the air escapes, the pressure on the inside of the balloon pushes it forward. In jet planes, gases are compressed inside the engine. As they escape out the back, the greater pressure on the inside pushes the plane forward.

5. **PADDLEBOAT**. Transfer the pattern of a boat and paddles to thin Styrofoam (see figure 3.3); cut out one boat and two paddles. Slot together the two paddles at right angles, and fix them to the body of the boat with a rubber band. Wind it up and place it into a tub of water. Although real paddleboats use steam rather than rubber bands to make them go, this illustrates the use of the paddle. Perhaps some of the children have ridden on paddleboats they powered by pedaling.

6. **SHIPS**. Show children pictures of large ships. How can something so large and heavy float? The answer is that the ship is made to hold a lot of air, which is lighter than water. With a tub of water or an aquarium without fish, one can illustrate this idea:

   a. Show the children how a lump of clay sinks. Shape the clay into a boat form, and it floats. The hollow shape, filled with air, takes up more space in the water than the lump did so it floats.

   b. Place a small inflatable toy on the surface of the water before you inflate it. Eventually it starts to sink. Blow it up and it floats much better.

   c. Double a piece of aluminum foil and fold it into the shape of a boat. Float it on the water. Put some paper clips or pennies in the boat and watch what happens. How many can the boat hold? Was it more than expected? Now flatten the boat, folding it tightly together, and watch it sink.

   d. Take a sponge and let the children feel how light it is. When put on the surface of the water it floats because it has many small holes, all filled with air. Squeeze the sponge under the water and watch the air bubbles escape to the surface of the water. Filled with water instead of air, the sponge sinks. Lift the sponge out of the water and let the children feel how heavy it has become.

7. **RAMPS**. Experiment with blocks and ramps made out of boards. Use small toy cars to travel down the ramp. Adjust the boards to different heights and angles to see what works best. Have races with the toy cars, one per board, to determine how the ramps can be changed to make the cars go faster or farther. Can you find anything else that will roll down the ramp?

8. **FRICTION**. For this activity, collect a stack of books, some string, and a skate or a skateboard. Ask the children to pretend they are people who lived five thousand years ago when their only mode of transportation was their feet. If they wanted to move something, they had to carry it or drag it. Wrap the string around the books. Have the children take turns pulling the books across the floor. Next, place the stack of books on the skate. Tie the string to the skate so that the books don't fall off. Now have the children pull the stack of books. With the invention of the wheel they have just cut in half the friction of the books being dragged across the floor.

9. **ROLLING VERSUS PUSHING**. Fill two coffee cans with sand and replace the lids. Put the two cans on the floor, placing one can on its side and one flat on the floor. Ask the children to predict which one will be easier to move. Is it easier to push the flat can across the floor, or to roll the can on its side? Explain that when we roll the can, we have cut down on friction by placing less surface area on the floor. More surface is covered by the flat can, causing more friction.

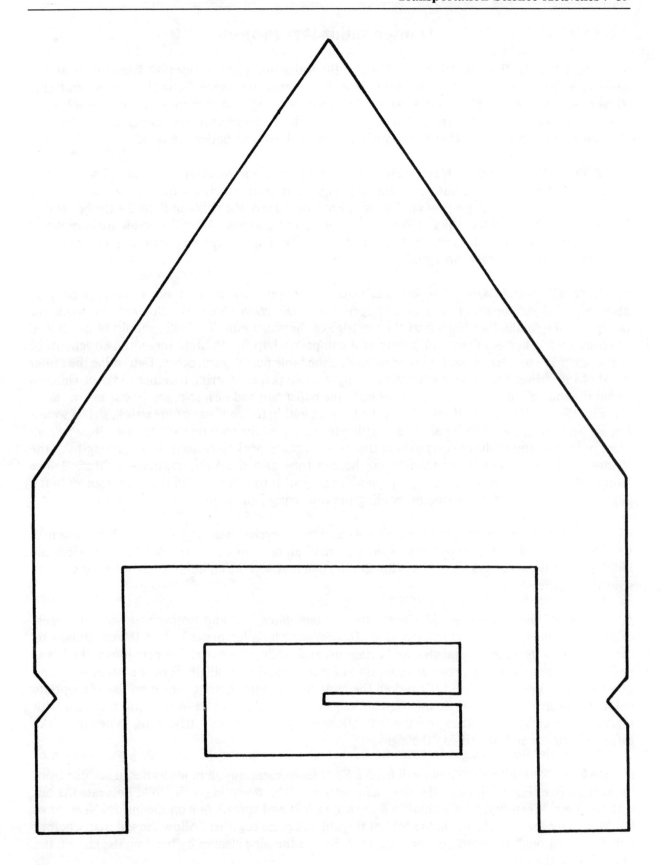

Fig. 3.3.

Transportation Art Projects

1. **UNDER THE HOOD**. *Materials*: Plenty of construction paper shapes cut from the given patterns (see figures 3.4 to 3.8a), one large piece of construction paper for each student, and glue. *Directions*: Give each child a large piece of construction paper and some glue, placing all of the precut shapes within reach. Instruct the children to make a collage using the shapes and explain that the end result is a view of what their family car might look like under the hood.

2. **BOX CITY**. *Materials*: Have each child bring a shoe box or cereal box from home. Other materials include poster paint, construction paper cut into small squares for windows, glue, markers, and a large, flat piece of cardboard. *Directions*: Have the children decorate the boxes they brought from home to look like houses, stores, or other buildings. After the boxes are completed, attach them to the large sheet of cardboard to form a city. The city can be put on display or used on the floor to drive toy cars through.

3. **HOT AIR BALLOON**. *Materials*: Each child will require one balloon, one 6-ounce paper cup, about 9 feet of yarn or string, tape, and a paper punch. *Directions*: Show the children how to use the paper punch to make four holes near the top edge of the paper cup. The holes should be positioned opposite each other as in the four points of a compass. Help the children measure two lengths of string, each 3½ to 4 feet long. Lay both strings on the table next to each other. Determine the center point of the strings and make a knot there, tying the two pieces of string together. Ask the children to put the ends of the string through the holes in the paper cup and tie into place, one string per hole. Blow up the balloon and tie it shut. Place the balloon within the confines of the string, as if it were a hot air balloon. Tie an additional piece of string to the top of the balloon for hanging. Place a small piece of tape on top of the balloon to hold the string in place. Make adjustments in the lengths of the strings if necessary by untying them from the cup (one at a time) and reknotting them. Before hanging the balloon from the ceiling, the children may wish to place a small plastic passenger in the cup and give the passenger a ride by holding the top string and running with the balloon.

4. **TIRE TRACKS**. *Materials*: Miniature cars and motorcycles, paint, pie tins or other containers to hold paint, and paper. *Directions*: Spread a small amount of paint into each pie tin. Give the children the toy cars or motorcycles to dip into the paint. Allow the children to "drive" their vehicles over the paper.

5. **TRAFFIC SIGNS**. *Materials*: Cardboard for templates, red and yellow construction paper, craft sticks, black marking pens, and glue. *Directions*: Make templates out of the cardboard by drawing circles, rectangles, triangles, and octagons, and cutting them out. The octagons will serve as patterns for stop signs, the circles are for railroad crossings, the rectangles for speed limit signs and other warning signs, etc. Give the children the template of their choice to trace on the appropriate color of construction paper. Assist the children in cutting them out and printing on them with markers. The children will then glue the craft sticks to the back of the traffic signs. When dry, take turns holding up and identifying the signs.

6. **RAFTS**. *Materials*: Each child will need a Styrofoam meat tray, a pipe cleaner, a sail cut from the pattern (see figure 3.9, page 43), glue, and markers. *Directions*: Have the child decorate the sail with markers. When dry, let the child fold the sail in half and spread glue on the inside. Next, have the child place the pipe cleaner in the fold of the sail and press together. Allow the sail to dry before punching it through the center of the meat tray. Secure the pipe cleaner by bending the end on the underside of the raft.

(Text continues on page 44.)

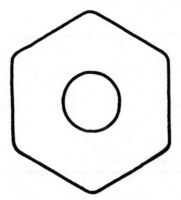

Fig. 3.4.

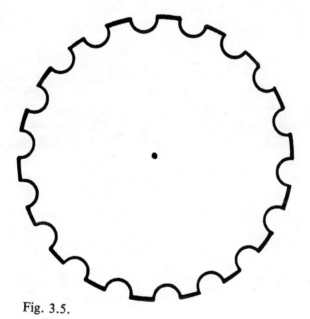

Fig. 3.5.

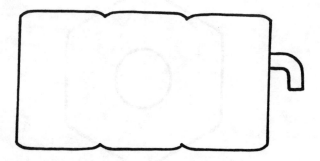

Fig. 3.6.

Fig. 3.7.

Fig. 3.8.

Fig. 3.8a.

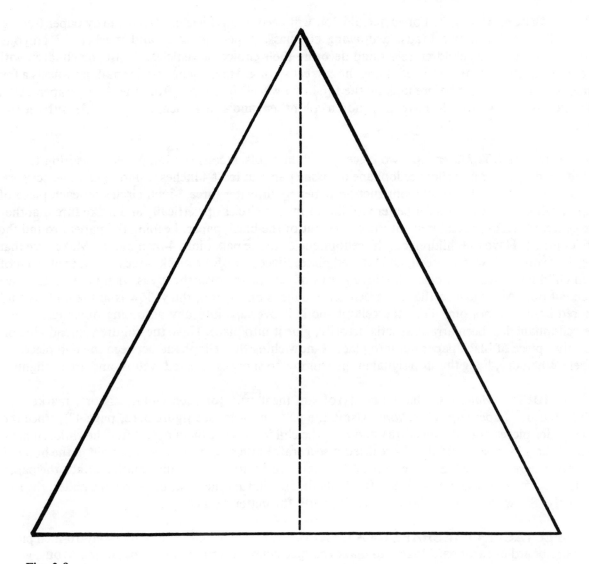

Fig. 3.9.

7. **WHEELS**. *Materials*: For each child you will need one vehicle cut from sturdy paper (see figures 3.10 and 3.11), two brads, a drawing compass, paper, scissors, and markers or crayons. *Directions*: Have the children select and decorate their choice of vehicles. Assist the children with the compass, helping them to determine the correct setting. Have them practice making wheels a few times with the compass before making the final two wheels to cut out from the sturdy paper. After they cut out the two wheels, have the children color them and attach them to the vehicle with the two brads.

8. **STOPLIGHT**. *Materials*: Two pieces per child of black construction paper measuring 12 by 6 inches; red, green, and yellow cellophane or tissue paper at least 4 inches square; glue; and scissors. *Directions*: Prepare the black construction paper by drawing three 3-inch circles on each piece of paper, using a white crayon for better visibility. Line the circles up vertically and make sure that they are centered. Help the children cut the circles out of the black paper, keeping the paper around the circles intact. Have the children cut the cellophane or tissue paper into 4-inch pieces. Make sure that they have one yellow, one green, and one red piece. Place one of the black pieces of paper in front of each child and have them place the three pieces of cellophane over the areas where the circles have been cut out. Arrange it so that the green cellophane is on the top, the yellow is in the middle, and the red is on the bottom. Trim the cellophane if it overlaps into any adjoining openings. When the cellophane has been arranged satisfactorily, glue it into place. Have the children spread glue on the other piece of black paper put into place, sandwiching the cellophane between the two pieces of paper. When dry, hang the stop signal in the window to show off the red, yellow and green "lights."

9. **GLIDERS**. *Materials*: One large Styrofoam meat tray for each child, scissors, markers or paint, and one paper clip. *Directions*: Using the pattern given (see figure 3.12, page 47), trace the three glider pieces onto the meat tray and help the children to cut them out. After the children have painted the glider parts and they have dried, use a craft knife or box cutter to cut a slit in the body of the craft where indicated. Slip the wing and the tail into position. Have the children attach the paper clip to the nose of the glider, and let it fly! Note that the harder the children throw the glider, the less it will fly. Show the children how to toss it gently for better results.

10. **SPECTACLES THE SHAPE OF A CAR**. *Materials*: Each child will need a 4-by-16-inch piece of poster board or cardboard, paper to make the spectacles pattern, markers, paint or crayons, glue, and glitter. *Directions*: To make a template for the spectacles (see figure 3.13, page 48), fold a 4-by-16-inch piece of paper in half. Place the center fold line of the pattern on the fold of the paper. Trace and cut out. Use this template to transfer the spectacles pattern onto the poster board. Cut out one pair of spectacles for each child. Ask the children to decorate the specs with paint, markers, or crayons adding headlights and door handles. When dry, help the children write their names across the side of the spectacles with glue. Have the children sprinkle glitter over the glue. Shake off the excess glitter and let dry. When the spectacles are dry, bend the earpieces back to fit each child.

(Text continues on page 49.)

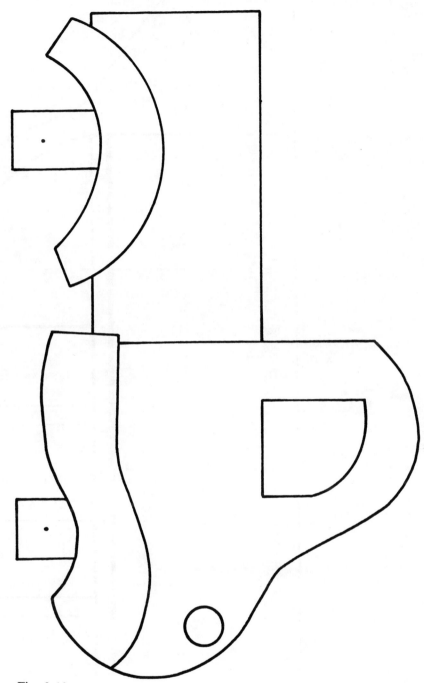

Fig. 3.10.

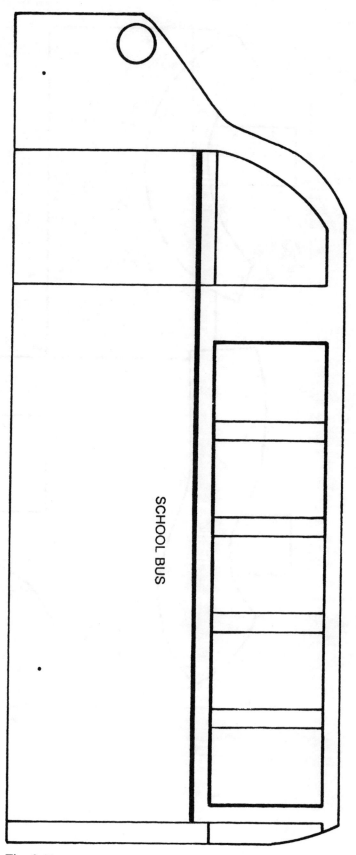

Fig. 3.11.

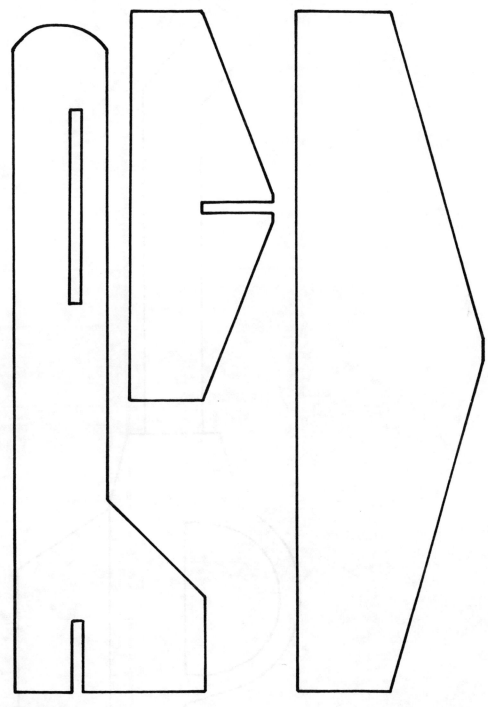

Fig. 3.12.

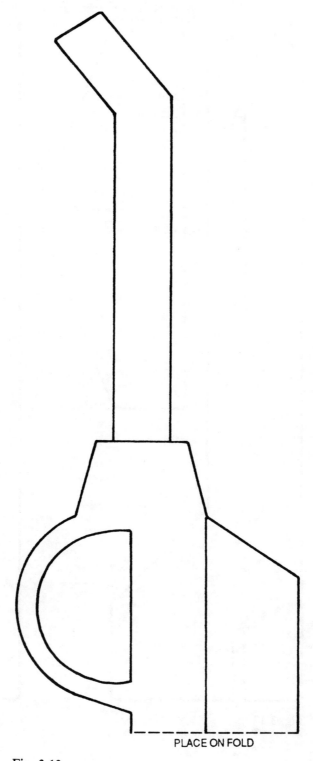

PLACE ON FOLD

Fig. 3.13.

Transportation Class Project

The Long, Long Train

Have each child bring a box to class from the grocery store. Stress that the boxes must be large enough to stand inside. Remove the box bottoms and decorate the boxes to look like train cars. The teacher could decorate his or hers to look like the engine. One of the teacher's aides could bring up the rear as a caboose. Punch two holes in the sides of the cars and pass cord through the holes to serve as handles or straps. If desired, the cars could be strung together with more cord. When the train is ready and the children are positioned in their own cars, go chugging out the door and all through the school.

Transportation Story Time

1. **COLORING BOOKS.** After the children have had time to become familiar with the books you have kept on display, ask them to point out their favorites. Discuss why they find the books appealing. On plain white paper, trace each child's favorite pictures. Place a plain sheet on top of the sheets with pictures and staple them together to make a coloring book. Help the children to write the name of the books on the plain top sheet.

2. **TO BE CONTINUED...** Often a picture book, although entertaining, is just too long for some children. Instead of struggling to read through books like *Curious George Rides a Bike* and *The Little Engine That Could* at once, read only a portion of the book. Later in the day, come back to the same book. Ask the children questions about the part that you have already read. Start reading again a page or two before your prior stopping place. You will be helping children develop their memories and concentration.

Another tactic for getting through longer than normal books is to paraphrase it. Read the book beforehand and decide what you are going to say. Instead of reading the book word-for-word, tell the story in your own words while showing the pictures. Children themselves often paraphrase books with which they have become familiar. Ask if some of the children would like to share one of their favorite books with the class in this manner.

Transportation Songs, Poems, Fingerplays

1. This is a freight train chugging down the track.
   (*Extend arm, run down and back with fingers*.)
   The whistle toot-toots, (*pull chain*.)
   And the wheels clack clack. (*bicycle arms*.)
   It carries wood and oil, and grain in a sack. (*heft sack onto back*.)
   Everyday it goes up north and then comes back. (*Extend arm again, run fingers up and down it*.)

2. **OLD BOMBAY.** (*Fill in the blanks*.)
   Ready, set, go! We're on our way,
   Off to visit old Bombay. First we'll ride on a _____ going on our way,
   As we travel to old Bombay.
   Next we'll catch a _____ going on our way, on our journey to old Bombay.

Then we'll hop aboard a _____ going on our way,
As we travel to old Bombay.
At last we'll jump on a _____ going our way,
On our journey to old Bombay.
Here we are at last in old Bombay. Traveling can be fun, if you know your way!

3. "Stop" says the red light
    "Go" says the green
    "Wait" says the yellow light (*blink*)
    Blinking in between.
    That's what they say (*stop*)
    That's what they mean (*go*)
    We all must obey them (*blink*)
    Even the queen. (*crown on head.*)

4. Engine, engine, Number Nine
    Running on Chicago Line.
    If she's polished, how she'll shine.
    Engine, engine, Number Nine.

5. A peanut sat on a railroad track,
    His heart was all a-flutter, (*flutter hand over heart.*)
    The Five-Fifteen came rushing by,
    Toot! Toot! (*pull chain.*)
    Peanut butter!

6. Dad goes on a train,
    It runs on the track.
    It takes him to town,
    And brings him back.

7. Up, up and away (*point up.*)
    I go in my balloon (*make a large circle with arms.*)
    I lean out and touch the clouds (*lean and touch.*)
    But wish to reach the moon! (*reach up.*)

8. Humblety Bumblety Pie!
    A plane can touch the sky.
    And if I knew how to fly
    Then so could I!

9. Unicycle, bicycle, tricycle, car.
    (*Hold up appropriate number of fingers for each.*)
    Whichever one you ride,
    It will take you far.

10. To the tune of "He's a Jolly Good Fellow":

I drove over the mountain, I drove over the mountain
(*Drive car*.)
I drove over the mountain to see what I could see.
(*Put hand on forehead to shade eyes*.)
But all that I could see, but all that I could see
Was the other side of the mountain, the other side of the mountain. The other side of the mountain was all that I could see.

Repeat with the following verses:

I sailed over the ocean. (*boat*)
I flew over the clouds. (*airplane*)
I rolled through the tunnel. (*train*)

Finish with:

I think I'll go back home, I think I'll go back home. I think I'll go back home, I've seen all I want to see!

Transportation Music List

Cassettes

"A Bicycle Built for Two." *Disney's Children's Favorites, Vol. 1*. Walt Disney Music Co. 606054, 1979.

"Down by the Station." *Disney's Children's Favorites, Vol. 4*. Walt Disney Music Co. 606084, 1990.

"Dump Truck Song." *Disney's Children's Favorites, Vol. 2*. Walt Disney Music Co. 606064, 1979.

"I've Been Working on the Railroad." *Disney's Children's Favorites, Vol. 1*. Walt Disney Music Co. 606054, 1979.

"Michael, Row the Boat Ashore." *Disney's Children's Favorites, Vol. 3*. Walt Disney Music Co. 606074, 1986.

"Row, Row, Row Your Boat." *Disney's Children's Favorites, Vol. 1*. Walt Disney Music Co. 606054, 1979.

"Wabash Cannonball." *Disney's Children's Favorites, Vol. 4*. Walt Disney Music Co. 606084, 1990.

"Wheels on the Bus." *Disney's Children's Favorites, Vol. 4*. Walt Disney Music Co. 606084, 1990.

Transportation Book List

Fiction

Burningham, John. *Mr. Gumpy's Motor Car.* Thomas Crowell, 1973.
   Mr. Gumpy takes the locals for a ride, only to be rained on and stuck in the mud.

Calhoun, Mary. *Hot Air Henry.* Illustrated by Erick Ingraham. William Morrow, 1981.
   This is a beautifully illustrated story about a cat who accidentally solos in a hot air balloon.

Ehrlich, Amy. *The Everyday Train.* Illustrated by Martha Alexander. Dial Press, 1977.
   Jane watches the local train go by every day as she waves to the engineer.

Gay, Michel. *Take Me for a Ride.* William Morrow, 1983.
   This is a charming and simple story about a toddler and his stroller.

Newton, Laura P. *William the Vehicle King.* Illustrated by Jacqueline Rogers. Bradbury Press, 1987.
   William uses all of his toys to make a bustling city in his own bedroom.

Piper, Wally. *The Little Engine That Could.* Illustrated by George Hauman and Doris Hauman. Platt and Munk, 1954.
   Little Engine saves the day when the dolls and toys need help bringing good food to eat over the mountain to all the good little boys and girls on the other side.

Rey, H. A. *Curious George Rides a Bike.* Houghton Mifflin, 1952.
   That mischievous little monkey rides again!

Thomas, Jane Resh. *Wheels.* Illustrated by Emily Arnold McCully. Clarion Books, 1986.
   Wheels is the story of a little boy's first bike race.

Nonfiction

The following nonfiction books provide simple illustrations and text about vehicles (and their trappings) that children want to know more about. These books are extremely useful if put on display in the reading area of the classroom.

Barton, Byron. *Airport.* Harper and Row, 1982.

Crews, Donald. *Bicycle Race.* Greenwillow, 1985.

_____. *Flying.* Greenwillow, 1986.

_____. *Freight Train.* Greenwillow, 1978.

_____. *School Bus.* Greenwillow, 1984.

_____. *Truck.* Greenwillow, 1980.

Gibbons, Gail. *Boat Book*. Holiday Press, 1983.

_____. *Trucks*. Thomas Crowell, 1981.

Rockwell, Anne. *Bikes*. E. P. Dutton, 1987.

Poems and Rhymes

Siebert, Diane. *Truck Song*. Illustrated by Byron Barton. Harper and Row, 1984.

Stuart, Doris. *All Aboard*. Western Publishing, 1988.

4
DOWN ON THE FARM
(Farm)

Focus on the Farm

From the first time children hear "Old MacDonald Had a Farm," they are hooked on farm animals and the sounds the animals make. The learning experiences in this chapter will expand the children's knowledge of farm animals and introduce the concept that food does *not* grow on supermarket shelves!

Consider discussing these subjects:
    Farm animals: babies, sounds, homes
    Farm products
    Agriculture
    Farms end nomadic lifestyle of our ancestors
    Farm chores
    Plant growth
    Planting and harvesting

Farm Motor Skills

1. **DRIVE THE PIG TO MARKET.** Use a large ball for the pig, and a sturdy ruler or stick to push the "pig" forward. Ask the children to take turns pushing the ball along with the stick, driving the pig to market. Once they have mastered the basics, see if the children can manage to maneuver the pig along a designated path or through a simple obstacle course.

2. **FARM CHORES.** Sing the following song while vigorously acting out jobs one might need to do while working on a farm:

> This is the way we _____.
> This is the way we _____.
> So early in the morning.

Some possible chores to perform might include mowing the hay, feeding the chicks, sow the seeds, pull the weeds, hoe the field, etc.

3. **FARM TAG.** One child is "it." The other players line up along one side of the play yard. The child who is it yells a command, such as "Strut like a turkey," or "Skip like a lamb." The players must cross to the other side of the yard in such a manner, trying not to be caught by the person who is it. The first child to be caught becomes it.

4. **THE FARMER IN THE DELL.** Have all but one of the children join hands in a circle. The extra child is the "farmer" and stands in the center of the circle. The children circle to the right and begin singing:

> The farmer in the dell, the farmer in the dell,
> Hi Ho the Derry-O, the farmer in the dell.

The farmer in the center of the circle selects a child to stand in the center with him or her as the song continues:

> The farmer takes a wife, the farmer takes a wife,
> Hi Ho the Derry-O, the farmer takes a wife.

Continue the song, each time the latest addition to the center of the circle selecting the next child.

> The wife takes the child, the wife takes the child,
> Hi Ho the Derry-O, the wife takes the child.
> The child takes the nurse...
> The nurse takes the dog...
> The dog takes the cat...
> The cat takes the rat...
> The rat takes the cheese...
> The cheese stands alone...

On the last verse, all of the children encircle the "cheese," clapping hands and jumping up and down in time to the song. If there are children who had no turn as a character in the song, the cheese becomes the farmer as the game begins again.

5. **WHEELBARROW.** Have the children each select a partner. One child will be the farmer, the other will be the wheelbarrow. The child who decides to be the wheelbarrow rests on the floor on hands and knees. The child's ankles become the handles of the wheelbarrow as the farmer grasps them and stands up. The activity is set in motion when the pair start walking forward, the wheelbarrow using his or her hands while the farmer holds up the child's feet. When the wheelbarrow tires out, have the children trade roles.

6. **RELAY RACES.** Divide the children into teams of five or six children each. Place a line on the floor with chalk or masking tape for the teams to stand behind. Designate a spot several yards away for the children to race to before returning to those next in line. Continue the race until each child on the team has had a turn. Some common relays include the potato sack race in which each child steps into a cloth bag and hops, the wheelbarrow walk listed in the previous activity, and the potato relay. The potato relay consists of each child using a spoon to carry a potato to the line and back without dropping it.

7. **ANIMAL TAG.** Place a different farm animal sticker or cutout on the arm of each child where it can be seen. Select one child to be "it." The remaining children stand in a circle around the child who is it, who calls out the names of two farm animals. The children with those animals on their sleeves must quickly leave their homes in the circle and try to trade places with each other. The child who is it tries to get to one of their homes first. The child left without a home starts the next round as it.

8. **DUCK, DUCK, GOOSE.** All of the children but one sit in a circle on the floor facing the center. The one child left standing goes around the outside of the circle, tapping each child on the head, each time saying "duck." After several times, the child must say "goose!" as he or she taps one last child. This child must jump up and chase "it" around the outside of the circle. If it reaches the "goose's" spot first and sits down, he or she is safe and the goose becomes it. If the goose reaches home first, it must start over again.

9. **TURKEY STRUT.** Use masking tape to make turkey footprints on the floor as illustrated (see figure 4.1). Put the footprints all over the room. Play a tape of the song "Turkey in the Straw" or some other farm music. Invite the children to act like turkeys, strutting around the room and gobbling as the music plays. When the music stops, the turkeys must quickly find a pair of turkey prints on which to stand. When the music resumes, the turkeys strut around the room again. If you wish, play this game as you would musical chairs, removing a set of prints each time the music stops.

Fig. 4.1.

10. **PETER RABBIT.** Use the pattern (see figure 4.2) given to make a rabbit on stiff cardboard, about 12 inches tall. Cut the rabbit out and punch a hole just below the rabbit's head. Thread a 10-foot piece of string through the hole. Tie one end of the string to a chair leg just high enough for the rabbit's back legs to rest on the floor. Ask a child to hold the other end of the string, and slide the rabbit to that end. The child can make the rabbit hop by pulling on the string.

Farm Language Activities

1. **RHYMING.** Say a simple word such as egg, cow, hen, or pig, and ask the children to call out words that rhyme. Write the words on the blackboard. To extend this activity, read or tell the story of Chicken Little, in which all the characters have rhyming names.

Next, say a word and ask the children to say as many words as they can that start with the same sound. Write that letter or consonant blend on the blackboard.

2. **BABY ANIMAL SOUNDS.** Select one child to be the mother or father farm animal. The best animals to choose would be sheep, chickens, or cows. Take the mother farm animal to a remote corner of the room and have the animal hide its eyes. Choose one or two of the remaining children to be the babies. All of the children must cover their mouths, as the mother returns to find her babies. The children chosen to be the babies make tiny baas or peeps or moos. The mother or father must listen very carefully to find the babies.

3. **FARMER'S TRUCK.** Place several plastic fruits and vegetables on the table. Using a toy phone, pretend to be the grocer and place a call to the child, who pretends to be the farmer. Name two or three specific items for the farmer to place in his or her toy truck for delivery. The better the child becomes at the game, the more items the grocer can request for delivery.

4. **SPEAK!** Select one child to be the farmer. The remaining children are the animals. The farmer sits on a chair with his or her back to the other children. Quietly choose one animal to tap the farmer on the shoulder. The farmer says, "Speak, _____, speak," filling in the blank with the name of an animal. The animal who tapped the farmer on the shoulder makes the appropriate animal sound until the farmer guesses the child's name. That child becomes the farmer for the next round.

5. **EGG CARTON LETTERS.** In an egg carton, write one lowercase letter in each section. On Ping Pong balls or plastic eggs, write the corresponding uppercase letter. The child's task is to place the egg in the section with the corresponding lowercase letter.

6. **EGG CARTON COLORS.** To help with color identification, paint each section of an egg carton a different color. Provide small items in corresponding colors such as marbles, crayons, small plastic toys, or plastic eggs. The child's job will be to place each item in the matching section of the egg carton, and then say the color out loud. To spice up the game, use unusual colors such as magenta or turquoise, and provide more than one item per color.

7. **FARM SOUNDS.** Ask the children what sounds different farm animals and machines make, such as a chicken, chick, rooster, pig, tractor, horse neighing, horse galloping, etc. Have all the children give their own renditions of the sounds.

ENLARGE

Fig. 4.2.

8. **FARM SHAPES**. Cut out shapes of farm items that go together such as: hen and nest, chick and egg shell, horse and wagon, pig and trough, cow and milk bucket, etc. Protect the cutouts by covering them with clear adhesive paper. Mix up the items and see if the children can find the correct pairs. Discuss why the pairs go together.

9. **SING ALONG**. Using farm animal sounds, sing a simple phrase. Ask the children to imitate you. For more fun, sing songs such as "Happy Birthday to You" or "Mary Had a Little Lamb" using animal sound voices.

10. **HOW NOW, BROWN COW**. Make a different cow for each child and a duplicate set for yourself. Give each child a cow. Pick one from your stack and pin it to the bulletin board. Have the children look at their cows. If the children think that they have a match to the one on the board, let them bring them up and pin them next to your cow. Have the children examine the cows closely. If they match, have the children say, "How now, brown cow!" If the cows do not match, the children should take the cow back and continue to watch for a match.

Farm Math Activities

1. **BIG RED BARN**. Cut a barn shape from a large sheet of red poster board. Cut five to ten flaps or doors on the front of the barn, depending on how much room you have. Glue the barn sheet to another sheet of poster board the same size or larger. On the top of each flap, draw a set of chicks, hens, roosters, cows, horses, or other animals. Farm animal stickers may also be used. Under the flap, on the back sheet, write the numeral that corresponds to the number of animals on the flap. Ask the children to count how many animals are on each flap. They can check their answers by lifting the flap and revealing the numeral underneath.

2. **EGG TOSS**. Number the sections of an egg carton with a marking pen. Choose the numbers 1 through 12, or any other numbers you wish to teach. If teaching very young children, use only a few numbers and repeat them two or three times. Pretend a Ping Pong ball is an egg. Ask the child to toss the egg into any section of the egg carton, and have the child call out the number of the section in which the egg lands.

3. **HOW MANY?** Give the child two to three sets of small plastic farm animals to sort by species, putting each group into a corral or pen made from blocks. Help the child count the number of animals in each pen and write the numeral down on an index card.

4. **A DOZEN EGGS**. Number twelve eggs or Ping Pong balls 1 through 12 with paint or a marking pen. Have the child place the eggs in numerical order in an egg carton. To make the activity easier for younger children, write the appropriate numeral in the bottom of each section of the egg carton. Talk about the word "dozen." What other items are sold by the dozen?

5. **BAG IT**. Use brown paper bags and food items such as small pieces of fruit (crab apples, tangerines, or plums), new potatoes, or carrots. Place the fruit or vegetables in the bags, giving each a different amount, and have the children identify which bags contain the most and the fewest items. Ask them to count the items and then write the appropriate numeral on the outside of the bag.

6.   **MATCH 'EM UP.** Make number cards by writing the numerals 1 through 10 on index cards. Using stickers of farm animals, make picture cards with sets of items to match the number cards. Mix the cards up. The child's task will be to match the number card to the picture card containing the appropriate number of items.

7.   **HENNY HEN.** Make a nest by placing Easter grass in a basket or box. Place a number of Ping Pong balls or plastic eggs in the nest, and top them with a toy chicken. Ask the children to guess how many eggs Henny Hen has laid. Lift her up and have the children count the eggs. How many are there? Was the guess more or fewer than the actual number? Have the children close their eyes while you change the number of eggs in the nest.

8.   **FEED THE ANIMALS.** Place a toy animal of your choice on the table. In front of the animal, place a tin pie plate. Provide the child with a pan containing uncooked oats or popcorn, and a scoop to feed the animal. Consult with the child on how many scoops of food the animal should eat, then help the child place that many scoops of food into the pan. Pretend the animal eats all of the food. How many more scoops should the animal be fed?

9.   **FRUIT TREE.** Make a large tree out of felt and place it on the flannel board. Cut out several small red circles to represent apples; other colored circles can represent oranges, plums, lemons, etc. Place one of the types of fruit on the tree and a felt numeral on the flannel board next to it. Ask the children to identify the number, and then "pick" that many pieces of fruit from the tree.

10.   **NUMBER NECKLACE.** Use animal cookie cutters as patterns to cut farm animal shapes from construction paper. Ask each child to select 10 cutouts. Using a paper punch, help the children punch a hole in the top of each shape. Have the children write the numbers 1 through 10, one number per cutout, or have them write the numbers 1 through 12 for an even dozen. Help the children string the shapes in numerical order on a length of yarn. Tie the yarn around their necks to make necklaces.

Farm Science Activities

1.   **BEES, PLEASE!** Most people think of bees as pests thanks to their painful sting. Bees are important to flowering plants, however. Without bees, flowering plants would have to rely on the wind for fertilization. By providing man-made hives for them to live in and flowering plants for them to get food from, many farmers take pains to attract bees. The bees in turn, do the farmer a favor. A bee flies from flower to flower, collecting nectar and ripe pollen on its hairy legs. Eventually the bee flies home with this burden, but not before dropping some of the pollen on the sticky tip of a plant's stigma. The pollen then moves down into the ovary of the plant, finds the ripe ovum, and joins with it, making a new seed.

Flowering plants attract bees with their bright colors and sweet fragrance. Try attracting some of your own bees. Obtain some freshly cut, newly opened, sweet-smelling flowers. Place them in a jar or bowl of water on the outside windowsill. If one bee finds the bait, it will fly back to the hive and tell the other bees about it. From the safety of the classroom, children will soon see many bees collecting nectar and pollen.

2.   **THE INCREDIBLE, EDIBLE COW.** Cows provide many food and other products to humans. Assemble as many of these products as possible in the classroom to sample: milk, various cheeses

from cottage cheese to cheddar, hamburger or other cuts of cooked meat, cold cuts such as beef bologna or hot dogs. Display a piece of cowhide and leather shoes or clothing for the children to touch and feel.

3. **ANIMAL MATCH.** Make animal cards by gluing or drawing pictures of adult farm animals, their babies, and the products they provide on separate index cards. Examples: adult cow, calf, dairy products; sheep, lamb, wool clothing; hen, chick, eggs.

Mix up the cards and ask the children to match the adult animal to the baby animal, and to match the animal to the product it provides. Can the children say the name of the adult animal? The baby animal? Imitate the animal sound? Think of more animal products?

4. **LET'S EAT!** Most of our food is grown on farms. The foods and vegetables we eat come from all the major plant parts: roots, stems, flowers, leaves, ovaries, and seeds. Make a poster of a plant showing all of its parts. Bring foods to class that represent these parts. Help the children to classify the foods according to their edible parts.

Roots: Onions, garlic, carrots, potatoes, beets, yams, peanuts. Show the children the root of the plant on the poster. Point out any feeder roots still clinging to the vegetables. When tasting the root foods, ask the children if they notice that the roots taste sweet. This is due to the stored starches in the root.

Stems: Rhubarb, asparagus, celery. Show the children the long, thin stem of the plant on the poster. Explain how water travels through the root and up the stem of the plant to the leaves. If you wish, place a stalk of celery in a glass of colored water and watch the celery change color.

Leaves: Lettuce, spinach, cabbage. Show the children the leaves of the plant on the poster. What color are the leaves of the plant? They are green because they contain chlorophyll, which turns light into food for the plant. You will notice that the spinach leaves are all very green because they sit loosely together and are all exposed to the light. The cabbages and lettuce, however, have their darkest leaves on the outside layers and fade to white on the inside. The leaves on the inside are tightly packed and see little or no light. The darker green the leaves are, the more nutritious they are.

Flower: Broccoli, cauliflower, artichokes. Point out the flower on your poster. These vegetable flowers hardly look like flowers at all because they are barely budding. If they were left in the ground to grow, you would see some flowers that seem more familiar. Sometimes broccoli is picked a little late and tiny yellow flowers appear. Look at these tiny specks with a magnifying glass.

Ovaries: The ovary is the part of the plant that holds the seed. The fruits we eat are ovaries: oranges, apples, peaches, pears, grapes, etc. Pumpkins, squashes, cucumbers, green beans, and tomatoes all hold the seed of the plant and are all fruits.

Seeds: Corn, peas, nuts, lima beans. Some seeds we eat, others we discard. We eat corn, peas, the seeds in strawberries, all types of beans, etc. We discard the seeds from watermelons, oranges or grapefruit, and apples. These seeds would not hurt us if we did eat them since they are actually nutritious. The seeds of a plant are nutritious because they contain all the stored up food a tiny plant will need to continue life outside the ovary.

5. **ROOTS AND STEMS.** To illustrate that stems always grow up toward the sun and roots always grow down into the earth, place a square of fine gauze over the top of a glass and fasten it on with a rubber band. Place the glass in a dish to catch the extra water that spills over. Fill the glass to the brim with water, and sprinkle some fast-growing seeds on the gauze. For the first few days, make sure that there is enough water in the glass to keep the gauze wet. After three or four days the seeds will sprout. Observe that the stems grow upward and the roots grow downward.

To extend this activity and show that the plants cannot be tricked into growing the wrong way, place the seedlings on a wet paper towel. Place the paper towel between two panes of clear glass measuring at least 6 inches in diameter. (Borrow the glass from two picture frames, if necessary.) Use rubber bands to hold the glass panes together. Place the apparatus in a shallow dish of water in a sunny window. Every two days, turn the glass to a different side. The plant stems and roots will switch direction.

6. **LITTLE SPROUTS.** There are a variety of creative ways to germinate seeds for a garden to be planted later. Some of these include:

Sponge plant: Securely staple a piece of string to each corner of a square or rectangular sponge. Place seeds on the sponge and dampen it, then tie the strings together and hang in a sunny window. Water as needed. (Or simply keep the seeds on a damp sponge on the window sill.)

Potato plant: Place a potato on its side in a dish. Scrape out some of the potato, forming an indentation on one side. Sprinkle seeds in the indentation and place near a sunny window. The seeds should germinate in a few days, before the potato has dried out. If the potato dries out, add a little water.

Jar method: This works well with popcorn or lima beans. Soak the seeds overnight. The next day, place crumpled paper towels in an open glass jar. Pour ½ inch of water into the jar. Place the seeds between the glass and the towel so that you can observe them as they grow. Place in a sunny area. Add water as needed to keep the paper towels moist.

Paper cups: Fill a paper cup with potting soil, sprinkle fine seeds over the top of the soil. Add water. Seeds the size of apple seeds may be planted about 1 inch deep, and larger seeds should be planted 3 to 4 inches deep. Two or three of the medium seeds may be planted in one cup. If it is a large seed, plant only one per cup.

Plants from cuttings: It is important for the children to realize that plants do not always have to be grown from seeds; they may also grow from cuttings or by planting the root. Start a sweet potato plant by placing three or four toothpicks around the middle of a sweet potato. Place the bottom half of the potato in a clear jar filled with water. In a sunny area, the roots will start to grow immediately, followed soon by new shoots springing from the top half of the potato.

A regular potato that has sprouted eyes may be planted. Cut the potato into sections, including at least one eye in each section. Plant 4 to 6 inches deep in potting soil.

Many houseplants may be grown from stem clippings. Try placing cuttings from a pothos aureus or arrowhead philodendron or coleus in a clear jar of water. After the roots sprout and become several inches long, replant in a new pot of soil.

7. **LITTLE FARMERS**. Now that the class has sprouted its own seeds (check with your nursery to find out which vegetables grow quickly in your area), it is time to transplant them in soil. You may choose to send the seedlings home with the children or start a classroom garden. If a garden plot is not part of your school's outside area, or if it is too cold for a garden outside, plant a container garden inside. For each type of vegetable you wish to plant, fill a plastic tub or wooden box with the following soil mixture: half potting soil, one quarter soil from outside, one quarter sand. Make sure that there are drainage holes in the bottom of the container before planting, or place a 1-inch deep layer of gravel in the bottom of the tub. For each little sprout, have the children make a hole as deep as the root of the plant and place the sprout into the soil, patting the soil firmly around the base of the plant. Place the sprouts 3 or 4 inches apart, depending on the plant. Place the containers in a sunny area and water them regularly. The children's patience will be rewarded some day with a school-grown snack.

Farm Art Projects

1. **SEED COLLAGE**. *Materials*: Provide each child with one large piece of green construction paper, glue, and several types of inexpensive dried seeds and beans, such as popcorn, lima beans, pinto beans, and navy beans. *Directions*: Ask the children to squeeze out a long stripe of glue along the length of their paper. Have them spread the glue slightly, keeping the long thin shape, and sprinkle one type of seed along the glue stripe. They should make two or three more stripes of glue, adding different types of seeds to each. The finished collage should remind one of the rows of seeds planted in a garden.

2. **SEED JAR**. *Materials*: Each child will need one tall glass jar with a lid, paint, a paintbrush, and several types of dried seeds or beans such as popcorn, lima beans, pinto beans, or barley, and a scoop or small cup. *Directions*: Ask the children to paint the jar lids the color of their choice. While the lid dries, ask the children to fill the jar with several layers of seeds. Have them scoop enough seeds into the jar to cover the bottom to about 1 inch high. Without shaking or moving the jar, have them select a different type of seed for the second layer. When the second layer is about 1 inch high, have them choose a third type of seed. Have the children continue until the seeds reach the top of the jar. Place the dried lid on the jar and screw tightly shut. This decoration looks good on a kitchen counter and also makes a fine bookend.

3. **MILK CARTON BARN**. *Materials*: Each child will need a ½- or 1-pint cardboard milk carton, red paint, a paintbrush, and black paint or marker. The teacher will need a box cutter or craft knife. *Directions*: Have the child paint the entire milk carton with red paint. After it has dried, use the box cutter to cut a door and window in the carton. When the window and door are cut, the child may complete the barn by painting the roof black and outlining the door and window in black. When completely dry, the child may use the barn as a home for small plastic farm animals.

4. **BARNYARD MURAL**. *Materials*: A long sheet of butcher paper, paint, a paintbrush for each child, markers or crayons, glue, and rice. *Directions*: Draw a barn and the surrounding barnyard on the butcher paper. Paint the children's palms the color of their choice, and ask them to press it onto the mural in the appropriate area. Quickly wash the paint off the children's hands. When dry, ask the children to draw a face and feet onto each handprint, transforming it into a rooster or a turkey. After the paint has dried, have the children add more color by coloring the ground and sky with crayons or markers. Have the children glue the rice onto the mural near the poultry. This is their chicken scratch. When dry, hang up on the wall.

If you wish, individual poultry pictures may be created in the same manner. Provide small barns cut from construction paper to glue to a 9-by-11-inch sheet of plain paper, and add handprints and rice as directed above.

5. **CAROL CATERPILLAR.** *Materials*: Various colors of construction paper cut in circles 2 to 3 inches in diameter, glue, scissors, markers, and one pipe cleaner per child. *Directions*: Ask the children to select as many circles as they would like to glue together. Have them glue the circles end to end to make a caterpillar's body. On the first circle they will draw a face with the markers. Finally, have them cut two short lengths of the pipe cleaner to glue onto the head as antennae. Younger children may have an easier time of the gluing if they can glue the circles onto a sheet of construction paper, rather than making a free-form caterpillar.

6. **BABY CHICK.** *Materials*: Each child will need one cotton ball and one eggshell, glue, powdered yellow paint, a zippered plastic bag, a paper punch, scissors, and black construction paper scraps. *Directions*: Place some powdered yellow paint and several cotton balls into the plastic bag. Shake the bag, coating the cotton balls with the yellow paint. Ask the children to glue one yellow cotton ball onto their eggshells. Show them how to use the hole punch to punch two black circles to use for the chick's eyes. Ask them to cut a tiny triangle from a corner of the paper to make a beak. With small drops of glue, have them glue the eyes and beak in place on the cotton ball. Let the chick dry in a section of an empty egg carton.

7. **LAMBKIN.** *Materials*: Each child will need one lamb (see figure 4.3, page 66) cut from cardboard, cotton balls, glue, markers, and two spring-type clothespins. *Directions*: Provide each of the children with one cardboard lamb cut from the given pattern. Next, have the children color in the lamb's facial features with markers. Ask the children to spread glue over one side of the lamb, except for the head. That side of the lamb should be covered with cotton balls. Let the lamb dry slightly before repeating the process on the other side. Show the children how to clip the clothespins to the lamb's belly to make four legs for it to stand on. Stand the lamb up to dry completely.

8. **POP UP CORN.** *Materials*: Each child will need a craft stick, a 6-ounce or larger paper cup, a Styrofoam meat tray with a textured surface, paint, glue, and green construction paper. *Directions*: Use the patterns given (see figure 4.4, page 67) to cut leaves out of construction paper and ears of the corn out of the Styrofoam for each child. (The "good cutters" of the class might try their own cutting.) Ask the children to paint their ears of corn yellow and their craft stick green. Next, glue the ears of corn and leaves to the craft stick as illustrated. When these have dried thoroughly, cut a small slit in the bottom of the paper cup for the craft stick to fit into snugly. The children may then surprise friends by having them look into the cups only to see an ear of corn pop right up from it. Another option would be to make flowers rather than ears of corn.

9. **PIG PUPPET.** *Materials*: Each child will need 1½ paper plates, pink paint, a paintbrush, markers, pink construction paper, scissors, and a stapler. *Directions*: Ask the children to paint the entire outside of their paper plates pink. When the plates have dried, ask them to use the markers to create the facial features of a pig on the whole plate. Ask them to cut two triangular ears from the construction paper and glue into place. Fold the ears forward for a three-dimensional effect. (A picture of a pig would be useful as an example for the children to model their own pigs after.) When the pig's ears have dried in place, supervise the children in stapling the half paper plate to the back of the whole paper plate, forming a pocket. The children can put their hands in the pocket and use the pigs as puppets.

Fig. 4.3.

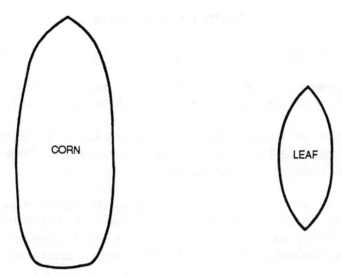

CORN

LEAF

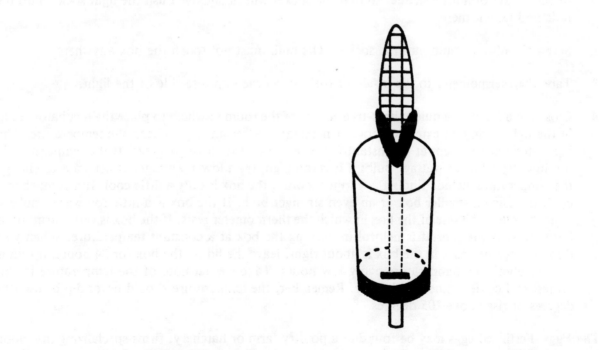

Fig. 4.4.

Farm Class Project

Hatching Chicks from Eggs

Hatching chicks from eggs may sound like a complicated project, but with a little advance planning, it makes a very satisfying activity. The chicks are the ones doing the work, after all!

The first and most important item is to make sure that you have a home for the chicks once they have hatched. Do not even consider this project until arrangements have been made for the babies to live at the school indefinitely, or to be adopted or sent to a farm.

The Incubator. The incubator may be purchased or made from scratch. Natural Science Industries, a company in Far Rockaway, New York, sells an inexpensive incubator stocked with quail eggs.* Baby quails make wonderful pets! Incubators may also be found in the Sears Roebuck catalog. If you do not wish to purchase one, an incubator is a simple item to make yourself. Here are the basic directions:

Materials: One cardboard carton in which you have replaced one side with glass so that the children may view the chicks, a light socket containing a 60-watt bulb, electrical tape, a thermometer, a small dish of warm water, a large wad of cotton, and thermostat (optional).

1. Cut a hole in the center of one end of the box, near the bottom. The hole should be the size of the socket or a little smaller so that the socket will fit snugly. Push the light socket into the hole and tape it there.

2. Screw the 60-watt bulb into the socket. The bulb must not touch the box anywhere.

3. Tape the thermometer to the inside of the box on the opposite side of the light.

4. Close the lid. Select a quiet, draft-free corner of the room in which to place the incubator. Plug in the light, using an extension cord if necessary. After an hour, check the temperature. The incubator must be kept at a constant temperature of 101 to 104 degrees. If the temperature is too low, try a higher-wattage bulb; if it is too high, try a lower wattage. Other ways to change the temperature include finding a warmer room if the box is only a little cool. If it is much too cool, try using a smaller box or an even stronger bulb. If the box is a little too warm, poke a ½-inch hole in the side of the box in which the thermometer rests. If the box is very warm, try a larger box. A thermostat is helpful in keeping the box at a constant temperature. When you think the temperature in the box is about right, leave the lid on the box for 24 hours, opening only to check the temperature every few hours. Take special note of the temperature in the hottest and coldest times of the day. Remember, the temperature should never dip below 100 degrees or rise above 105 degrees.

The Eggs. Fertilized eggs may be found at a poultry farm or hatchery, firms specializing in school science projects, or possibly pet shops. A feed store may know of a supplier or allow you to post a notice on their bulletin board. Obtain a minimum of six eggs, since all of them may not hatch. Find out from your supplier when the eggs were laid. The projected hatching day will be 21 days from that day. Listen to any advice the egg supplier might give you.

---

*Natural Science Industries, 15-17 Rockaway Beach Boulevard, Far Rockaway, NY 11691, (718) 945-5400.

1. Treat the eggs very gently and do not handle them more than necessary. It is a good idea to wash your hands before touching the eggs since oils from your skin may block the pores of the egg shell. Do not wash the eggs or the chicks inside will drown.

2. Place the eggs together in a wad of cotton placed in the middle of the box. Using a pencil, make a small dot on each egg, on the side that is currently facing up. Place a small dish of warm water in the box with the eggs. The eggs need the humidity which is normally supplied by the mother's body.

3. After placing the eggs and water in the box, close the lid and leave them alone for 24 to 48 hours. (If the eggs are a day or two old, skip this step.) Do not tape the lid or seal it too tightly, as the chicks need air to survive.

4. After the 24- to 48-hour period, turn each egg over. The pencil mark will now be facing down. Add warm water to the dish if any has evaporated.

5. Turn the eggs over twice each day, once in the morning and once in the evening. Arrange for someone to turn the eggs on the weekend. It may be wise to keep a chart, logging each time the eggs have been turned. After one week, the box may be opened for 20 minutes once each day to allow them to cool a bit. This cooling time would correspond to the length of time the mother hen would leave the nest to feed. Remember to add water when necessary, to not handle the eggs more than necessary, and to wash hands before handling!

6. On day 20, leave the eggs alone. They will begin to hatch in the next 24 hours.

The Chicks. Do not help the chicks hatch; the struggle is necessary. The chicks need this exercise to help make them strong. Also, a chick that cannot get out of the egg by itself would probably be too weak to survive anyway.

1. After the chicks have had ample time to hatch using a tiny tooth on the top of their beaks, throw away the broken shells and the unhatched eggs. Leave the chicks alone for 24 hours. They will use this time to finish eating the yolk which has been nourishing them for the past three weeks and to dry off.

2. The chicks will be fragile at first and need your help to survive. If you will be keeping the chicks at the school, make a brooder for them. If they will be given away, provide instructions for the adopting parents and make sure they have assembled the brooder before sending the chicks home with them.

   To make a brooder, use a roomy, tall carton. Take the light from the incubator and change to a 15-watt bulb. Suspend it from a yardstick or dowel taped across the top of the box. Wind the cord around the yardstick until the light bulb is perched two inches above the bottom of the carton. Tape it into place. Line the bottom of the box with several layers of newspaper, and place a shallow water dish or a pet water bottle in the box as well. Change the newspaper every day to keep the box clean. Change the water often.

3. When the chicks are dry, place them in the brooder. The chicks are too cold if they huddle near the light. They normally will only gather around the light when they sleep or periodically to warm up. If the chicks seem to be too cold, put in a 25-watt bulb. The temperature near the light should be in the 90-degree range.

4. After 24 hours the chicks may start pecking and scratching. This means that they are hungry! Scatter a small bit of chicken scratch (found at feed stores) on the bottom of the box.

5. After two days, feed the chicks a small dish of chick mash (found at feed stores) twice a day. Take the dish away after 10 minutes. If they eat all the chick mash sooner than in 10 minutes, increase the amount that you feed them.

6. After one week, find a place for the chicks to run around. Exercise is essential to their good health. If they start to huddle together, however, they have become chilled and should be placed in their box to warm up. Also after one week, you may feed the chicks some chopped lettuce and tiny bits of cooked egg yolk.

7. When the chicks have reached two weeks old, let them exercise outside as much as the weather permits. At one month, the chicks will have their adult feathers. They can now live on their own outside with no brooder, unless you are in a very cold climate. Provide the chickens with shelter, food, and a place to perch and they will live happy, healthy lives!

Farm Story Time

1. **BIG RED BARN.** In many farm books, the main action takes place in the big red barn. Cut a large red barn from paper and staple it to the bulletin board within reach of the children. Make paper cutouts of the animal characters who live in the barn. When introducing the farm story, give a cutout to each child. When the story is over, the children may tack their animal characters to the bulletin board, in or around the big red barn.

2. **OLD MACDONALD.** After reading a farm story, join in a rousing rendition of "Old MacDonald Had a Farm," using the animal characters in the book you have just read. This is a good way to review the story, and the song may be used as an introduction the next time you read the book.

3. **BOOK TAPE.** Select a book in which the animal characters squawk, crow, oink, and neigh. Tape yourself as you read the book, letting a different child provide each different animal sound effect. Leave the tape and the book in the reading corner for the children to listen to as they turn the pages.

Farm Poems, Songs, Fingerplays

1. The big brown hen and Mrs. Duck
    Went walking out together,
    They talked about all sorts of things,
    The farmyard and the weather.
    But all I heard was:
    "Cluck! Cluck! Cluck!"
    And "Quack! Quack! Quack!"
    From Mrs. Duck.

2. Chook, chook, chook, chook, chook,
   Good morning Mrs. Hen.
   How many chickens have you got?

   Madam, I've got ten.
   Four of them are yellow, (*hold up four fingers.*)
   And four of them are brown, (*hold up four fingers of other hand.*)
   And two of them are speckled red, (*add thumbs.*)
   The nicest in the town.

3. Said the first little chicken, (*hold up first finger.*)
   With a queer little squirm, (*squirm.*)
   "I wish I could find a fat little worm."
   Said the next little chicken, (*hold up second finger.*)
   With an odd little shrug, (*shrug.*)
   "I wish I could find a fat little bug."
   Said the third little chicken, (*hold up third finger.*)
   With a sharp little squeal, (*squeal when you say, "squeal."*)
   "I wish I could find some nice yellow meal."
   Said the fourth little chicken, (*hold up fourth finger.*)
   With a small sigh of grief, (*sigh.*)
   "I wish I could find a little green leaf."
   Said the fifth little chicken, (*hold up fifth finger.*)
   With a faint little moan, (*moan.*)
   "I wish I could find a wee gravel stone."
   "Now see here," said the mother, (*shake index finger at chicks.*)
   From the green garden patch,
   "If you want your breakfast,
   Just come here and scratch!"

4. Sing to the tune of "For He's a Jolly Good Fellow":
   We've got a pig in the parlor,
   We've got a pig in the parlor,
   We've got a pig in the parlor,
   And he's a good one, too!
   He's a good one, too!
   He's a good one, too!
   We've got a pig in the parlor,
   And he's a good one, too!

5. Here is the beehive, (*cup left hand to form hive.*)
   Where are the bees? (*shrug.*)
   Hidden away where nobody sees. (*hide fingers of right hand in the left.*)
   Soon they will come creeping, (*fingers creep out.*)
   Out of the hive.
   1-2-3-4-5. (*show each finger.*)
   Buzzz! (*fingers fly away.*)

6. This is the rooster. (*point to head*.)
   This is the hen. (*point to chin*.)
   This is the pullet. (*point to nose*.)
   What did I say this is? (*point to nose*.)
   "Pullet." (*pull child's nose*.)

7. Mr. Turkey took a walk one day
   In the very best of weather.
   Along came Mr. Duck
   And they both talked together.
   Gobble, gobble, gobble,
   Quack, quack, quack,
   Good-bye, good-bye,
   And they both walked back.

8. Five little peas in a pea pod pressed, (*make a fist*.)
   One grew, two grew, and so did the rest. (*show respective fingers*.)
   They grew and grew and did not stop, (*spread fingers wide*.)
   Until one day the pod went POP! (*clap hands*.)

9. In the heart of a seed,
   Buried down so deep,
   A little plant lay fast asleep.
   (*Lay head on hands with eyes closed*.)

   "Awake," said the sun,
   "Come up through the earth." (*head pops up*.)
   "Awake," said the rain,
   "We are giving you birth."

   The little plant heard
   With a happy sigh,
   And pointed its petals
   Up to the sky. (*stretch up to the sky*.)

10. This mooly cow switched her tail all day, (*hold up first finger*.)
    And this mooly cow ate the sweet meadow hay. (*second finger*.)
    And this mooly cow in the water did wade, (*third finger*.)
    And this mooly cow chewed her cud in the shade. (*fourth finger*.)
    And this mooly cow said, "Moo! The sun's gone down." (*hold up last finger*.)
    "It's time to take the milk to town." (*walk two fingers along forearm*.)

11. When the farmer's day is done,
    In the barnyard everyone,
    Beast and bird politely say,
    "Thank you for my food today."

    The cow says "Moo."
    The pigeon, "Coo."
    The lamb says "Maa."
    The sheep says "Baa."

"Quack," says the duck.
Says the hen, "Cluck, cluck."
The dog, "Bow wow,"
The cat, "Meow."
The horse says, "Neigh,"
"I love sweet hay."
The pig nearby
Grunts in his sty.

When the barn is locked up tight,
Then the farmer says, "Good night,"
And thanks his animals, every one,
For the work that has been done.

12. Oats, peas, beans, and barley grows.
Oats, peas, beans, and barley grows.
How, you nor I nor anybody knows.
Oats, peas, beans, and barley grows.

Thus the farmer sows his seed,
Stands erect and takes his ease.
Stamps his foot and clasps his hands,
And turns about to view his lands.
(*Perform actions stated. May be sung to "Twinkle Twinkle Little Star."*)

Farm Music List

Cassettes

"Baa, Baa, Black Sheep." *Disney's Children's Favorites, Vol. 3*. Walt Disney Music Co. 606074, 1986.

"Baby Bumble Bee." *Disney's Children's Favorite Silly Songs*. Walt Disney Music Co. 2528B, 1988.

"Bingo." *Disney's Children's Favorites, Vol. 2*. Walt Disney Music Co. 606064, 1979.

"Farmer in the Dell." *Disney's Children's Favorites, Vol 2*. Walt Disney Music Co. 606064, 1979.

"Mairzy Doats." *Disney's Children's Favorite Silly Songs*. Walt Disney Music Co. 2528B, 1988.

"Old MacDonald." *Disney's Children's Favorites, Vol. 1*. Walt Disney Music Co. 606054, 1979.

Farm Book List

Fiction

Brown, Margaret Wise. *Big Red Barn*. Illustrated by Felicia Bond. Harper and Row, 1989.
  Rhymed text and illustrations introduce the many different animals that live in the big red barn.

Bulla, Clyde Robert. *Dandelion Hill*. Illustrated by Bruce Degen. E. P. Dutton, 1982.
  Violet, the new cow at Red Barn Farms, causes trouble when she kicks up her heels on Dandelion Hill.

Jewell, Nancy. *Calf, Goodnight*. Illustrated by Leonard Weisgard. Harper and Row, 1973.
  Too many distractions cause Mother Cow problems when she tries to herd her calf into the barn for the night.

Krauss, Ruth. *The Carrot Seed*. Illustrated by Crokett Johnson, Harper and Row, 1945.
  This is the well-loved story of a boy patiently waiting for a carrot to grow from the seed he planted.

Martin, Bill, and John Archambault. *Barn Dance*. Illustrated by Ted Rand. Henry Holt, 1986.
  Unable to sleep, a young boy follows the sound of music to the barn, where he finds something very unusual happening.

Nakatani, Chiyoko. *My Day on the Farm*. Thomas Crowell, 1976.
  A child's day on the farm can hold many new experiences.

Provensen, Alice, and Martin Provensen. *The Year at Maple Hill Farm*. Atheneum, 1978.
  A large amount of information is packed into this month-by-month account of the happenings at Maple Hill Farm.

Rabinowitz, Sandy. *The Red Horse and the Blue Bird*. Harper and Row, 1975.
  This book relates a simple tale of farmyard friends helping each other.

Rogers, Paul. *Sheep Chase*. Illustrated by Celia Berridge. Viking Kestral, 1986.
  Flossie the sheep leads the farmers on a merry chase through the countryside.

Rojankovsky, Feodor. *Animals on the Farm*. Alfred Knopf, 1967.
  This picture book contains large drawings of many farm animals.

Rylant, Cynthia. *Night in the Country*. Illustrated by Mary Szilagyi. Bradbury Press, 1986.
  You'll love the artwork in this book describing what you might see and hear at night from the safety of your little house in the country.

Scarry, Richard. *Richard Scarry's Egg in the Hole Book*. Western Publishing, 1967.
  Henny the Hen looks everywhere for her lost egg.

Stoeke, Morgan. *Minerva Louise*. E. P. Dutton, 1988.
  The reader is treated to a cock-eyed house tour when a silly hen pays a visit to the farm house.

Tafuri, Nancy. *Early Morning in the Barn*. Greenwillow, 1983.
    Meant for very young children, this simple picture book relates the sounds various farm animals make as they wake up in the morning.

Nonfiction

Dunn, Judy. *The Animals of Buttercup Farm*. Random House, 1981.
    This book contains many large color photographs of common farm animals.

Dunn, Phoebe. *Farm Animals*. Random House, 1984.
    More than 15 farm animals are introduced in simple text for young children.

Rockwell, Anne, and Harlowe Rockwell. *How My Garden Grew*. Macmillan, 1982.
    A young child explains how a garden grows.

5
DEEP IN THE WOODS
(Forest)

Focus on the Forest

A unit on the forest is especially useful in introducing environmental issues such as conservation and recycling.

Consider discussing these subjects:
>   Coniferous and deciduous trees
>   Forest products
>   Good forest habits
>   Forest animals and their homes
>   Recreation: hiking, skiing, camping
>   Conservation, recycling to save trees
>   Trees as producers of oxygen

Forest Motor Skills

1. **BIG BAD WOLF**. Choose one child to be the wolf. The wolf stands with its back to the other children pretending to be asleep. The other children are the pigs. They stand at a starting line about 12 feet from the wolf. When the teacher says, "Go!" the pigs try to creep up to the wolf without waking it. The wolf counts to 10, shouts, "Freeze!" and turns around. The pigs must stop and be very still. Anyone the wolf sees moving must go back to the starting line. Repeat the game until one of the pigs reaches the wolf. This child may start a new round, becoming the next wolf.

2. **CROSSING THE STREAM**. Place two long pieces of string parallel to each other, about 12 inches apart. The strings represent the banks of the stream. Between the two strings lies the water. Have the children line up on one side of the stream. The object of the game is for the children to take turns jumping over the stream without touching the strings or the space in between them. Once every child has had a turn, move the strings farther apart to make the next crossing more difficult. Those children who "fall into the stream" may sit on the sidelines, moving the strings.

3. **ANOTHER CROSSING**. Another way to cross the stream is to do it on "rocks." Tape sturdy paper plates to the floor in a wavy path across the room. They should be placed about 2 to 3 feet apart from each other, for the children to hop from rock to rock. The children should cross the room trying not to touch the floor. If they "fall in," the children may sit on the floor, pretending to tread water.

4. **OBSTACLE COURSE**. Arrange furniture or play equipment into an obstacle course. With a long piece of string, mark the path you want the children to take through the course. Drape the string loosely, passing it under, over, or between objects. The children's task is to follow the string through the course.

5. **A-HUNTING WE WILL GO**. Pick two children to face each other, clasping hands and raising them over their heads to form an arch. The rest of the children form a line and walk under the arch, singing the following song:

>   A-hunting we will go,
>   A-hunting we will go,
>   We'll catch a fox, put him in a box,
>   And then we'll let him go.

At "we'll catch a fox," the two players forming the arch drop their hands to trap a child between them. At the end of the song, the "fox" is released.

6.   **CHARADES**. Hold up a picture of a forest animal. The children pretend to be that animal with sounds and movement.

7.   **FOREST HIDEOUTS**. Make rabbit holes from short cardboard boxes. Turn them upside down and cut a large hole in the top of each box. The children may hop in and out of these shelters. Caves can be made from large cartons or barrels turned on their sides. The children can pretend to be bears or other animals hibernating, waiting for a chance to jump out of their hiding place when spring finally arrives.

8.   **FOREST WALK**. Pantomime a walk through the forest. The children choose an animal they would like to imitate. Caves and animal homes can be under chairs and tables, or use the props from activity 7, Forest Hideouts. Let the children crouch, hide, or scamper about. Forest music such as "Peter and the Wolf" makes a wonderful accompaniment to this activity.

9.   **FOLLOW THE LEADER**. When taking the children out for a walk or to the play yard, have them take turns giving each other instructions to follow, such as "Sit on the grass," "Hug that tree," or "Scamper like a squirrel."

10.   **LEAF PUZZLES**. Make easy puzzles by tracing leaf shapes onto a piece of construction paper. Use preserved leaves from science activity 1 or leaves that you have drawn on construction paper and then cut out. Have the children place the leaf shape onto the appropriate leaf outline.

Forest Language Activities

1.   **WOOD**. Place a box of objects on the table. The objects should be either wood (spool, pencil, toothpick, block) or nonwood (plastic toy, scrap of fabric, a magnet, a crayon). The children must select an item and tell if it is wood.

2.   **SEQUENCE CARDS**. Make sequence cards of three, four, or five frames each. Some possible story lines include a seed sprouting into a flower, a tree losing its leaves, the four seasons, a partial Three Bears story. Help the children to place the sequence cards in their correct order, if necessary, then ask the children to "read" the story to you.

3.   **ANIMAL PINUP**. On a bulletin board decorated to resemble a forest, pin up pictures of animals. Some should be of forest animals, and the rest should be animals that do not belong in the forest. The children's task will be to take down the pictures of the animals that do not belong. Another way to make use of these materials is to leave the forest bulletin board blank and to ask the children to select and pin up only the forest animals.

4.   **BIG STICK, LITTLE STICK**. Collect sticks and twigs of different lengths and thicknesses. Trim off or sand down any sharp edges or rough spots. Help the children to compare the dimensions of the sticks. Which are taller, shorter; longer, shorter; thick, thin; thinner, wider; tall, taller, tallest, etc.

5.   **WHO AM I?** Think of a forest plant or animal and give the children clues as to its identity. The children take turns guessing until the correct answer is given.

6.   **FOREST COLORS.** Make cutouts of forest items such as trees, leaves, animals, etc. Use light green, medium green, and dark green construction paper. Also use different shades of brown, red, or blue paper. Let the children explore the paper cutouts. Discuss the concept of dark and light, darker than, and lighter than. Ask the children to arrange one color's cutouts from light to dark. Place the cutouts of another color in random order on the table and then select one. Ask the children to pick one of the same color that is either darker or lighter than the one you hold.

7.   **WIGGLE OR JIGGLE.** Hold up a picture or an item. If the item relates to the forest, the children wiggle their ears. If it does not, the children jiggle their feet.

8.   **FEELIE GAME.** Place various objects into a sack or box. Leave a hole big enough for a child's hand. The objects could be rocks, pine cones, rabbit fur, a pine bough, etc. Have the children reach in and describe the items they feel as rough, smooth, hard, or soft. See if they can identify the object.

9.   **FOREST SOUNDS.** Make a tape of sounds for the children to identify. Different animal or insect sounds, sounds of wind or water, or even human sounds are appropriate. Use pictures to provide clues. Have the children pick out the correct picture from a group of three or four. Example: for the sound of a bird chirping, display a picture of a bird, a rock, a squirrel, and some hikers. The children would then point to the picture of the bird.

10.   **THE HIKE.** Collect a bag of props to keep hidden from the children. In the bag place a pine cone, a rock, pine boughs, a stuffed toy rabbit, and anything else pertaining to the forest. Have the children sit in small chairs, or on the floor with their feet extending out in front of them. Make up a story about a hike in the woods. Use the props in the bag to illustrate things that you talk about. Ask the children to participate by stomping their feet in front of them while they "hike," shade their eyes with their hands when they need to look around, etc.

Here is an example of how the story could go: "One day I decided to take a walk in the woods." (Start to stamp feet.)

"Suddenly, I heard a strange noise above me." (Look up.) "There was a small, round object hanging from a tree. Suddenly, plop! A pine cone hit me on the head! (Pull a pine cone from the bag and bounce it off your head in a comical manner.)

"I started to run, since more could fall off at any moment..." (Stomp feet quickly.)

Forest Math Activities

1.   **SORTING ANIMALS.** Cut pictures of forest animals and birds out of magazines or coloring books. Place them on a table in front of the children. Help the children go through the pile, counting the legs on each animal. Then have the children group the pictures by species, size, or color, and then count the number in each set. The children can also divide the animals according to those with long tails, short tails, or no tails. There are endless sets to be defined and counted.

2. **PLANT A FOREST.** Cut 10 slits into the bottom of a shoe box or other similar-sized box. Paint the box if you wish. With a marking pen, number the slits 1 through 10. Using a craft stick for the trunk of each tree and green construction paper for the leaves, assemble 10 trees by gluing the paper to the stick. Use a marker to number the trees 1 through 10. The child's task is to place each tree into its matching numbered slot (see figure 5.1).

Fig. 5.1.

3. **LARGE AND SMALL.** Select leaves from nearby trees. Collect a large and small leaf from each tree. Press the leaves between two large books to flatten them. Protect the leaves by preserving them in wax or by placing them between two sheets of clear adhesive paper and trimming to within ¼-inch of the leaf. Place the larger leaves on the table. Place the smaller leaves in a box. Ask the child to select a leaf from the box and match it to its partner on the table.

4. **TRACK MATCHING.** Draw pictures of different animal tracks on index cards. Make two cards with each type of track. Mix the cards up and ask the children to find the pairs of matching tracks. The children can also play "Concentration" with the cards.

5. **STEPPING STONES.** Make stepping stones from heavy brown construction paper, cardboard, or sturdy paper plates. Number the stepping stones 1 through 10. Tape the stepping stones in a pattern on the floor in numerical order. They should be far enough apart so that the children must jump from stone to stone. The children should read aloud the number of each stone as they jump on it. Another way to play this game is to place the stepping stones in a random order and to instruct the children to jump on the numbered stone you call out.

6. **LEAFLESS TREE.** Use a flannel board for this activity. Cut a large, leafless tree out of brown flannel. From green flannel, cut out at least 50 small green leaves and the numerals 1 through 5. To begin the activity, place the leafless tree on the flannel board and the leaves in a pile within reach. Select a numeral and place it on the flannel board next to the tree. Ask the children to come forward to place that many leaves on the tree. Continue until the tree is filled and no leaves remain. (For older children, cut out more leaves and use larger numerals. Cut out a felt zero and put *no* leaves on the tree to explain the empty set.)

7. **NUTTY BASKETS.** Paint the numerals 0 through 10 on the front of 10 small baskets. Give the child a large basket, filled with acorns or peanuts. The child must place the appropriate number of nuts in each numbered basket.

8. **SORTING NUTS.** Place several types of nuts (still in the shell) in a large bowl or basket. There should be at least one of each type of nut, but not more than 10. Peanuts, walnuts, filberts, Brazil nuts, almonds, or pecans are good choices that can be eaten later during snack time. The child's job is to sort the nuts, putting each type into a separate pile or basket. After the nuts are sorted, assist

the child in counting the number in each set. As you help the child count, talk about the nuts' colors and textures, the plant or tree which each nut came from, and its taste.

9. **SHORT TO TALL TREES**. Cut five tree silhouettes from green or brown construction paper. The first tree should be only 3 inches tall. The second one should be 4 inches, the third 5 inches, etc. Mix them up and place them on the table in front of the child. The child must put the trees in order from the shortest to the tallest.

Forest Science Activities

1. **PRESERVING LEAVES**. Place two cups of water in a small saucepan. Drop in the wax of one white votive candle. Heat over a small burner until the wax melts completely. Remove from the heat and let cool slightly. Using tweezers, help the children to carefully dip green leaves into the pan to coat them with wax. Dry them on newspaper. The leaves will stay soft and supple, but will take a long time to change color.

2. **LEAF PRINTS ON FABRIC**. Help the children place green leaves on wooden boards and cover the leaves with pieces of muslin or light cotton fabric (such as a square cut from an old sheet.) Hold the cloths down with some pushpins, if desired. Using hammers, have each child pound on their leaves so that the color is driven into the fabric. Set aside to dry. Help the children answer the following questions:

Does the stain wash out? Are there some leaves that will not make prints? Do some leaves leave their mark more readily than others? Would a dry brown leaf make a print? How do the different leaves smell when being hammered?

Note: To extend this activity into the realm of art, try making prints on a handkerchief or scarf once the children have practiced on scraps.

3. **MAKING PAPER**. Have the children help with the process of recycling by assembling the following materials: one piece of window screening, slightly smaller than 9 by 13 inches, a 9-by-13-inch cake pan, newsprint, and an iron (on cotton setting), a blender, and scrap paper such as newspaper or magazine pages.

    a. Fill the blender with 2 cups of water.

    b. Tear the scrap paper into 1-inch squares.

    c. Add as many of the 1-inch squares of paper to the blender as it can easily handle. Puree the mixture until the paper is in tiny pieces.

    d. Fill the cake pan half full of water.

    e. Pour the paper mixture into the pan and stir gently until the paper fibers float.

    f. Slide the screen gently under the floating fibers. Pull up carefully so that an even layer of fibers form on the screen. If the first try is no good, try again.

    g. Allow the excess moisture to drip off.

    h. Place the screen on a stack of newspapers to absorb the moisture.

    i. Lay plain newsprint over the screen and iron it. Let the paper cool every few minutes. Iron it until dry. The homemade paper will lift up evenly when it is dry.

4. **IS IT ALIVE?** Collect pictures of living things such as plants, animals, insects, etc. Collect pictures of nonliving things such as rocks, water, sand, or dry leaves. Mix up the pictures and have the children sort the pictures into two groups: living and nonliving.

5. **LOGS.** Bring a small pine log into the classroom. Observe the bark around the outer edge, and the rings in the cross section of the log. Explain that in spring, a tree grows more quickly and produces light-colored wood, but that during the summer, the tree does not grow as fast and the wood looks much darker. The dark areas look like rings. Count the rings and find out how many summers old the tree is. Saw the log lengthwise down the middle and observe. The lighter wood toward the outside of the log is called "sapwood." It is young and carries water and minerals from the roots up through the tree. The minerals gradually harden the sapwood until it gets darker and darker. The harder, darker middle part is called the "heartwood." What kind of wood would you build a house or furniture from? Observe the knotholes where limbs had started to grow. Observe the rough bark, which is there to protect the soft inner tree. Let the children take turns feeling the bark, the knotholes, and the inner tree. Are there other types of wood they are familiar with? How are they different from the pine log?

6. **TERRARIUM.** For each terrarium, you will need a large glass jar with a wide mouth such as a peanut butter or pickle jar. Put a layer of gravel, then a layer of sand in the jar. On top, put a deep layer of potting soil. Transplant low-growing plants collected from the area. If no plants are available, buy some small, suitable plants from a nursery. Ferns, mosses, and fungus plants do well in a jar. After the plants have been planted in the jar, pour in some water until it reaches halfway up the gravel. Cover the jar with a piece of plastic wrap and fasten it on with a rubber band. Poke one or two air holes in the plastic wrap. Place the terrarium in the brightest possible indirect light. If it dries out, add more water; if it seems too wet, open the top for awhile. It might be interesting to place some forest seeds such as acorns into the terrarium to see what happens over the course of the school year. (Soaking the seeds in water overnight before planting might help them sprout.) Observe that the plants will thrive as long as they have rich soil, indirect sunlight, and enough water.

Forest Art Projects

1. **TORN PAPER TREES.** *Materials*: Brown or green construction paper cut into tree shapes about 6 inches tall; green, brown, orange, red, or yellow construction paper scraps; scissors and glue. *Directions*: Provide each of the children with a tree cutout and let them choose the color of paper scraps they want to use for leaves. Have the children cut or tear the scraps into small round pieces resembling leaves, and glue them onto the tree shape, making a beautiful collage-style tree.

2. **PLAY-DOH BUG.** *Materials*: Play-Doh (either homemade or manufactured), colored toothpicks, and pipe cleaners. *Directions*: Cut the pipe cleaners into 3- to 4-inch lengths. Provide each of the children with a small amount of Play-Doh. Ask the children to roll it into a ball or egg shape for the bug's body. They can add toothpicks and pipe cleaners to the dough for the bug's legs and antennae.

3. **LITTER BAG.** *Materials*: Each child will need one paper lunch sack, a construction paper handle (1½ by 12 inches), crayons or markers, and a stapler. *Directions*: Fold over the open end of the lunch bag two or three times to make a cuff. Let the children decorate their own litter bags with crayons or markers. Assist them in stapling the construction paper strip to the top of the bag to form a handle.

4.   **NATURE RUBBINGS**. *Materials*: One 8-by-10-inch sheet of lightweight paper for each child; crayons; construction paper; newspaper; and objects such as leaves, dried flowers, flat pieces of bark from a tree, ferns, etc. *Directions*: Have the children arrange several nature objects on a sheet of newspaper, then place the lightweight paper on top of the objects and rub over them with the broad side of a peeled crayon. The children may choose different colored crayons on each object or one color for the whole picture. The different textures of the objects will be apparent on the paper after they rub it. To make a frame for the nature rubbing, use a ruler to measure off strips on the construction paper. Each child will need two 1-by-8-inch strips and two 1-by-10-inch strips. Assist the children in cutting these out if necessary. After the strips have been cut out, glue the strips around the edges of the rubbing to make a frame. Place on newspapers to dry.

5.   **BIRD FEEDER**. *Materials*: For each bird feeder you will need a cardboard milk carton (pint size to half-gallon size), acrylic paints, paintbrushes, string, a box cutter, a sharp scissors or pick for punching holes, and birdseed (optional). *Directions*: Using the box cutter, cut rectangular openings in two opposite sides of the milk carton. Be sure to leave about a 1-inch base on the bottom of the carton so that the birdseed will not fall out. With the pick or scissors, poke a hole in the top of the carton through which to thread the string. After this initial preparation, the child's task will be to paint the entire outside of the milk carton. Set it on newspapers to dry when the painting is complete. After drying, help the child put a string through the hole in the top of the feeder so that it can hang from a tree. Give each child birdseed in a zip-topped plastic bag for later use.

6.   **NATURE PRINTS**. *Materials*: Different shapes and types of leaves, paint, sponges cut into small pieces; newspaper; paper for printing on; and a cookie sheet or pie tin to hold the paint. *Directions*: After covering a table with newspapers, put a large dab of paint (perhaps a few different colors) on the cookie sheet. The thicker the paint, the better it works. To begin making prints, the children will choose a leaf from the collection and place it on the newspaper in front of them, then they dab it with a sponge dipped in paint. The children should cover the entire side of the leaf with paint. Have the children lift the leaf up by the stem while you place some clean newspaper over the place in front of them. After the leaf is set down on the clean newspaper, painted side up, help the children place a sheet of paper (to be printed on) on top of the leaf. The children will rub the paper with the palms of their hands to make the leaf print. Carefully peel off the printed paper and place it on newspaper to dry. Dispose of the painted leaf and wet newspapers.

7.   **PRESSED NATURE PICTURE**. *Materials*: Leaves, small flowers, ferns, grasses, newspapers, scissors, glue, crayons or markers, and construction paper (one piece 8 by 10 inches, another piece 10 by 12 inches, for each child). *Directions*: Collect the nature materials a week ahead of time and press between pieces of newspaper. Place heavy books on top of the materials to press them flat. Make sure the materials are dried thoroughly before using.

Provide each of the children with two sheets of paper, glue, and crayons. Each child will make a collage with the dried nature materials by gluing them onto the smaller piece of construction paper. After the glue has dried, crayon designs can be added. Mount the collage by centering it on the larger piece of construction paper and gluing it into place. This forms a nice frame around the collage and also serves to make it sturdy.

8.   **NEWSPAPER TREE**. *Materials*: Each child will need two sheets of newspaper, masking tape, and scissors. *Directions*: Open up a newspaper and spread two sheets on the floor, one on top of the other. The children will roll up the newspaper as tightly as possible to form a tube. Fasten this with a

piece of masking tape. Make four marks on the tube (see figure 5.2) where indicated and have the children cut at the marks as deep into the tube as possible. The deeper the cut, the fluffier the tree will appear. After the cuts have been made, hold the base of the tree loosely and undo the masking tape. Help the children to gently pull the top of the tree up, releasing the leaves where the cuts have been made. Continue until the tree cannot be pulled any higher. Retape the tree so that it will retain its tube shape.

9.   **CARDINALS AND BLUE JAYS.** *Materials*: Each child will need one or more bird shapes cut from red or blue construction paper, red or blue tissue paper, markers or crayons, string, and a hole punch. *Directions*: Using the pattern given (see figure 5.3, page 86), trace and cut out at least one bird shape per child. Cut a slit in the bird's body where indicated. Cut red and blue tissue paper into 6-inch squares.

Fig. 5.2.

Provide each child with a bird shape and a square of tissue paper the same color. Let the children draw faces on the birds with crayons or markers. Show the children how to fold the tissue paper accordian-style and help them slide folded tissue through the slots in the birds' bodies. After the wings are fluffed, show the children where to punch a hole so that they can thread string through it. Hang the finished forest birds from the ceiling of the classroom.

10.   **BEAR CHAIN.** *Materials*: Lightweight paper, and markers or crayons. *Directions*: Cut the paper into strips 4 inches wide and at least 12 inches long. Make a mark on the paper about every 2 inches so that the child can see where to fold the paper. Help the child fold his or her strip of paper accordian-style at the 2-inch intervals. On the top leaf, the child will trace the bear pattern (see figure 5.4, page 87). Make sure that the bear's paws overlap the edges of the paper. Without unfolding the strip, assist the child in cutting out the bear figure. Be sure that the paws are left uncut to hold the chain intact. Lift the top bear gently until the whole chain opens. The child may then draw faces and other features on each bear.

11.   **PINECONE OWL.** *Materials*: Each child will need a large, clean pinecone, construction paper, scissors, markers, and glue. *Directions*: Help each child to trace the owl feature patterns onto a piece of construction paper (see figure 5.5, page 88). Ask the children to color them and cut them out. Fold the beak along the dotted line for a three-dimensional effect. Placing the glue on the paper cutouts, help the children glue their cutouts to the pine cones by attaching the beak and eyes near the top and by setting the base of the pine cone on the feet. After drying, the tail may be curled by rolling it around a pencil and then releasing it.

(Text continues on page 89.)

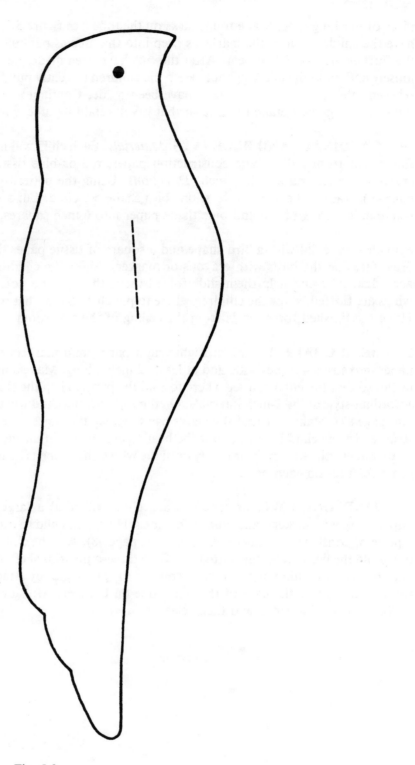

Fig. 5.3.

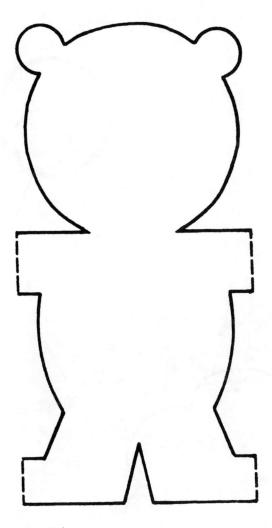

Fig. 5.4.

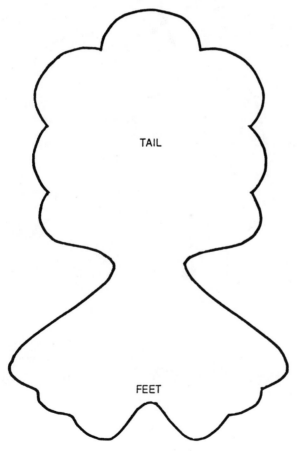

Fig. 5.5.

12. **ANTLERS.** *Materials*: Each child will require a large brown paper grocery sack, markers, scissors, string, a paper punch, and a cardboard template made from the given antler pattern (see figure 5.6, page 90). *Directions*: Prepare a cardboard template of the antler pattern by placing the pattern on a folded piece of paper. Line up the fold line of the pattern with the fold of the paper, trace, and cut out. Using the pattern you have just made, trace around it on a sheet of cardboard and cut out.

Provide the children with the cardboard antler pattern. Let them trace around the pattern onto the grocery sack and help cut out the antlers. Show the children where to punch holes with the paper punch. Help thread string through the holes to tie the antlers onto the children's heads. The antlers may be decorated with the markers.

Forest Class Project

Planting a Tree

From the nursery you will need to purchase a tree popular with the children. Select one in a 5-gallon container. Other items to purchase are a bag of mulch (1½ cubic feet), a small bag of sulfur, and fertilizer.

Distribute digging utensils to all of the children. Dig a hole in the ground two times as wide and two times as deep as the tree's root ball. Using half of the soil from the hole, mix in the mulch, 1 cup of soil sulfur, and fertilizer according to the instructions on the container. Start to fill the hole back up with this soil mixture, tamping it down lightly about every 6 inches. Place the tree in the hole when it is about half full. You will need to judge the correct depth at which to place the tree. When it is in place, use the rest of the "good soil" to finish filling the hole. Leave a 3-inch well around the tree to hold water. Keep the new tree damp for 10 days to 2 weeks and then water as needed after that. Once the tree is established, plan a picnic around its base to celebrate.

Forest Story Time

1. **IN THE FOREST.** The forest is the setting for many children's stories. "The Three Bears," "Little Red Riding Hood," "Hansel and Gretel," and "Snow White" are only a few of them. After reading such a story, ask the children if they would like to act out a small portion of the most exciting part. Assign characters to one or two of the children and ask the remaining children to be the trees of the forest. If the children have made paper trees during the week, each child can hold up a tree during the story, either standing straight and still or blowing in the wind.

2. **BREAD CRUMBS.** In keeping with the forest mood, hide two or three picture books such as "Hansel and Gretel" around the room right before story time. Use popcorn or paper cutouts to represent the famous bread crumbs in the Hansel and Gretel story. Make a trail of bread crumbs leading to each hidden book. Ask the children to use the trail of bread crumbs to locate the story books, just like Hansel and Gretel used them to try to find their way home.

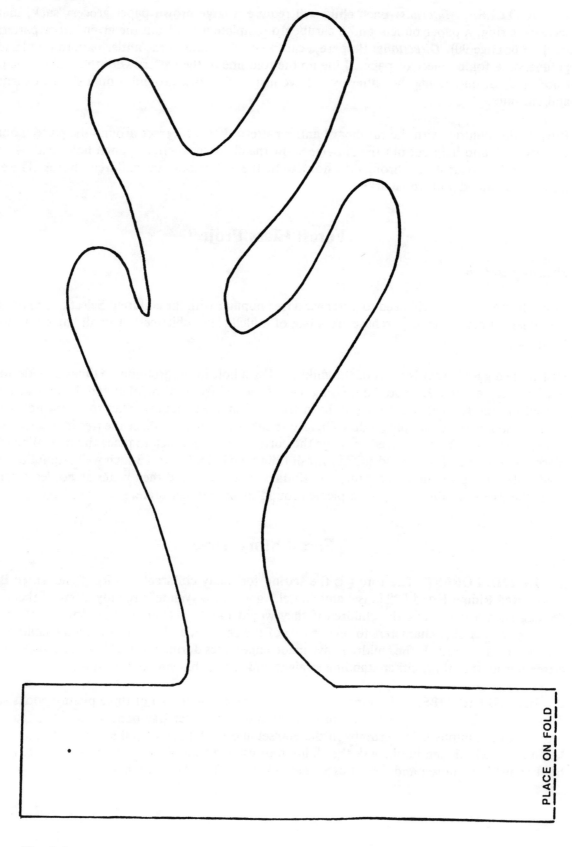

PLACE ON FOLD

Fig. 5.6.

Forest Poems, Songs, Fingerplays

1. Hop, old squirrel, Eideldum, Eideldum.
   Hop, old squirrel, Eideldum dee.
   (*Repeat*.)

   (*Variations: Replace hop with run, walk, skip, hide, peek, etc. Replace "squirrel" with little bird, green frog, Mister Stag*.)

2. Little cabin in the woods
   Little man by the window stood,
   Little rabbit hopping by
   Frightened as he could be.
   "Help me, help me, help me," he cried,
   "Before the hunter shoots me dead."
   Little rabbit come inside safely to abide.

   (*Dramatize as you recite poem*.)

3. Whiskey, friskey, hippity hop:
   Up he goes to the tree top. (*hold arm upward*.)
   Whirly, twirly, round and round: (*move arm in a circle*.)
   Down he scampers to the ground. (*bring arm down*.)
   Furly, curly, what a tail:
   Tall as a feather, broad as a sail. (*extend arms vertically, then horizontally*.)
   Where's his supper?
   It's in the shell. (*cup hands*.)
   Snappity crackity, out it fell. (*open hands*.)

4. I stuck my head in the old skunk's hole
   And the old skunk said, "Well bless my soul!"
   "Take it out, take it out, take it out, take it out, REMOVE IT!"
   I didn't take it out and the old skunk said,
   "If you don't take it out you'll wish you had!
   Take it out, take it out, take it out, take it out, REMOVE IT!"
   SSSSSSSSS! I removed it too late!

5. Under the spreading chestnut tree
   We danced as happy as could be.

   (*Point hands down when you say "under." Put arms straight out sideways when you say spreading. Touch your chest when you say chest. Touch your head when you say nut. Put your arms straight up when you say tree. Begin very slowly, and repeat, faster each time*.)

6. 1, 2, 3, 4, 5 (*show appropriate fingers*.)
   I caught a hare alive. (*clasp hands together*.)
   6, 7, 8, 9, 10 (*show appropriate fingers*.)
   I let him go again. (*unclasp hands*.)

7. This little squirrel said, "Let's run and play."
This little squirrel said, "Let's hunt nuts today."
This little squirrel said, "Yes, nuts are good."
This little squirrel said, "They're our best food."
This little squirrel said, "Come, climb this tree."
"And crack these nuts: one, two, three."

(*Start with your palm open. On each line, close one finger, until you make a fist. On the last line, rap your head when you count 1, 2, 3.*)

8. This little bear has a soft fur suit.
This little bear acts very cute.
This little bear is bold and cross.
This little bear rests his head on moss.
This little bear likes bacon and honey.
But he can't buy them, he has no money.

(*This is done on the fingers or toes the same way as "This Little Piggy."*)

9. A big black bug bit a big black bear.

10. How much wood could a woodchuck chuck if a woodchuck could chuck wood?

11. Fuzzy Wuzzy was a bear. Fuzzy Wuzzy had no hair. Fuzzy Wuzzy wasn't fuzzy, was he?

12. (*For this fingerplay, it is best to sit on a chair in front of your audience. Instruct the children to repeat each line that you say. Alternate slapping your hands on your thighs to keep a beat and dramatizing the story with hand motions.*)

Goin' on a bear hunt. I'm not afraid. Got my gun. Coming to a river. Everybody swim.
Goin' on a bear hunt. I'm not afraid. Got my gun. Coming to a tree. Everyone climb the tree.
Is there a bear over there? (*look to the right*.) No. Is there a bear over there? (*peer to the left*.)
No. Climb down the tree.
Goin' on a bear hunt. I'm not afraid. Got my gun. Coming to a clearing. Walking across the clearing.
Goin' on a bear hunt. I'm not afraid. Got my gun. Coming to a cave. Is there a bear in the cave? YES!
(*very quickly*:)
Running through the clearing, climbing up the tree, climbing down the tree, swimming through the river, run home and lock the door.
(*very slowly*:)
Went on a bear hunt. Had my gun. I wasn't afraid.

Forest Music List

Cassettes

"The Bear Went Over the Mountain." *Disney's Children's Favorites, Vol. 2.* Walt Disney Music Co. 606064, 1979.

"Camping." *Disney's Children's Favorites, Vol. 4*. Walt Disney Music Co. 606084, 1990.

"The Green Grass Grew All Around." *Disney's Children's Favorites, Vol. 1*. Walt Disney Music Co. 606054, 1979.

Forest Book List

Fiction

Beskow, Elsa. *Children of the Forest*. Adapted from the Swedish by William Jay Smith. Delacorte Press, 1969.
Tiny people no larger than a mushroom play with fairies, encounter ogres, and talk with owls.

Brown, Margaret Wise. *The Little Fur Family*. Illustrated by Garth Williams. Harper and Row, 1946.
The little fur family lives in the trunk of a tree in the wild, wild woods.

Carroll, Ruth, and Latrobe Carroll. *The Picnic Bear*. Illustrated by Ruth Carroll. Henry Z. Walck, 1966.
Fuzzy Bear loves ant picnics, buttercup picnics, and wild strawberry picnics, but finds human picnics irresistable.

Coats, Laura Jane. *The Oak Tree*. Macmillan, 1987.
A day in the life of an oak tree is depicted in this picture book for young children.

Fisher, Aileen. *Animal Jackets*. Designed and illustrated by Muriel Wood. Lettering by Paul Taylor. L. A. Bowman, 1973.
Many different forest animals keep warm in different ways.

Galdone, Paul. *The Three Bears*. Seabury, 1972.
This is the classic Goldilocks tale, retold and comically illustrated by Paul Galdone.

Hawkinson, John, and Lucy Hawkinson. *Robins and Rabbits*. Illustrated by John Hawkinson. Albert Whitman, 1960.
Who lives in the woods? This book names many who do, but explains that rabbits abound because they have so many relatives!

Krauss, Ruth. *The Happy Day*. Illustrated by Marc Simont. Harper, 1949.
What a happy day it is when spring returns to the forest!

Pfloog, Jan. *The Fox Book*. Western Publishing, 1965.
This simple book for very young children introduces the fox.

Pfloog, Jan. *The Squirrel Book*. Western Publishing, 1965.
The squirrel is introduced in this simple book designed for very young children.

Ryder, Joanne. *Chipmunk Song*. Illustrated by Lynne Cherry. E. P. Dutton, 1987.
Let your imagination take you into the forest with the chipmunks as you burrow under the ground, gather food, and climb trees.

Udry, Janice May. *A Tree Is Nice*. Illustrated by Marc Simont. Harper, 1956.
    There are many reasons why people love trees and this classic picture book names some of the reasons.

Nonfiction

Ertl, James. *Adventures of a Squirrel*. Encyclopaedia Britannica Press, 1962.
    Color photos and text chronicle the life of a squirrel from his birth to an exciting day when he is captured by a little boy.

Hazen, Barbara Shook. *Where Do Bears Sleep*? Illustrated by Ian E. Staunton. Addison Wesley, 1970.
    Forest and other animals sleep in many unusual places.

6
BY THE BEAUTIFUL SEA
(Ocean)

Focus on the Ocean

The vast oceans of the world surround us wherever we may live. Surrounding the children with information and activities from a chapter on the ocean will help them learn more about our global environment.

Consider discussing these subjects:
    Marine life: plants, fish, shellfish, mammals
    Parallels to life above water
    Islands
    Shells
    The beach
    Properties of water: solid, liquid, gas
    Salt water versus fresh water
    Ocean products
    Recreation
    Pollution and possible solutions

Ocean Motor Skills

1.   **BEACH BALL BOWL.** Include enough children to form a large circle. Form the circle with the children's feet spread far apart, touching the feet of the child next to them. The child chosen to be "it" stands in the center of the circle with a large beach ball. The object of the game is to prevent the child who is it from rolling the ball between the legs of the other children. The children must use only their hands to deflect the ball and cannot move their feet. The child who is it gets to trade places with any child who allows the ball to roll through his or her legs.

2.   **ROW, ROW, ROW.** Each child must find a partner and sit on the floor, facing each other. The partners position themselves by straightening their legs, hooking their feet together, and holding hands. Once in position, the children start "rowing" and singing:

> Row, row, row your boat, gently down the stream.
> Merrily, merrily, merrily, merrily,
> Life is but a dream.

After the song is sung, the children jump up and quickly find another partner. Repeat.

3.   **CRAB WALK.** Form three or four lines of children for a relay race. The children perform the relay race walking on their hands and feet, tummies facing up.

4.   **SEASHELLS.** Bury seashells or small toys in a sand box. Let the children count the ones that they find and then bury them again for the next shell seekers.

5.   **SARDINES.** Have all of the children but one close their eyes. The other child has until the count of 20 to hide. The "seekers" search for the hiding child. Any child who finds the hiding child

quietly slips in with him or her and hides from the others. The children continue packing themselves in together until only one "seeker" remains. The last child becomes the next person to hide first.

6. **SEA PUZZLES**. Outline several shells on a piece of cardboard. Have the child place each shell on the correct outline. Also use seashore shapes such as sailboats and fish that have been cut out of colored paper and laminated.

7. **TIDDLYWINKS**. Place a shallow dish of water in front of two to four children. Provide each child with a set of tiddlywinks bought at the store: one shooter and four smaller discs. If you cannot find such a set in the toy store, use a quarter as the shooter and pennies as the smaller ones to be shot. The children line up their four small tiddlywinks in front of themselves, each maintaining an equal distance from the dish of water. In order to shoot the tiddlywinks, the children hold their shooter and use it to depress the edge of the smaller disc. This causes it to jump forward. Pretend that the tiddlywinks are baby fish trying to jump into the water. The object of the game is to see who can get all four tiddlywinks into the water first.

8. **CHARLIE OVER THE WATER**. The players form a circle around one child chosen to be "Charlie." Say the following chant:

> Charlie over the water
> Charlie over the sea
> Charlie catch a blackbird
> Can't catch me!

On the last word of the chant, all the players should squat. Charlie tries to tag them before they squat. If Charlie is successful, the tagged player becomes Charlie.

9. **SAILOR, SAILOR**. Recite the following chant:

> Sailor, sailor, over the sea,
> All he could see was the sea, sea, sea.
> How many days was he sick?
> One, two, three, etc.

Provide the child with a ball. Using the last line of the verse, see how many times the child can bounce the ball before missing it. This verse may also be used with children who know how to jump rope.

10. **FISHERMAN TAG**. One child is chosen to be the fisherman. The other children are fish. The "fisherman" tries to catch the fish by tagging them with his or her hand. The fish are tricky, though. If they stoop down (as if under the water) they are safe. They can only stay under the water as long as they can hold their breath. Then they must stand up again and once again become fair game. When the fisherman catches a fish, that fish then becomes the fisherman. Repeat.

Ocean Language Activities

1. **SWITCH.** Use three different objects pertaining to the ocean for this activity. Shells or small plastic beach toys work well. Line the objects up on the table in front of the children. Let them study the objects for 10 seconds, and then have the children close their eyes for 10 seconds. While the children's eyes are closed, switch the order of the objects. After they open their eyes, the children must then put them back in their original order. Do this activity again, adding more objects as the children master the old number of objects.

2. **"S" WORDS.** Obtain pictures of the beach from magazines and books; use posters or make your own beach scenes. Have the children look for objects in the picture that start with the letter "s." Some vocabulary words to look for include: sand, surf, sea, shovel, sun, sky, seashore, shore, suntan, suntan lotion, shells, swimmer, starfish, etc.

3. **FISHING FOR LETTERS.** Cut fish shapes out of construction paper and print a letter of the alphabet on each fish. Fasten a paper clip to each fish, then spread the fish out on the floor. Make a fishing pole from a ruler and a piece of string. Attach a magnet on the end of the string where the fish hook would be. Let the children take turns fishing for letters. When the child catches a "fish," ask him or her to identify the letter on the fish. After the children have practiced catching the fish and have gained some control over the fishing pole, call out specific letters for them to target. Call out letters to spell simple words or the child's name. Younger children can also have a good time with the fish if they are made from several different colors. Instead of identifying letters, they can focus on the colors of the fish.

4. **SAND WRITING.** Pour 2 inches of sand or cornmeal into a large dishpan. (The advantage of using cornmeal is that it dissolves if it accidentally gets into a child's eye.) If using sand, add a little water and smooth it out to make a good writing surface. (Do not add water if using cornmeal.) Using a deck of flash cards with letters or numbers on them, have the children first trace a letter on the flash card with their fingers and then trace the same letter in the sand. If dissatisfied, they can smooth out the sand and try again. Younger children can make simple geometric shapes.

5. **LAND OR SEA.** Name items related either to land or to the sea. If the item relates to land, the children should all pretend to hike. If the item relates to the sea, the children should pretend to swim.

6. **ECHO.** Ask the children to copy whatever you say. Start with a short sentence, and add on to it each time. For example:

> I went to the ocean.
> I went to the ocean to swim.
> I went to the ocean to swim and to surf.
> I went to the ocean to swim and to surf and to sunbathe.

Use this activity to teach consonant sounds like above or to teach rhyming: "I played with a pail, a snail, and a whale." Numbers in sequence may also be the object: "In the ocean swam one seahorse, two whales, three sharks...."

7. **SURPRISE BOX.** Place a surprise object in a shoe box with a lid. Use items relating to the ocean such as shells, a container of sand, beach toys, a towel, sunglasses, etc. (You can even use a picture of the object instead of the real thing, such as a picture of a shark or a whale.) Have the children pass the box around and try to guess what is inside. The children may shake the box but may not open it. Give clues about the contents of the box until someone guesses correctly what is inside.

8. **TREASURE HUNT.** Hide a "treasure" in the classroom or the playground. Also hide four or five clues written on a piece of paper. Give verbal clues to find the first piece of paper. Read the clue to the children. The first piece of paper found should indicate where the second clue can be found, the second clue should indicate where the third one can be found, and so on. The final clue should lead to the treasure.

For example: The "treasure" could be a box containing one lollipop for each student. Tell the children to find the first clue under something that goes back and forth. (The clue is taped to the underside of one of the swings in the playground.) The piece of paper that the children find has this rhyme written on it:

> Seesaw, Margery Daw
> Sold her bed and laid upon straw.

The second clue is hidden near the seesaw. Perhaps a few more clues can lead to other playground equipment, a bush or flowerbed, and then finally to the sandbox where the treasure is actually buried.

9. **SHELL SENSATIONS.** Obtain as many seashells as possible and group them according to their traits. Sort the rough from the smooth and group certain colors, shapes, or sizes. Let the children touch the shells and tell why the shells are grouped as they are.

10. **DISCRIMINATION.** For each discrimination card, cut a piece of tagboard to 4 by 16 inches. With a marker, divide the card into four sections, each 4 by 4 inches. The first dividing line should be extra thick to set off the first section from the other three. The first section should contain a simple word, picture, or shape. (Use stickers with pictures of shells or fish on them to make the cards easily and quickly.) Pick a word, shape, or picture for the first section. Repeat it in one of the other sections. The remaining two sections should contain words, pictures, or shapes that are similar to the others but not exactly the same. The children's job is to find the word or picture on the right side of the card that matches the one defined in the first section (see figure 6.1). Make as many cards as you like, using words for the older children and pictures and shapes for the younger ones.

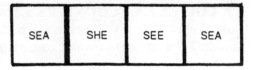

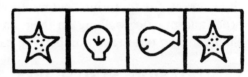

Fig. 6.1.

Ocean Math Activities

1. **GEOMETRIC FISH.** For each child, provide construction paper on which a small circle, a small triangle, and a large triangle have been drawn. Provide a contrasting color of paper on which a large circle has been drawn. Discuss the differences in these shapes as you assist the child in cutting them out. Give the child verbal instructions as to how to glue the shapes onto another piece of paper to form a fish. The child should be able to identify and to count the different shapes (see figure 6.2).

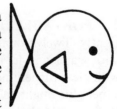

Fig. 6.2.

2. **FISH BOWL.** Obtain a fish bowl, a small aquarium, or a large mixing bowl. Give the children measuring cups or small plastic containers, and have them count how many containers of water it takes to fill the fish bowl.

3. **GROUPING SHELLS.** Present the children with shells varying in color, type, and size. Ask the children to sort the shells by color, then by size, then by shape. Help count how many shells are in each set. Select one of the shells and ask the children to find one that matches it. Finally, make a set of a small number of shells. See if the children can make sets of shells with the same number in it.

4. **GO FISH.** Use cards you make yourself in the shape of fish. Either number the fish as playing cards or use geometric shapes on them. Make four cards each of every number or shape used; you will need 10 to 13 sets in all. Two to four children may play. Deal each child five cards and put the rest of the cards face down on the table. The child who goes first asks any player for a card to match one in his or her hand. If the player has such a card, it must be given to the child. If not, he or she tells the child to "go fish." The child then draws one card from the deck. If the child has obtained a match either way, it is laid on the table. Play proceeds to the right. If all the cards in the child's hand are used, he or she picks one from the deck. The children keep playing until all of the cards are used up. At the end, the children count to see how many matches they each have.

5. **SANDY FINGERS.** For this activity, you will need a tub with some wet sand in it and shells for counting. Put any number of shells in front of the children. Have them count the shells and then trace the numbers in the sand with a finger. If the children don't like the way their numbers turn out, they can smooth the sand over and try again. Shapes and letters can also be drawn in the sand.

6. **COFFEE CAN COUNTERS.** Obtain five coffee cans or other large metal cans. With a nail, poke from one to five holes in the bottom of each can. The children can use them in water play, counting the streams of water coming out.

7. **FOOTPRINTS IN THE SAND.** Trace around a child's foot on cardboard 10 times. Help the child cut out the footprints and number them 1 through 10. The child should then arrange them in order and practice walking on them and counting. The footprints can also be mixed up, and the child can hop onto each number you call out.

8. **MYSTERIOUS SAND SHAPES.** Cut out some simple geometric shapes of rough sandpaper and glue them onto pieces of cardboard. Have the children close their eyes and trace the shape with their fingers. Can they tell you what the shape is?

Ocean Science Activities

1. **PORTABLE OCEAN.** Give each child a small, clear, unbreakable container that can be sealed tightly. Twelve-ounce beverage containers work well. Have the children fill their containers half full with water and let them add one or two drops of blue food coloring. Fill the container to the top with clear turpentine and seal them tightly enough so that the children cannot open them. (A dab of super glue might help make the seal permanent.) Have the children hold their bottles sideways. With just a gentle shake, waves will fill their little oceans.

2. **WATER MAGNIFYING GLASS.**
Explain to the children that water has many properties. One of the more interesting things that water can do is magnify objects. To make a water magnifying glass, cut a bleach bottle or other container as shown in figure 6.3.

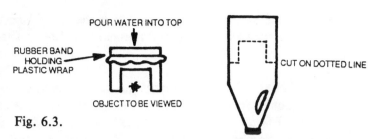

Fig. 6.3.

Place a sheet of clear plastic wrap over the opening on top, using a rubber band to hold it in place. Pour as much water onto the plastic wrap as it will hold. Place objects to be magnified in the opening directly under the water magnifier. Look through the water to the object below to see it magnified.

3. **WAVES.** Waves are ridges of water on top of the ocean. They follow each other, one after the other, across the water. The wind causes most waves; it blows the top of the water and makes ripples in it. If the wind keeps blowing in the same direction, the ripples get bigger and bigger until they become waves. The longer and harder the wind blows, the larger the waves become. To illustrate the motion of a wave, conduct the following experiment.

Float a rubber ball in some water in a large sink or tub. Make waves by holding your hand flat on top of the water and moving it up and down in a slow, steady motion. Try not to splash the water. Make the waves at one end of the tub and float the ball at the opposite end. Have the children observe that the ball floats up and down in a circular path, not back and forth along with the waves. The ball illustrates that the water does not move back and forth along with the waves, but up and down as the wave passes by.

4. **SAILING, SAILING.** Make a tiny paper boat and have a child try sailing around the oceans on the globe in your classroom. The child can start the trip in any ocean. Keep the paper boat traveling in the water. Does it ever get land locked? No! The globe names four oceans, the Pacific, Atlantic, Indian, and Arctic, but there really is only one gigantic ocean.

5. **BUOYANCY.** This experiment illustrates the difference in salt and fresh water buoyancy. You will need two glasses, some salt, water, and one egg.

Fill both glasses with water. Add 2 tablespoons of salt to one of the glasses. Float the egg in the salt water. What happens? Try floating it in the fresh water. What happens? The egg sinks in the fresh water and floats in the salt water because the denser the liquid, the greater the chances an object will float. Have the children look for other differences between the salt and the fresh water. One big difference is in the taste. Have them taste both kinds of water. Do the waters look any different? Can they be identified without tasting them or floating objects in them?

6. **SOLID, LIQUID, GAS.** Show the children the Arctic and the Antarctic regions on a globe. Explain that it is so cold there that the water of the oceans freezes and becomes ice. Show the children some ice, explaining that ice is water in a solid form.

Point out the equator. Explain that the sun's rays hit directly at the equator and it is very hot there. Put some water in an electric pan. Tell the children that the water is liquid now, but watch what happens when it starts to boil. Can the children see the water turn to a gas when it starts to boil?

Hold a pan lid over the steam and watch the water condense. Explain the parallels between the steam being trapped by the lid and rain clouds. Review the three forms of water: liquid, solid, and gas.

7. **DIFFUSION.** Fill a gallon glass jar with water and place it where the children can see. Let the jar sit untouched for at least an hour to get rid of the water currents that were made while it was being filled. Place one drop each of red, yellow, and blue food coloring in the water. Watch the colors as they slowly spread. This is called diffusion. Notice that after a long time the colors are all mixed with the water and no discernible streams of color remain. The dye has diffused. Now pour ¼-cup of vegetable oil on top of the water. Does it act the same way that the dye did? How can you make it diffuse like the food dye did? Try shaking the jar. What happens? Does the oil mix with the water the way that the food coloring did? If you wanted to clean up the oil, how could you do it? Explain to the children that oil will not mix with water, causing problems with cleanup. When an oil tanker spills oil in the ocean, it is disastrous because it coats the shoreline and all the animals that live there. After ecologists skim what oil they can from the surface of the water, the main problem is to wash it from the beach and diffuse it. Nature's tides and storms will eventually wash most of the oil away from the shore, but it will take years. To clean up the mess more quickly, the oil is sprayed off the shore with a high powered hose (like a firehose) and then mopped up with pom-poms made of specially absorbant fibers.

Detergent can also be used in addition to the hoses to aid diffusion of the oil. Place a drop of detergent in the middle of the oil in the jar. What happens? If you keep adding more detergent, what happens? Try absorbing the oil with cloth, tissue, or paper towels. Which one works best?

The oil that is skimmed off the surface of the water can be recycled, but the dirty pom-poms or mops must be stored in a toxic waste dump. We must all learn to be very careful when dealing with substances such as oil. The mess never gets totally cleaned up.

Ocean Art Activities

1. **MEAT TRAY PRINTING.** *Materials*: A Styrofoam meat tray for each child, scissors, tempera paint, paintbrushes, colored paper, and markers or crayons. *Directions*: Draw large fish shapes on the smooth side of the Styrofoam trays and help the children cut out the shapes. Have the children paint the textured side with tempera paint. Print the shape by having the children carefully press it to the surface of the colored paper. Have the children finish their design with more paint, markers, or crayons.

2. **SHINE-THROUGH PAINTINGS.** *Materials*: Paper, tempera paint, paintbrushes, salad oil, construction paper cut into narrow strips, and glue. *Directions*: Have the children paint a picture and then let it dry. Spread salad oil over the dried picture, and dab off any excess oil. Give the children construction paper strips to glue around the edge of their paintings to make a frame. Hang the paintings in the window to let the light shine through.

3. **POPSICLE RAFT.** *Materials*: Craft sticks, glue, paint, paintbrushes. *Directions*: Have each child place two craft sticks 3 inches apart and parallel to each other for the raft base. Have the children glue more sticks across the base to form the top of the raft. Paint and let dry. Do the rafts float?

4.   **STARFISH**. *Materials*: Each child will need one brown paper bag, star shape to trace around, glue, markers, scissors, a paintbrush, and sand. *Directions*: Give each child a paper bag, star shape, and marker. Have the children trace the star shapes onto the brown paper bags, cut them out, paint the star shapes with glue, and sprinkle sand over them. Remove the excess sand and let dry. Faces or other designs may be added to the dry starfishes with marking pens.

5.   **CRAYON RESISTS**. *Materials*: White paper, white crayons, and water colors. *Directions*: Have the children draw a design on the paper with their white crayons and then paint over it with water, tinted with water colors. Let dry.

6.   **TUB TOYS**. *Materials*: Styrofoam, a scissors or knife, and waterproof markers. *Directions*: Cut out the shapes of fish, turtles, life preservers, starfish, etc. Let the children decorate them with the waterproof markers to make their own bath toys.

7.   **SEASCAPE**. *Materials*: Each child will need one piece of blue construction paper; fish and underwater plants you have cut out of paper beforehand; several small rocks, aquarium gravel, small shells, and shell macaroni; glue; and some sand. *Directions*: Have the children glue the collage materials to the construction paper to make a seascape. Make sure they understand that the sand and rocks belong along the bottom of their pictures and that the fish and plants float above them.

8.   **SANDCASTING**. *Materials*: Each child will need one small disposable foil baking pan, damp sand, a plastic spoon and knife, shells and pebbles to decorate shapes with, and plaster. *Directions*: Fill the baking pans with sand that is just wet enough to hold its shape. Have the children draw outlines of the sea creatures of their choice, then scoop the sand from the outlined shapes. They can decorate their shapes by pressing shells or pebbles into it. Mix the plaster to the consistency of heavy cream and pour it into the molds. Let stand 24 hours. Remove the mold and brush away the excess sand.

9.   **TACKLE BOX**. *Materials*: Each child must have a cardboard egg carton, string or yarn, paint, a paintbrush, paper clips, and s-shaped Styrofoam packing bits (optional). *Directions*: Have the children paint the outside of their egg cartons. Let dry. Make two holes in the lid of the egg carton about 3 inches apart. Help the children thread the yarn through the holes and then tie to make a handle. Let the children put paper clips in the compartments for fish hooks and the Styrofoam bits or cut up string for worms to make their own tackle boxes.

10.   **OCTOPUS WIND SOCK**. *Materials*: A 6-by-16-inch piece of construction paper, scissors, a hole punch, string, crayons or markers, and crepe paper streamers. *Directions*: Have the children draw octopus' faces on the middle of pieces of construction paper. Help them cut the crepe paper into eight long arms, somewhat equal to each other in length. Have the children glue the ends of each streamer to the bottom inside edges of the construction paper, spacing them equally apart. Let the glue dry for a few minutes and then glue or staple the octopus' heads into a cylindrical shape (see figure 6.4). Let dry. Show the children how to use the hole punch to make two holes near the top of the heads, on opposite sides. Thread pieces of string through the holes to make handles for hanging the wind socks.

Fig. 6.4.

Ocean Class Project

Saltwater Aquarium

These instructions for the saltwater aquarium are for all children, those who live near the ocean and can obtain fresh sea water and those who live far from the sea and must visit a pet shop for their supplies. Either way, a saltwater aquarium is a fun addition to any classroom.

Materials: A glass or plastic aquarium (5- to 10-gallon size), hydrometer for checking saltiness of the water, under-gravel filter, an air pump, a glass thermometer, and seawater or chemicals for making seawater. Be sure that anything you buy to go into the aquarium is plastic or glass. Do not use anything made of metal; it will corrode and cause major problems.

If you are collecting your own seawater, use several clean plastic containers with tight lids and some cheesecloth or nylon material to filter the water.

Directions: **Clean the aquarium**. Wash the aquarium, the gravel, and all the equipment with clean running water. Do not use soap as residue from it may kill your creatures.

Collect the water: Collect seawater in plastic containers as far from shore as possible. Take twice as much as you will need to fill the aquarium so you will have a reserve supply. Filter the water before putting it in the aquarium. Store the extra filtered water in a cool, dry place.

To make the artificial seawater, purchase salt at a pet shop. (Table salt does not work!) Mix the special salt according to the directions on the label. Usually 1 pound of the salt makes about 3 gallons of artificial seawater.

Assemble the aquarium: Place the under-gravel filter in the bottom of the aquarium. A plastic tube attaches to the filter at one end and the air pump at the other end. Cover the filter with 2 inches of clean gravel. Fill the aquarium with the prepared water. Insert the hydrometer and the thermometer. Cover the top with a glass or plastic lid to keep evaporation at a minimum and to keep dust out. Mark the water level on the outside of the aquarium with a crayon or piece of tape. Replace the water that has evaporated weekly with fresh water. Optimal temperature for the aquarium is 65 degrees. Use the hydrometer to check the salinity of the water. If natural, maintain the same salinity and if artificial keep at about 1.025.

Add creatures: Hermit crabs, shrimp, sea horses, and small starfish are some interesting animals to try in the aquarium. Add one or two at a time to see if they adjust to the environment.

If you have collected your own shells and sand from the beach and want to put them into the aquarium, make sure they are clean by placing them under running water for at least two hours. Place them in a different container of salt water for a few days to make sure they will not decay and foul your water. Rinse one more time before adding to the aquarium. Sea plants usually do not fare well and should be avoided.

Feed the animals: Feed the animals with purchased food or bits of lean meat. Feed twice a day and remove any uneaten food after 10 minutes.

Troubleshooting: Remove animal droppings and any other debris often. If the water becomes fouled, possibly due to any shells or other materials you may have used, replace it with your emergency supply. If questions about your aquarium come up, the pet store where you may have purchased some of your materials is usually a good source of information.

Ocean Story Time

1. **FISHING FOR STORIES**. For each book you plan to read aloud, make a small facsimile of its cover out of sturdy paper. Fasten a paper clip to each of these and place on the floor. Use a fishing pole made from a ruler with a piece of string tied to it. Attach a magnet to the end of the string where the fish hook should be. Let the children take turns "fishing" for a book. The book that has been "caught" is the one that will be read during storytime.

2. **SEA SOUNDS**. Make a sound effects tape to enhance the books that are to be read at story time. Either make one ahead of time using a sound effects record, or enlist the children's help in making their own sound effects. If the children are to help, have them sit down near the tape recorder. Read the first page of the book, then discuss what sound effects to use. Can the children imitate the sound of the waves coming to shore, sea birds calling, or fog horns bellowing? Books about the ocean offer a wealth of opportunities for accompanying sounds. After practicing the sound effects to be used for the first pages of the book, record them. Make sure the sounds being recorded last as long as they need to during the reading of the book. Go on to the next page or series of pages which will require sound effects, practice the sounds, and record them. Continue until the book is completed. Play the sound effects tape as you read the book. When you have finished, make the tape available to the children in the reading corner.

Ocean Poems, Songs, Fingerplays

1. To the tune of "Frere Jacques":

   Fish are swimming, fish are swimming,
   In the sea, in the sea,
   A-splishing and a-splashing,
   A-splishing and a-splashing,
   Look and see, look and see.

2. Little drops of water
   Little grains of sand
   Make a mighty ocean
   And the pleasant land.

3. My brother was a sailor.
   He sailed across the sea,
   And all the fish that he could catch
   Were one, two, three. (*hold up appropriate number of fingers.*)

4. Three wise men of Gotham
   Went to sea in a bowl
   And if the bowl had been stronger
   My song would have been longer.

5. A sailor went to the sea, sea, sea
   To see what he could see, see, see
   And all that he could see, see, see
   Was the bottom of the deep blue sea, sea, sea.

   (*Each time "sea" or "see" is said, hold hand up to brow in a saluting fashion.*)

6. 1, 2, 3, 4, 5 (*hold up appropriate number of fingers.*)
   I caught a fish alive. (*make fishing gestures.*)
   6, 7, 8, 9, 10 (*hold up appropriate number of fingers.*)
   I let him go again. (*toss fish.*)

   Why did I let him go? (*shrug.*)
   Because he bit my finger so. (*make biting motion with hand.*)
   Which finger did he bite? (*shrug.*)
   The little finger on the right. (*hold up appropriate finger.*)

7. "Mother, may I go out to swim?"
   "Yes, my darling daughter.
   Hang your clothes on a hickory limb
   But don't go near the water."

8. A B C D goldfish?
   L M N O goldfish.
   O S A R!

9. She sells seashells by the seashore.

10. The slowly sinking ship sank.

11. One fish, two fish, three fish, four, (*hold up one finger for each fish.*)
    Swimming on the ocean floor. (*fold hands together and make wavelike motion.*)
    Big fish, little fish, long fish, short, (*make a large circle with arms overhead; make small circle with forefinger and thumb; stretch arms out horizontally; then bring together with small space between hands.*)
    Swim together just for sport. (*repeat wave-like motion.*)

    —Carol Holland

12. Behold the wonders of the mighty deep,
    Where crabs and lobsters learn to creep,
    And little fishes learn to swim,
    And clumsy sailors tumble in.

Ocean Music List

Cassettes

"Blow the Man Down." *Disney's Children's Favorites, Vol. 2.* Walt Disney Music Co. 606064, 1979.

"My Bonnie Lies Over the Ocean." *Disney's Children's Favorites, Vol 2.* Walt Disney Music Co. 606064, 1979.

"Sailing, Sailing." *Disney's Children's Favorites, Vol. 2.* Walt Disney Music Co. 606064, 1979.

"There's a Hole in the Bottom of the Sea." *Disney's Children's Favorite Silly Songs.* Walt Disney Music Co. 2528B, 1988.

"Three Little Fishies." *Disney's Children's Favorite Silly Songs.* Walt Disney Music Co. 2528B, 1988.

"Way Down Here Beneath the Ocean." *Disney's Children's Favorite Silly Songs.* Walt Disney Music Co. 2528B, 1988.

Ocean Book List

Fiction

Domanska, Janina. *I Saw a Ship a-Sailing.* Macmillan, 1972.
    Intricate illustrations highlight the traditional rhyme that tells about mice who sail a ship on the sea.

Freeman, Don. *The Seal and the Slick.* Viking, 1974.
    Children help a baby seal who accidentally wanders into an oil slick.

Gerstein, Mordicai. *The Seal Mother.* Dial Press, 1986.
    This is an unusual folk tale about a seal who sheds her skin and lives on land as a human.

Gretz, Susanna, and Alison Sage. *Teddy Bears at the Seaside.* Illustrated by Susanna Gretz. Macmillan, 1989.
    Five bears and their dog fish, swim, and snorkel at the beach.

Haas, Irene. *The Maggie B.* Atheneum, 1984.
    Maggie sails away with her baby brother on her imaginary ship.

Lionni, Leo. *Swimmy.* Pantheon, 1963.
    The little fish, Swimmy, teaches his friends how to swim in such a way that the hungry sharks won't be tempted to eat them.

Lund, Doris Herold. *The Paint Box Sea.* Illustrated by Symeon Shimin. McGraw-Hill, 1973.
    Two children vacation near an ever-changing seashore.

Rockwell, Anne, and Harlowe Rockwell. *At the Beach.* Macmillan, 1987.
    A little girl spends the day at the beach.

Ryder, Joanne. *Beach Party.* Illustrated by Diane Stanley. Frederick Warne, 1982.
    Rose's family spends a fun filled day at the beach, celebrating Uncle Tom's birthday.

Winnick, Karen B. *Sandro's Dolphin.* Lothrop, 1980.
    A young boy befriends a dolphin.

Nonfiction

Florian, Douglas. *Discovering Seashells.* Macmillan, 1986.
  This picture book illustrates families of shells and tells where they can be found.

Goudey, Alice. *Houses from the Sea.* Illustrated by Adrienne Adams. Charles Scribner's Sons, 1959.
  Children find many shells at the beach.

McGovern, Ann. *Sharks.* Illustrated by Murray Tinkelman. Four Winds Press, 1976.
  Using a question and answer format, this book gives information about sharks' habitat and eating habits.

Salsam, Millicent. *See Along the Shore.* Harper and Row, 1961.
  This interesting book explains what the average child would see and experience at the seaside.

Tresselt, Alvin. *Rain Drop Splash.* Illustrated by Leonard Weisgaard. Lothrop, 1946.
  The journey of a rain drop as it makes its way from the mountains to the ocean is explored.

7
ZOO SAFARI
(Zoo)

Focus on the Zoo

Children and adults love to visit the zoo to learn about wild animals. In addition to helping children recognize common zoo animals, the activities in this chapter will help the children understand the difference between wild and tame animals and to become sensitive to the four basic needs of any animal.

Consider discussing these topics:
    Wild animals
    Tame animals
    Animal habitats
    Basic needs of animals: food, water, shelter, space
    Zoo keepers
    Methods for acquiring animals
    Zoo babies' names

Zoo Motor Skills

1. **FEED THE ELEPHANT**. "Feed the elephant" by having the children take turns tossing peanuts through a hole in a piece of cardboard. The piece of cardboard should be made to look like an elephant (or other zoo animal), the hole being the elephant's mouth.

2. **SHELLING PEANUTS**. Children love to shell peanuts, crunching them up and finding an edible treasure inside. Give the children only three or four at a time and place a dropcloth under the table to make cleanup a breeze.

3. **MONKEY AND THE PEANUT**. Have all but one child sit on the floor in a circle. The child standing is the monkey. He or she walks around the outside of the circle, holding a peanut. The monkey picks a child to chase him or her by dropping the peanut in the child's lap. The sitting child jumps up and chases the monkey around the circle. If the monkey can get to the child's place and sit down before being tagged, the monkey then takes the child's place on the floor. Now a new monkey is holding the peanut and the game continues.

4. **SNAKE TAG**. Here is a new twist to the standard game of "tag." Choose someone to be "it." It tries to tag the other children. When it tags another child, that child must hold it's hand. Now the two children, who are starting to form a "snake," try to tag someone. The next child who is caught must hold hands with the first two, all three trying to tag the rest of the children. Continue until all of the children have been caught and added to the snake. The last child to be caught is it when the game begins again.

5. **ZOO RACES**. Divide the class into two teams. Ask the children to walk on their hands and feet, pretending to be bears. See which team can get all of its members across the finish line first. Have more races using bunny hops, snake crawls, flying birds, swinging monkeys, and so on.

6. **CURIOUS GEORGE**. Hide a toy monkey somewhere in the classroom or playground. Make a trail of paper banana peels leading to the monkey. Make the trail go along the floor and over and around various obstacles. Give one or two children a yellow hat to wear (to portray the Man in the Big Yellow Hat) while they follow the trail, looking for Curious George. Change the hiding place and the trail several times to keep the rest of the children from knowing in advance where Curious George can be found.

7. **THE MONKEY AND THE LION**. Draw a line on the ground. The lion stands behind the line. Other players (the monkeys) taunt the lion. The monkeys can go near the line, but not touch it. If the lion catches the monkeys, or if they accidentally touch the line, they must trade places with the lion.

8. **MONKEY SEE, MONKEY DO**. Choose one child to be the leader. He or she pretends to be a monkey in a cage at the zoo. The monkey performs any type of action, such as combing hair, chewing food, or making funny faces. The other children should mimic the monkey as closely as possible. Let the first monkey choose someone to be the next monkey.

9. **THIS IS THE WAY**. Sing these lyrics to the tune of "This Is the Way We Wash Our Clothes":

> This is the way the elephant walks, the elephant walks, the elephant walks.
> This is the way the elephant walks
> At the zoo.

Portray an elephant walking using one of your arms as the trunk. Think of other animals to sing about and portray, such as this is the way to slither like a snake, this is the way to swing like a monkey, this is the way to swim like an otter, and this is the way to stretch like a giraffe.

Zoo Language Activities

1. **WHERE IS IT?** Mount 6 to 10 interesting pictures on tagboard or construction paper, and place a paper clip at the top of each. Using a cookie cutter as a pattern, cut a small animal shape out of another piece of construction paper. Without letting the children see, clip the animal cutout behind one of the pictures. Let the children take turns guessing which picture the animal is hiding behind. They must ask if the animal is behind a particular picture by describing the picture. The animal cutout may be kept as a reward for the child who guesses correctly where the animal was hiding.

2. **ANIMAL PARTS**. Obtain large pictures of zoo animals. Use a page from a self-sticking note pad to cover up one part of the animal's body, such as an elephant's ear or a giraffe's neck. Hold the pictures up one at a time and ask the children to tell you what body part is hidden.

3. **ANIMALS IN ORDER**. Name three animals, and have the children repeat the animals in the order you gave them. Increase the number of animals you say as it gets easier for the children. Include other uncommon animal names.

4. **PEEKABOO**. Collect several interesting pictures of animals. For each picture, cut a piece of sturdy paper the same size. Cut several small doors in the piece of sturdy paper. Clip the paper to the picture so that when the children peek behind the little doors, they see part of the picture. Have the children see if they can guess what the picture is using as few peekaboos as possible.

5. **ZOO LOTTO**. For four players, use four large pieces of paper, two each of 32 different animal stickers, and index cards. Divide each paper into eight sections. Place a different animal sticker in each section, affixing its mate to an index card. Cut the index cards to fit on top of the lotto sections. To play, give each child one of the lotto boards that you have prepared. Mix up the index cards and place them facedown on the table. Select the top card and show it to the players. The child it belongs to should identify the animal and then place the card on his or her lotto board in the appropriate space. Continue until all the children have covered the spaces on their lotto boards.

6. **GUESSING GAME.** Ask the children to take turns pretending to be an animal at the zoo. Each child should tell something about the animal and see if any of the other children can guess what the animal is.

Another variation of this game is to think of an animal, and have the children ask questions until someone guesses the animal. The first child to guess correctly then thinks of and answers questions about a new animal.

7. **DR. DOOLITTLE.** Sing this to the melody of "Old MacDonald's Farm:"

> Doctor Doolittle had a zoo, E I E I O.
> And in that zoo he had a _____, E I E I O.
> With a _____ here and _____ there.
> Here a _____ there a _____.
> Everywhere a _____.
> Doctor Doolittle had a zoo, E I E I O.

8. **ANIMAL HUNT.** Hide pictures of zoo animals throughout the classroom, and have the children hunt for the pictures, like an Easter egg hunt. Have the children tell what animal they found. Ask each child a question about his or her animal, such as what it eats, what color it is, etc.

9. **ZOO BOOK.** Have the children cut pictures of animals out of magazines or coloring books, and ask them to mount their pictures on pieces of construction paper. Have each child dictate a statement about his or her animal and print the statement on the paper under the picture. Staple all of the papers together to make a book.

Zoo Math Activities

1. **ANIMAL SHAPES.** Use cookie cutters to trace some animal shapes onto colored construction paper, making at least 12 different colored animals, two of each color. Mix them up. Ask the children to match the colors. Make another set in which the children will match the shape of the animal instead of the color. Use three of the animals to lay out a simple pattern for the child to repeat. Numbers can be printed on the backs of the animals for more advanced students. The children can then identify the numbers, match numbers, or put in numerical order.

2. **PEANUTS.** Use peanuts and a set of number cards for this activity. Offer the child one or more peanuts and ask him or her to select the number card that tells how many peanuts the child has. Use the same materials for another activity. Line up the number cards on the table. Help the child place the appropriate number of peanuts near each card.

3. **MONKEY MIX-UP.** Obtain as many jars or plastic containers and their lids as possible. Remove the lids. Tell the children that a mischievous monkey escaped from its cage and mixed up all the jars and lids. Ask the children to put them back together. This activity not only provides good small-motor practice but also helps the children judge sizes and shapes. After the children have successfully topped each container, you may expand the activity by asking them to line the containers up from smallest to largest, or ask them to sort the containers according to shape.

4. **ANIMAL STEPS.** Draw a line on the floor for the children to stand behind; draw another line at least 10 feet away. Roll a die on the floor in front of the children, the larger the die, the better. The children take that many steps. Continue rolling the die and taking steps until the children have crossed the other line. Make the steps interesting: do elephant steps, bear steps, mouse steps, etc.

5. **MONKEY, MONKEY.** Have children sit in a circle on the floor. Say the following rhyme and count the children:

> Monkey, monkey, full of cheer,
> How many monkeys have we here?

Tap one child on the head and he or she leaves. Continue singing and counting until no children remain.

6. **MONKEY CHAIN.** Use the pattern given to make several monkeys out of poster board (see figure 7.1). Bend the arms and tails slightly so that they do not lay totally flat on the table. Have the child try to pick up the monkeys by hooking their arms and tails together. The children should count how many they can pick up in a continuous chain.

7. **DINNER TIME.** Number 11 bowls from 0 to 10, one number on each bowl, and set a toy animal near each bowl. Provide a large bowl containing unshelled peanuts, cereal, or Styrofoam pieces, and the children use scoops or large spoons to prepare the animals' dinners. The children should identify the numbers on the bowls and place that many scoops of food into the bowls. Zero, of course, represents the empty set and should have no food placed in it.

8. **ELEPHANT WHEEL.** Use one large and two small cardboard pizza wheels to make an elephant as in the illustration (see figure 7.2). Attach the small wheels (the ears) to the large wheel (the head) by using brads. Cut holes for the eyes in such a way that the ears show underneath. Draw the numerals 1 to 10 on the left ears so that they show through the eye hole. Do the same with the right eye, using an appropriate number of dots to match the numerals. The child's job is to turn the left ear and the right ear until the numeral showing in the left eye matches the number of dots showing in the right eye.

Zoo Science Activities

1. **ANIMAL CATEGORIES.** The purpose of this activity is to help the children distinguish wild animals from domesticated or tame animals, and to recognize that wildlife occurs in many different forms.

Provide children with magazines, coloring books, and newspapers, instructing them to cut out as many pictures of animals as they can find. Explain that animals are every living thing except plants.

Fig. 7.1.

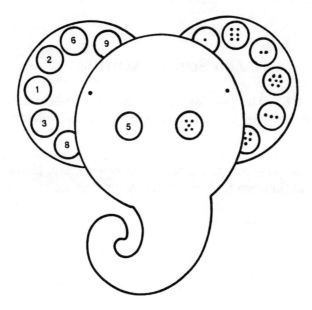

Fig. 7.2.

Divide a bulletin board into two sections, one labeled "Tame" and the other "Wild." Place an example of each type of animal under each label. Once the children have cut out a large number of animals, it is time to classify them. Discuss the fact that a wild animal lives freely, providing for its own food, shelter, and other needs. Wildlife does not refer to pets or farm animals. Wildlife includes fish, insects, birds, mammals, spiders, and reptiles. Some animals can be found in the wild but have cousins that live as pets, such as trout and goldfish, eagles and parakeets. Sometimes it may be difficult for a child to decide whether an animal is tame or wild. Encourage the children to think of what is *usually* the case. Have the children take turns holding up their pictures. Identify the animal and discuss whether it is tame or wild. Let each child tack or tape his or her animal picture in the appropriate space on the bulletin board.

Discuss zoos. Explain that a long time ago, zoos were mostly for entertainment. They gave people a chance to see wild and exotic animals that they would not normally have a chance to see. This is still the case today, although zoos often have a more important job, too. Nowadays the zoos are important to the breeding of and preservation of endangered animals. Zoos also serve to educate us about wild animals and issues concerning wild animals.

2. **ANIMAL HABITATS.** Another way to sort is to divide them into three groups according to their normal habitats. Divide the bulletin board into three sections, one for animals who live mostly on land, one for those in water, and one for those in the sky. Help the children decide to which habitat the animals belong and tack them to the bulletin board in the appropriate space.

Discuss the fact that it is the job of zoo designers to provide a suitable habitat for the animals that live there.

3. **ZOO BABIES.** On the top half of a bulletin board, wall, or large poster board, attach pictures of animal mothers. Underneath, attach pictures of matching baby animals. Mix up the order so that each baby is not directly underneath its own mother. Tape a piece of string near each mother, making sure that the string is long enough to reach the corresponding baby. Put another piece of tape near each baby. The child's job is to use the string to connect the mother animal to the baby animal.

4. **FOOD, WATER, SHELTER, SPACE.** For this activity you will need several different size boxes to serve as "cages," several stuffed toy zoo animals, water and containers to hold the water, zoo food such as fruit pieces and hay (or representations of these), and pieces of wood, tree branches, or small boxes to serve as shelter for the toy animals.

Explain to the children that all animals have four basic needs: food, water, shelter, and space. Explain that if people remove an animal from its wild environment where the animal provides for its own needs, people are responsible for meeting its needs. Most children will understand that animals (and humans) need food and water. Shelter and space may need some defining, however. Make sure the children can repeat and understand the four basic needs before proceeding.

The task the children will undertake in this activity is simple. Select one of the toy animals, identify it, and discuss what four basic needs it has. Use the items you have collected to make a habitat to suit its needs. Assemble as many habitats as supplies allow. Set up the habitats in an area where the children can have access to them for as long as possible before disassembling them. Pretend to be zookeepers who want to take good care of their animals.

If there is a classroom pet, discuss with the children how you are providing the pet's four basic needs.

Have children draw pictures of their own four basic needs. Stress that humans are animals too, and have the same four basic needs as other animals.

5. **CARRYING CAPACITY.** One of the four basic needs defined is space. Carrying capacity is the number of animals a certain habitat can support. The children may wonder, when visiting the zoo, why there may be only one or two animals in each habitat. This activity will help explain this.

Have the children sit very close together in a small area while you read a short story to them. Discuss how the crowding affects their behavior. Explain the fact that certain habitats can only support a certain amount of animals. If it gets too crowded, the animals will either stop having babies or move to another area in order to make it less crowded. One of the reasons that some animals are becoming rare is that their habitats in the wild are becoming too small to support a large number of animals. Scientists who work with animals in zoos take measures to ensure survival of these animals.

6. **PLEASE DO NOT DISTURB.** The goal of this activity is to illustrate the need to allow people and animals a "comfort zone." It may be especially appropriate to do this activity before a visit to the zoo.

Have a volunteer stand in front of the class. Approach the child slowly, asking the child to tell you when your presence makes him or her feel nervous or uncomfortable. Repeat with the other children, and observe that different children have different comfort zones. Do the children think that their comfort zones would be the same with a member of their family as it would be with a stranger? Introduce the idea that animals in the wild and also those in the zoo might be uncomfortable when approached by a stranger. Even animals we see in our own environment have need of their own space. It is wise to allow animals the space they need not only out of respect, but also for our own safety. Mother animals with their babies, animals that have no room for quick escape, and injured animals have comfort zones much larger than other animals. Have the children name some animals that they might encounter in their environment or at the zoo. Draw life-size outlines of some of these animals and pin them to the bulletin board. Have the children approach the animals, estimating how far away and how quiet they must stay to ensure an ample comfort zone for the animal. Stress that when in doubt, the more space provided, the better. If you wish, measure and record the estimated comfort zones, to verify with zoo personnel before visiting the zoo.

Zoo Art Projects

1. **SWINGING MONKEY.** *Materials*: Paper, markers or crayons, scissors, a hole punch, a drinking straw or unsharpened pencil. *Directions*: Transfer the monkey pattern (see figure 7.3) to a piece of paper for the child to cut out. The child may use markers and crayons to decorate the monkey. Help the child punch a hole in the monkey's hand and then slip the straw or pencil through the hole. By twirling the straw or pencil between his or her fingers, the child can make the monkey swing.

2. **JUNGLE SCENE.** *Materials*: One large piece of butcher paper or newsprint (mural size), animal shapes cut out of construction paper, green, brown, and yellow paints put into squeeze bottles; and markers. *Directions*: Ask the children to place the animal cutouts on the blank butcher

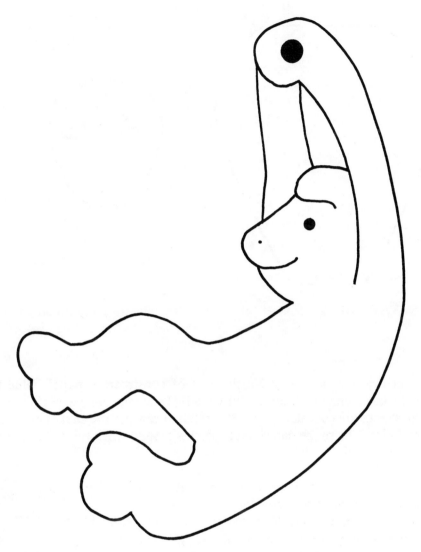

Fig. 7.3.

paper. With each child manning a squeeze bottle of paint, squirt the various colors all over the large paper, even on top of the animal cutouts. Carefully remove and discard the animal cutouts and let the mural dry. Once the mural has dried, hang it on the wall. Let the children use markers to fill in the details of the animals whose shapes are on the mural.

3. **STREAMER SNAKE**. *Materials*: Each child will need one template of the snake head pattern (see figure 7.4), one piece of colorful construction paper, pencil, scissors, glue, a small amount of glitter, and one length of crepe paper streamer about 3 feet long. *Directions*: Each child will trace around the snake-head pattern on his or her piece of construction paper, making sure the pattern's fold line is placed on the fold of the paper. Assist the children in cutting out the heads. Have the children place a dot of glue where each of the snakes' eyes should be. Before the glue dries, sprinkle glitter over the dots to form jeweled eyes. (Sequins can be used instead of glitter, if you prefer.) While the glue dries, help the children cut small forked tongues from scraps of construction paper. Have the children glue the tongue in place, and glue one end of the streamer between the two halves

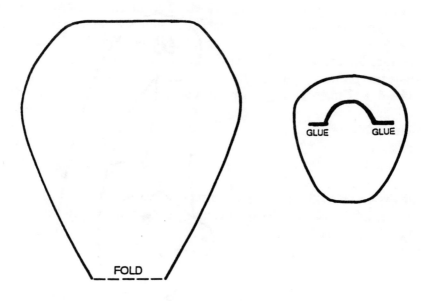

Fig. 7.4.

of the snakes' heads. Let dry. Cut a ½- by 2-inch piece of construction paper. Glue it to the underside of the snakes' heads, forming a loop, as illustrated. (Tape reinforcement of the loops may be necessary.) When the snakes are completely dry, the children can put the snakes on their hands, with fingers through the loops. The snake dances and squirms around when the children move their hands in wide circular motions.

4. **POCKET PUPPET**. *Materials*: One sheet of paper, crayons, markers, glue, and scrap paper for each child. *Directions*: Help the children fold their sheets of construction paper into thirds, lengthwise. Next, fold them in half. Fold back the top and bottom ends (see figure 7.5). The children can slip their thumbs and fingers into the slots to make the puppets move their mouths. Have the children glue on or draw eyes, noses, ears, etc.

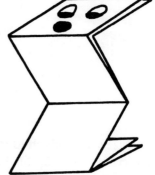

Fig. 7.5.

5. **ZOO MOBILE**. *Materials*: For each child you will need various-colored construction paper, yarn, animal-shaped cookie cutters, scissors, markers, and a coat hanger. *Directions*: Let the children trace outlines of animals onto construction paper, using the cookie cutters as guides. Help them cut out their animal shapes. If you wish, help the children identify the animals by helping to print the animal names on each one's side. Punch a small hole in the top portion of each animal. After the children have cut several lengths of yarn, help them string the yarn through the holes in the cutouts and attach them to the coat hangers. Hang the mobiles from the ceiling where a breeze can put the animals in motion.

6. **LION MASK**. *Materials*: Provide each child with a paper plate, a small triangle cut from brown construction paper, six pipe cleaners; yellow, orange, or brown yarn, yellow paint, a scissors, and glue. *Directions*: Hold the paper plate up to the child's face and mark where his or her eyes are. Cut out two eye holes, and let the child paint the mask yellow. While the paint dries, the child should

cut the yarn into as many 2-inch strands as possible. Let the child glue the brown triangle on the mask for the nose. Next, the child should put glue all around the outer edge of the mask, then apply the yarn pieces already cut out. This forms the lion's mane. Finally, the child can glue the pipe cleaners onto the face for the whiskers. A craft stick can be glued to the bottom of the mask as a handle, or it can be tied on with yarn. To attach yarn ties to the mask, poke a small hole on each side of the mask. Thread a 12-inch piece of yarn through each hole and tie into place.

To make a matching tail staple six 1-yard long lengths of curling ribbon together at one end. Help the child braid the tail, allow 3 or 4 inches at the end of the braid. Staple, and curl the ends, if desired. Tuck the tail into the top of the child's slacks or pin to the backside of the child's dress.

7. **CLOTHESPIN ANIMALS.** *Materials*: Construction paper, yarn, markers, glue, scissors, two clothespins for each child, and the animal patterns given (see figures 7.6 and 7.7). *Directions*: Help

BODY

Fig. 7.6.

Fig. 7.7.

each child transfer one animal body and one animal head to construction paper. The markers can be used to put facial features on the head. Assist in cutting the animals out, then have the child glue the head to the body. Cut a small piece of yarn for the tail and glue it to the body. Clip two clothespins onto the animal to form legs, allowing it to stand up.

8.   **DUCK HATS.** *Materials*: Each child will need a white paper plate, yellow and black construction paper, glue, and scissors. *Directions*: Cut the paper plate around the inner circle. Use the given pattern to trace and cut out the duck's bill, using yellow construction paper (see figure 7.8). Ask the children to cut two round eyes from the black construction paper. Show the children how to fold the top portion of the paper plate to make the duck's head (see figure 7.9). Have each child glue on the duck's eyes and bill. When dry, the hat will be ready to wear.

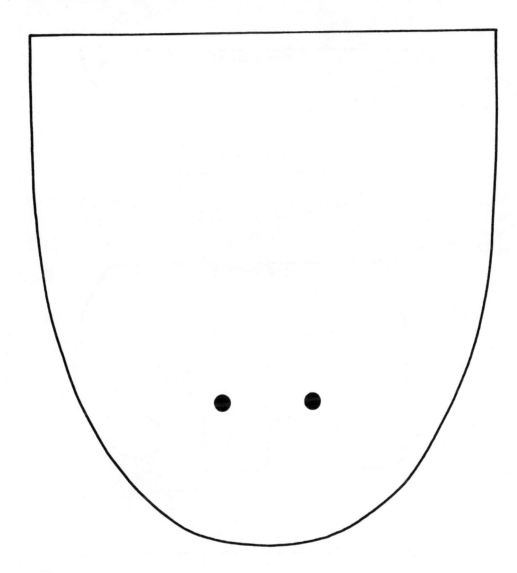

Fig. 7.8.

Fig. 7.9.

9. **FOLDING ANIMALS.** *Materials*: Construction paper, scissors, glue, and markers or crayons. *Directions*: For quick and easy standing animals, help each child transfer an animal pattern (see figure 7.10) to construction paper, making sure that the fold line of the pattern lies on the fold of the construction paper. Assist the children in cutting out their animals. The turtle looks best flattened out a bit, while the anteater and elephant should stand tall. After gluing the two ends of the elephant's trunk or the anteater's snout together, features may be added to the animals with pens or crayons.

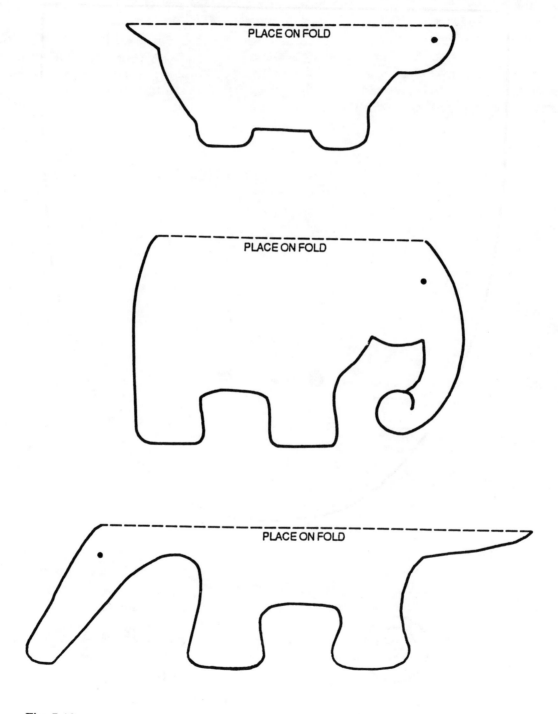

Fig. 7.10

Zoo Class Project

Zoo for a Day

Wouldn't it be fun to run your own zoo? With a little planning and some help from the children's parents, it could be possible to turn the classroom into a zoo for a few hours.

Lead a discussion in which children describe any pets or unusual animals they have at home or at a friend's house. Contact parents about bringing the animals (leashed or in cages) to school for a short observation period. Find out what kind of animals the local Humane Society or pet shop or zoo might be willing to bring to school for a short demonstration. Stress that you are interested in their most unusual animals. Research the animals that you know will be shown. Discuss the animals ahead of time, such as their four basic needs, how the animals look, their natural habitats, etc. Show pictures of the proposed visitors. It might be fun to plan one surprise animal visitor.

Plan a time and a place for your miniature zoo. Invite all parents. Make sure parents who are sharing their pets will stay and be responsible for supervising the pet. Arrange the animals in the classroom or outdoors. Have the children help make signs to hang near each animal for identification. The zoo should be set up in such a way that one or two children at a time can visit each animal, observe it for a short time, touch it or hold it (if possible), and be told a few facts about the animal. The children should be given time to ask questions, too. Every few minutes, the children can rotate to a different animal. It is not necessary to obtain a large number of animals, even five or six animals would do.

Serve refreshments, if feasible, and then talk about the animals shown. Were they what the children expected after doing their research? How were they different? What did the children learn? Did they learn more about the animal by actually observing it, as opposed to simply seeing it in pictures and talking about it?

If the school is in the market for a class pet, perhaps the "surprise" animal visitor would be a rabbit or goldfish that could live permanently at the school?

Zoo Story Time

1. **ANIMAL FAIR.** Use Janet Stevens' book *Animal Fair* to teach the song by the same name. Act out the events that happen in the song: the baboon combing his hair, the monkey getting drunk and stepping on the elephant's trunk, the elephant sneezing and falling on his knees. Open story time each day during zoo week by singing this song.

2. **ZOO CORNER.** Display the animal books that you have chosen with their stuffed counterparts. For instance, if you have chosen *Curious George* by H. A. Rey as a book to display, provide a toy monkey for the children to cuddle or play with while looking at the book.

3. **PUPPETS.** Animal puppets are easy to find. Use them to introduce the animal books you choose to read aloud. The puppets can also make comments as you read, or ask questions about the book afterward.

4. Activity 6 in the Zoo Motor Skills section is also a great extension activity to do after reading the book *Curious George.*

Zoo Poems, Songs, Fingerplays

1. Do your ears hang low? (*place hands by ears, fingers pointing down.*)
    Do they wobble to and fro? (*wiggle hands.*)
    Can you tie them in a knot? (*pretend to tie knot.*)
    Can you tie them in a bow? (*pretend to tie them in a bow.*)
    Can you toss them over your shoulder like a continental soldier? (*pretend to toss ears.*)
    Do your ears hang low? (*hands by ears as before.*)
    Do your ears hang high? (*place hands over head, fingers up.*)
    Do they reach up to the sky? (*stretch hands way up.*)
    Are they curly when they're wet? (*crunch up fingers.*)
    Are they shaggy when they're dry? (*wiggle fingers.*)
    Can you toss them over your shoulder like a continental soldier? (*pretend to toss ears over shoulder.*)
    Do your ears hang high? (*hands above head.*)

2. Five naughty monkeys bouncing on the bed, (*hold up five bouncing fingers.*)
    One fell off and bumped his head. (*rub head.*)
    Mother called the doctor, (*pretend to talk on phone.*)
    And the doctor said,
    "That's what you get for bouncing on the bed." (*shake finger in an accusatory way.*)

    Repeat verse, using four monkeys, then three, then two, then one. At the end of the last verse, say, "No more monkeys bouncing on the bed."

3. Eenie meenie minie mo. (*hold up hand and count off each finger.*)
    Catch a tiger by the toe. (*hold on to one finger.*)
    If he hollers let him go. (*let finger go.*)
    Eenie, meenie, minie, mo. (*count off each finger again.*)

4. All around the mulberry bush, the monkey chased the weasel.
    The monkey thought it was all in fun,
    Pop! Goes the weasel.

    (This song may be used as a game. For the verse, have children either sit in a circle or hold hands while walking in a circle. When they say "Pop! Goes the weasel," they all jump up.)

5. Five little elephants standing in a row. (*hold up five fingers.*)
    This little elephant stubbed his toe. (*fold down one finger.*)
    This little elephant said, "Oh, oh, oh." (*fold down next finger.*)
    This little elephant laughed and was glad. (*fold down next finger.*)
    This little elephant cried and was sad. (*fold down next finger.*)
    This little elephant so thoughtful and good, (*wiggle remaining finger.*)
    Ran for the doctor as fast as he could. (*make running motions with index and middle finger.*)

6. Five little monkeys swinging on the door, (*show five fingers.*)
    One fell off and then there were four. (*eliminate one finger.*)
    Four little monkeys hanging in a tree,
    One swung away and then there were three. (*eliminate another finger.*)
    Three little monkeys looking for the zoo,
    One went in and then there were two. (*eliminate third finger.*)

Two little monkeys looking for some fun,
One started laughing and then there was one. (*eliminate another finger.*)
One little monkey playing all alone,
He fell asleep and then there were none. (*fold hands and place under head as if asleep.*)

7. "Jenny, Jenny, do you have a penny
    for admittance to the zoo?"
    "Sorry, sorry,
    No, I don't.
    A picnic will have to do."

8. (For this poem, mime the animal mentioned in each verse.)

    I see a striped tiger as hungry as can be.
    I'm glad he's in his cage
    So he can't eat me.

    And there's a big fat hippo lying muddy in the sun.
    I'd like to wash him off,
    But I think he's having fun.

    I see the parrots squawking and flying about their cage.
    They talk and flap and flutter,
    Just like they're on a stage.

    I see lots and lots of animals at the zoo.
    I like to watch them having fun,
    And they like to see me, too!

9. (Sing to the tune of "Ten Little Indians" as you hold up the appropriate number of fingers.)

    One little, two little, three little elephants,
    Four little, five little, six little elephants.
    Seven little, eight little, nine little elephants,
    Living at the zoo.

    Ten little, nine little, eight little elephants,
    Seven little, six little, five little elephants,
    Four little, three little, two little elephants,
    One little elephant!

    (*Try these other animals for alternate verses: polar bears, buffaloes, bandicoots, crocodiles, hummingbirds, kangaroos, nightingales, pelicans, wallabies.*)

10. The elephant carries a great big trunk;
    He never packs it with clothes;
    It has no lock and it has no key,
    But he takes it wherever he goes.

Zoo Music List

Cassettes

"Animal Fair." *Disney's Children's Favorites, Vol. 1*. Walt Disney Music Co. 606054, 1979.

Candle. *Animals and Other Things*. Birdwing Records, BWC 2031A.
This is a collection of ten songs written about various animals.

"Do Your Ears Hang Low?" *Disney's Children's Favorites, Vol. 4*. Walt Disney Music Co. 606084, 1990.

Sing With Me Animal Songs. Random House 160149.
This cassette contains best-loved songs and a colorful song book.

Spangler, David. *Dancing Animals*. Caedmon Records CPN1834.
This is a collection of animal songs written by David Spangler.

Zoo Book List

Fiction

Barrett, Judi. *Animals Should Definitely NOT Act Like People*. Illustrated by Ron Barrett. Atheneum, 1980.
This book comically illustrates what would happen if animals tried to do some of the things that people do.

Barrett, Judi. *Animals Should Definitely NOT Wear Clothing*. Illustrated by Ron Barrett. Atheneum, 1981.
Animals would be a bit uncomfortable in human clothing.

Barrett, Judi. *A Snake Is Totally Tail*. Illustrated by L. S. Johnson. Atheneum, 1983.
This book describes various animals in a comical manner.

Campbell, Rod. *Dear Zoo*. Scholastic, 1983.
A child sends back pets requested from a zoo until the perfect pet finally arrives.

Rey, H. A. *Cecily G. and the Nine Monkeys*. Houghton Mifflin, 1942.
Lonely Cecily Giraffe teams up with Curious George and his friends.

Rey, H. A. *Curious George*. Houghton Mifflin, 1941.
The first Curious George story tells how George is captured and makes friends with the man in the yellow hat.

Rice, Eve. *Sam Who Never Forgets*. Greenwillow, 1977.
Sam the zookeeper feeds the animals every day at three o'clock.

Tafuri, Nancy. *Junglewalk*. Greenwillow, 1988.
   This is a wordless picture book. Vibrant artwork depicts a boy's imaginary walk through the jungle.

Nonfiction

Allen, Robert. *Zoo Book*. Photographs by Peter Sahula. Platt and Munk, 1968.
   This informational book contains a color photograph of each animal described.

Gibbons, Gail. *Zoo*. Thomas Crowell, 1987.
   This simply illustrated picture book takes a look behind the scenes at a large zoo, explaining the many tasks that zoo workers do every day.

Hoban, Tana. *Big Ones, Little Ones*. Greenwillow, 1976.
   Tana Hoban photographs mother animals and their babies.

Hoban, Tana. *A Children's Zoo*. Greenwillow, 1985.
   This book contains many photographs taken at a children's zoo.

Jacobsen, Karen. *Zoos*. Children's Press, 1982.
   This book is a very general introduction to zoos using simple language and large color photographs.

Munari, Bruno. *Bruno Munari's Zoo*. World Publishing, 1963.
   Vivid art accented by eloquent descriptions inform children of the animals introduced in this book.

Pfloog, Jan. *Zoo Book*. Golden Press, 1967.
   This book is a brief introduction to zoos, meant for very young children.

Rojankovsky, Feodor. *Animals in the Zoo*. Alfred Knopf, 1973.
   This book contains a description of one animal for each letter of the alphabet.

Roosevelt, Michele Chapin. *Zoo Animals*. Random House, 1983.
   This picture book contains a brief introduction to zoo animals for the very young.

Whitehead, Patricia. *Now I Know Monkeys*. Illustrated by Bert Dodson. Troll Associates, 1982.
   A large amount of monkey facts are contained in this picture book for young children.

Poems and Songs

Mullins, Edward S. *Animal Limericks*. Follett Publishing, 1966.
   This book contains many humorous poems about various animals.

Prelutsky, Jack. *Zoo Doings*. Illustrated by Paul O. Zelinsky. Greenwillow, 1983.
   This book contains short and silly animal poems.

Stevens, Janet. *Animal Fair*. Holiday House, 1981.
   Beautiful artwork and written music make it easy and fun to learn the favorite children's song.

8
UNDER THE BIG TOP
(Circus)

Focus on the Circus

Circuses are great entertainment. Why is it, then, that clowns sometimes frighten young children? A unit on the circus may be useful in helping to make children more at ease when confronted with masks and disguises.

Consider discussing these subjects:
    The big top
    Trained animals
    Clowns
    Circus acts
    Hard work behind the scenes
    Masks, makeup, disguises
    History of the circus

Circus Motor Skills

The following six exercises make use of balloons. Enlist the help of plenty assistants to help inflate them.

1. **KEEP IT UP!** Give each child one balloon or let two children share one balloon. The children will throw the balloon up in the air and try to keep it up as long as possible. If two children are sharing one balloon, ask them to take turns hitting. Experiment with hitting the balloon with different parts of the body. Make sure you have plenty of room to do this exercise.

2. **MUSICAL BALLOONS.** You will need one balloon per child, less one (as in musical chairs.) Have the children form a circle and pat the balloons around gently to music. If a balloon falls to the floor, have the child pick it up and get it started again. When the music stops, each child must grab a balloon. The child remaining with no balloon is out, but can be consoled by helping the teacher pop a balloon.

3. **BALLOONATICS.** Provide each child with a balloon or let two children share one balloon. Have the children bounce the balloon around or pat it in the air according to your directions. Tell them to use their feet, elbows, heads, or other body parts. Try asking them to hit it twice in succession or to try to hit it with their eyes closed. Play appropriate music while playing with the balloons. Tell the children they must stop when the music stops, as in musical balloons.

4. **JUMPING MONKEYS.** Blow up balloons and hang them from a string taped to the ceiling. Provide one balloon for each child, or let the children take turns sharing a few balloons. Adjust them to different heights for the different heights of the children. The balloons should be slightly out of reach. Tell the children that they are monkeys trying to reach a balloon that has been caught in a tree. First see if they can reach the balloon by standing on the ground and stretching their arms up. Next, let them jump for it. Adjust the heights of the balloons, if necessary.

5. **BALLOON STOMP.** Each child will need one balloon and a piece of string 24 inches long. Tie one end of the string to the balloon, and the other end to the children's ankles. Scatter the children around the room. Turn on some circus music, and tell the children to step on and pop each other's balloons, but to save their own balloon from being popped. Have the children stop when you stop the music, as in musical balloons.

6. **BALLOON VOLLEYBALL**. Inflate a balloon. Next, divide the children into two teams. Place a line of masking tape down the middle of the play area. One team stands on one side of the line, the other team stands on the other side. Have the children bat the balloon from one side to the other, trying to keep it in the air as much as possible. Keeping score is not necessary.

7. **BOWLING**. Use six 2-liter plastic soda bottles as bowling pins. Mark pin positions on the floor with some masking tape as illustrated:

X

XX

XXX

Make another mark on the floor which the children must stand behind to roll the ball at the pins. Have the children roll the ball at the pins and count how many they have knocked over. Let the children reset the pins themselves for each round of play.

8. **BEANBAG TOSS**. Use a cardboard box about 12 inches deep. Draw a clown face on the box, making holes for the eyes, nose, and mouth. Beanbags will be tossed into the holes. Make sure the holes are about twice the size of the beanbags. If the box that you have is too small for so many holes, make a clown face with a hole for the mouth only. Set the box at the correct angle for tossing the beanbags, weighting it with some books so it won't fall over. Put three masking tape lines on the floor for standing behind while throwing. Make one line "easy," one line "difficult," and one line a "real challenge." Have the children stand behind the "easy" line to start, and let them work their way up to the challenging one as they improve their skills at throwing.

9. **HUMAN PRETZELS**. Have the children sit around you on the floor. Ask them to perform the following daring feats: touch your left elbow to the opposite knee; pat your head and rub your stomach at the same time; put your fingers in your ears and wiggle your nose. Repeat.

10. **TIGHTROPE WALKER**. Put a masking tape line on the floor to act as your "tightrope." Ask the children to walk forwards, backwards, and sideways on the tightrope. Can they think of any stunts?

Circus Language Activities

1. **PAPER CUP SHELL GAME**. Turn six or more paper cups upside down and glue a different colored circle onto the bottom of each cup. Place a treat under each cup. Name a color and ask the child to tell you which cup that is. When the correct one is chosen, the child receives the treat under the cup. The same activity can be used to teach letters, shapes, or numbers.

2. **SAME AND DIFFERENT**. Use a large piece of tagboard or sturdy paper with pictures of clowns or other circus items glued or drawn on, one on each side. Some of the features should be the same, some should be different. Ask the children to tell how the clowns are the same and how they are different.

3. **ACTION!** Glue action pictures onto index cards, and ask the child to identify the action in each picture. Another way to do the same activity is to spread out the cards and ask the child to point to the one running, walking, jumping, etc. Larger pictures may be used if you wish to place them in a photo album rather than on cards.

4. **MATCHING CARDS**. Make two sets of cards, one set with one letter of the alphabet on each card, the other with a circus sticker on each one. Each picture card should have a corresponding letter card. For example, if you have a card with a clown sticker on it, also provide a card with the letter "c" on it. Place a few of the letter cards faceup on the table in front of the child. Place some of the appropriate picture cards in a pile facedown. Ask the child to select a picture card and try to match it to the appropriate letter card.

5. **THE RINGMASTER SAYS**. Tell the children that you are the ringmaster and to follow your instructions.

For example: hop on one foot, sit down, close your eyes, smile; touch your toes three times, whisper your name, and skip around the table.

Start with a few simple instructions and work your way up to more complex ones.

6. **TRAINED LION**. Find a box large enough for a child to fit into for this game. Put the box on the floor, and tell the child that you are the lion tamer and he or she is the lion. Give the child a number of instructions to carry out, all involving his or her position in relation to the box. For example: sit inside, stand beside, put a ball under, hide behind, etc.

7. **COLORED RIBBONS**. Obtain two to three ribbons each of many different colors. Tie a ribbon around each child's wrist. Tell the children to find the other children with the same color ribbon and hold hands. Do it again, asking the children to form pairs with children with *different* colored ribbons. Ask the children to identify their partner's color.

8. **SHELL GAME**. Use three nut shells or paper cups large enough to fit a marble or small treat underneath. Arrange the shells on a table with the treat underneath one of them. Show the child which shell the treat is under, and then mix them up so that the child must guess where the treat is. Tell the child to say which shell has the treat, the one on the left, right, or in the middle. If the child guesses, he or she receives the treat.

9. **CONCENTRATION**. For this game, you will need 16 index cards, and eight pairs of circus stickers to glue onto them. Each card will have one sticker glued to it, forming a deck of cards with eight pairs. Shuffle the cards and arrange them facedown on the table in four rows of four cards each. Ask the child to turn over two of the cards. If they are a match, he or she keeps the cards. If they are not a match, the child turns them back over. Now it is your turn to do the same. Continue until all the pairs have been found and the game ends. Once all the children are familiar with the game, have them play each other and add more pairs to the deck to make it more difficult.

Circus Math Activities

1. **PEANUTS**. Place a bowl of peanuts in the middle of the table. Have the children take turns guessing how many there are in the bowl. Count the peanuts. Give everyone a few to eat and try to guess how many are remaining in the bowl. Count them again, eat some more, guess again. Keep going until none remain.

2. **ODD MAN OUT**. For this exercise, obtain six 4-by-10-inch strips of tagboard. Draw six items on each strip, one of which is different than the other five. Ask the child to find the item that is different. Use numbers, shapes, or pictures for the six items.

3. **CIRCUS TRAIN.** Use a toy train or cardboard cutout of a train for this activity. On each car, place a number sticker. The numeral 1 goes on the engine, 2 on the next car, 3 on the third car, etc., until you reach the caboose which should be number 10. Show the child how the train looks when it is put together correctly. Take the train apart and mix up the pieces. Help the child put the train back in the correct order. Practice until the child can do it alone.

4. **CIRCUS SHAPES.** Show the children pictures of things pertaining to the circus that have geometric shapes. For instance, start with a picture of a clown with a round nose. Have the children assist you in finding five round items in the classroom. Lay them out in front of you in the order of their size. Do the same with squares, rectangles, and triangles.

5. **STRAWS AND CUPS.** Use paper cups and drinking straws to teach children one-to-one correspondence. Place 10 paper drinking cups in a row; give the child 10 drinking straws. Ask the child to determine if there are enough straws by placing one in each cup. Count as the child places each straw in a cup. Repeat, changing the number of cups and straws. Change it occasionally so that there are not enough straws. Help the child determine how many more are needed for each cup.

6. **COTTON CANDY.** Transfer 11 cone patterns to brown construction paper; then transfer 11 cotton candy patterns to pink construction paper (see figure 8.1). Cut the cone and cotton candy shapes out. Decorate the cones with the numerals 0 through 10, and affix gummed stars to the cotton candy. Leave one cotton candy blank (for zero), and place one star on the first one, two on the second one, etc. Cover the cones and cotton candy with clear adhesive paper to protect them and make them sturdier. Cut a slit in each cone so the tab on the cotton candy fits into it. Arrange the cones and cotton candy on the table in front of the child. Ask the child to match the appropriate cotton candy to the matching cone.

7. **POPCORN COUNTING.** You will need 11 paper lunch bags. Decorate each one with a numeral 0 through 10 and the word "popcorn." Crumple small pieces of white or yellow scrap paper to use as the popcorn. Place the "popcorn" in a large bowl. The child's job is to put the correct amount of popcorn kernels into each bag, leaving the one marked "zero" empty.

8. **EQUAL SETS.** You will need to assemble three sets of objects, each one having at least three items. Some objects to use might include small rubber balls, small plastic zoo animals, building blocks, etc. Demonstrate to the children how to form equal sets by putting three balls in a group, and then making a second set with the same number of balls. Make another set, and have each child make the matching set. Repeat, using a greater number of items each time.

Circus Science Projects

1. **DESCARTES THE DIVER.** Fill a clear plastic squeeze bottle approximately three quarters full of water. Place an eyedropper in the bottle vertically, sucking water up into the eyedropper until it floats upright. It may be helpful to practice this beforehand in a glass of water, as it takes a certain knack to getting the correct amount of water into the dropper. After the eyedropper is adjusted properly in the bottle, put the cap on tightly. If you squeeze the bottle, the eyedropper should sink. Allow the children to experiment with the bottle. With the right pressure on the bottle, the dropper should stay at the bottom of the bottle. After everyone has had a chance to practice with the bottle, take the dropper out. Refill the dropper, using colored water to show how the water exchanges in the dropper. Take the top off the squeeze bottle. Can anyone guess what will happen?

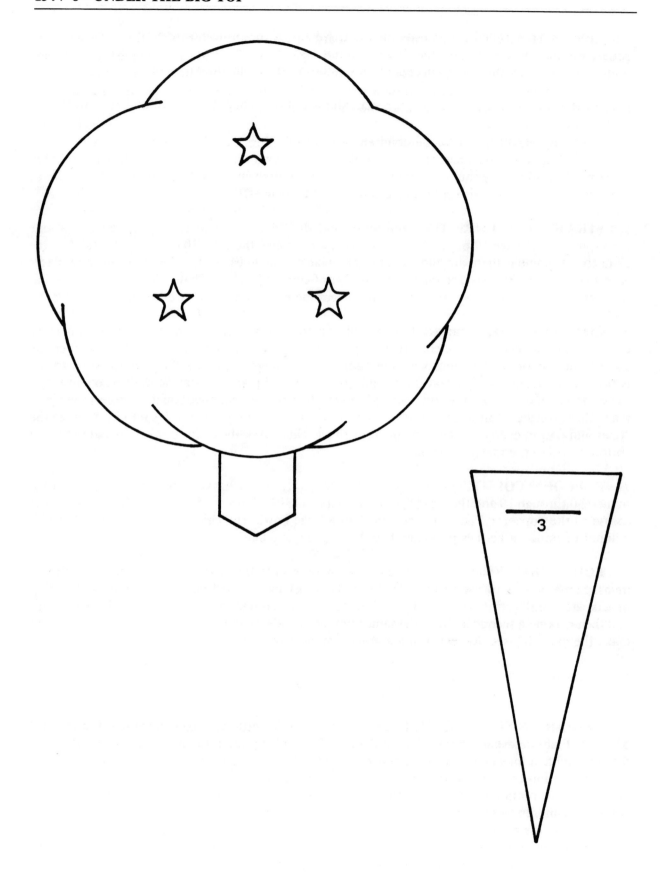

Fig. 8.1.

This eyedropper is called a Cartesian diver. It works on the principle of pressure equalization. Squeezing the bottle decreases the space inside it and therefore causes the pressure to increase. Water is pushed up into the eyedropper. This causes it to become heavier and to sink.

If you wish to make the experiment more entertaining, a face could be painted on the eyedropper's bulb to make it look like a little man doing diving tricks in the circus. Perhaps the children could bring their own eyedroppers and squeeze bottles to make their own diving toys.

2. **TRICKY RAISINS.** Tell the children that you are a circus magician and you are going to make raisins obey your commands. Fill a clear tumbler with water and add 2 tablespoons of vinegar. Stir well and add three raisins. Add a teaspoon of baking soda, but do not stir it. Say the magic words and watch the raisins rise from the bottom of the tumbler.

Why are they doing this? The vinegar and soda are combining to form carbon dioxide, a gas. The gas can be seen as it bubbles to the surface of the water. Some of the bubbles cling to the raisins and lift them with it up to the surface. Once the raisin has reached the top, the bubbles burst and the carbon dioxide is released into the air. With no bubbles holding up the raisin, it sinks again to the bottom until enough bubbles collect around it.

3. **BALANCING ACT.** Here are instructions for making your own tightrope walker. If you wish, make one for each child. For each balancing toy you will need one peg-type wooden clothespin, two large washers, and about 20 inches of wire. Center the piece of wire and wrap it around the base of the clothespin, and bend the wire so that you can attach a washer on each side. Place the clothespin on the child's finger and bend the wires, adjusting it until it balances. Try balancing the toy several different ways, on an elbow, a thumb, or the end of your nose. Explain to the children that tightrope walkers often use weight to help them balance.

4. **STICKY BALLOONS.** Inflate some balloons and rub them on nylon carpeting to build up a charge of static electricity. Show the children that the balloons will stick to the wall and to their hair. What happens? Why is electricity sticky? Explain that when you rub the balloon, you are accumulating an electrical charge on an insulated body. The wall and hair are not charged, so they are attracted to each other. Now rub two balloons on the nylon carpet. Try to stick them together and they pop away from each other. They have the same kind of electrical charge, so they repel each other. When you walk across a nylon carpet in the winter, you build up an electrical charge in your own body. What causes sparks when you touch something metal? There is an electrical discharge due to the fact that you have touched something that is a conductor.

Circus Art Projects

1. **ELEPHANT FINGER PUPPET.** *Materials*: Each child will need one piece of gray construction paper with the elephant pattern (see figure 8.2) transferred onto it, markers or crayons, and a scissors. *Directions*: Have the children decorate the elephant pattern with markers by coloring in the eyes and mouth, then cut the elephant out. The children may need help cutting out the round space intended for the trunk. After the elephant is cut out, the children can put their index fingers through the trunk hole, forming the elephant's trunk.

2. **FANCY HATS.** *Materials*: Each child will need two or three large squares of colorful wrapping paper, paste, a paintbrush for the paste, string, and decorations such as feathers, yarn, lace, or buttons. *Directions*: Have the child dip his or her paintbrush into the paste (you may want to water

Fig. 8.2.

it down slightly) and apply it to the first piece of paper. The child should lightly "paint" the whole surface, especially the edges. Help him or her apply the second piece of paper to the first piece. It does not need to be perfectly straight. If using a third piece, repeat the first step and apply the third piece on top of the second. Set the paper on top of the child's head and mold the crown of the hat around the child's head. Tie a string around the child's brow to hold the shape. Wait 10 minutes, take off the hat, shape it, and let it dry. Paste decorations on it and let it dry some more.

3. **FLYING FELLINIS.** *Materials*: Circus flyer patterns (see figures 8.3 and 8.4, page 137), paper, drinking straws, a paper punch, markers or crayons, scissors, and string or yarn. *Directions*: Transfer each circus flyer pattern onto paper for the children. Let them color the trapeze artists and cut them out. (Assist with the cutting as needed.) Allow the children to punch a hole in each flyer where indicated. Have the children cut the drinking straw in half and then use the holes to hang the flyers on the straws. Thread the string through the drinking straws and hang the Fellinis from the ceiling, within reach of each other.

4. **CLOWN SHOES.** *Materials*: Clown shoe pattern (see figures 8.5 and 8.6, page 138), brown paper grocery bags, markers or crayons, glue, glitter, scissors, and cotton balls or pom poms. *Directions*: Transfer the clown shoe pattern twice onto the paper sack, making sure to place the fold line of the pattern onto the fold of the paper. After cutting the shoes out, allow the children to decorate them with markers, crayons, glitter, pom poms, etc. Cut the slits in the back of the shoes as shown in the illustrations. These slits will fit together when the child wears the clown shoes, attaching behind his ankle. The clown shoes are made to fit over the child's own shoes, but may just as well be worn over stocking feet.

(Text continues on page 139.)

Fig. 8.3.

Fig. 8.4.

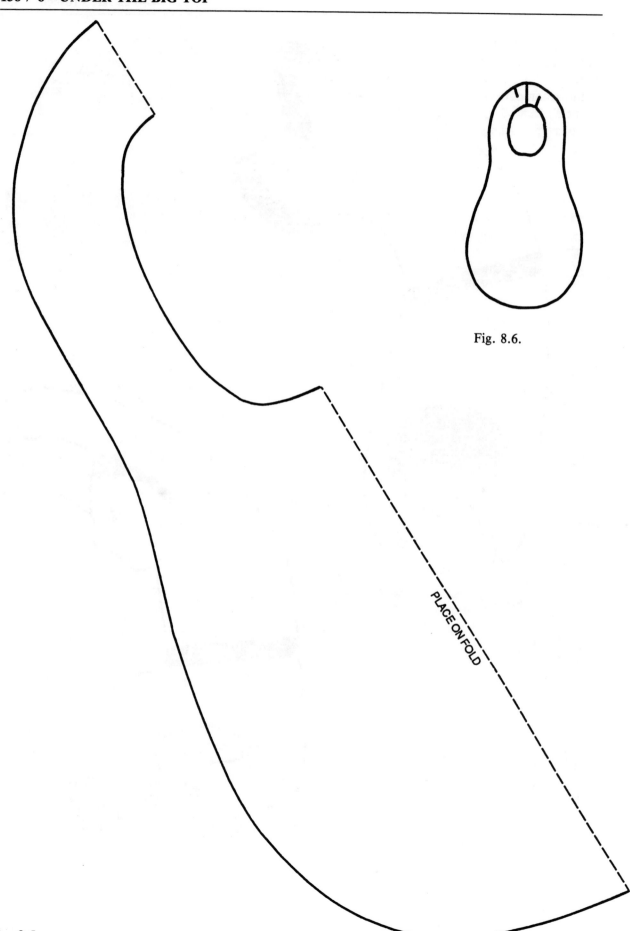

Fig. 8.6.

PLACE ON FOLD

Fig. 8.5.

5. **CANNON MAN**. *Materials*: For each child you will need one cardboard tissue paper roll, a pipe cleaner, a cutout of the cannon man pattern (see figure 8.7), a 7-by-10-inch piece of aluminum foil, glue, and crayons or markers. You will need a box cutter blade or nail file, and a stapler. *Directions*: Have the children wrap the foil around cardboard tubes, covering one end. The object is to cover all but one end of the tubes, making them look like silver cannons. Glue into place. Cut slits in the foil on the covered ends with the box cutter. This is where the cannon man will be sliding through. While the glue on the cannons is drying, let the children color the cannon man. When he is finished, fold him over on the dotted line and glue the pipe cleaner inside. When dry, the cannon man

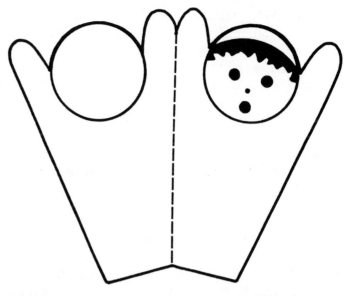

Fig. 8.7.

is ready to blast off. Simply insert him into the bottom of the cannon and gently slide him through the slit in the foil. He can slide up and down as often as he likes, as long as he never actually leaves the cannon.

6. **GEOMETRIC CLOWN**. *Materials*: Colorful construction paper, markers, scissors, and glue. *Directions*: Cut out many different geometric shapes for each child to use to construct a clown. A large oval can be used for the body; various size circles can be used for the head, eyes, nose, and buttons; a triangle can be used for the hat, etc. The child should glue the pieces together to form the clown and can add decorations to the clown's costume using the markers. Accordian-type arms and legs can be made from long, thin strips of paper. The child can simply fold the strips back and forth at 1-inch intervals before gluing them to the clown's body.

7. **TIN CAN STILTS**. *Materials*: Each child will need two sturdy tin cans with one end cut off and no ragged edges. Coffee cans or similar stout cans work well. Other materials include one triangular can opener, construction paper, markers or paint, scissors, and cord. *Directions*: Prepare the coffee cans by making sure they are clean and cutting two holes in the top with the can opener. The holes should be on opposite sides of each other. Provide each child with a piece of construction paper cut the same height as the can and long enough to go all the way around it. Have the children decorate the paper with the markers or paint, then helping them glue the paper to the can. Cut two pieces of cord. The length of the cord should be two times the measurement from the child's waist to heels. Thread the cord through the holes in the can and tie the ends together to make stilts (see figure 8.8).

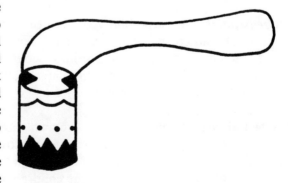

Fig. 8.8.

8. **CLOWN CUPS.** *Materials*: For each child you will need one small Styrofoam cup, several sandwich toothpicks with colored tassles on the end, two star stickers, and a red permanent marker. *Directions*: Have the child turn the Styrofoam cup upside down and glue the star stickers on it for the eyes. The child then uses the marker to make a mouth and nose. Poke the toothpicks through the cup on the sides or top to make the hair. Other embellishments may also be added.

9. **CLOWN HATS AND RUFFLES.** *Materials*: Three pieces of 9-by-12-inch construction paper for each child, scissors, glue, cotton balls, markers or crayons, glitter, a paper punch, string or yarn, and the hat pattern made into a template for tracing around (see figure 8.9). *Hat Directions*: Give the children the hat pattern and have them trace around it on pieces of construction paper. Let them decorate the hats with markers, crayons, glue, and glitter before cutting them out. If you wish to allow some drying time for the glue and glitter, the children can work on the ruffles in the meantime. After the children cut out the hats, assist them in rolling the cutouts into cone shapes. Glue, tape, or staple into place. Have the children glue cotton balls on top of the cones and down one side, if desired. Staple a piece of string to each side of the bottom of the hats for tying under the chins. *Ruffle Directions*: Have the children fold each of the two remaining pieces of construction paper in half, lengthwise. Ask them to cut along the fold. Have the children glue them end to end, resulting in one long strip of paper. The children can decorate this with crayons, markers, or glitter. Allow time to dry. Help the children fold the strips of paper accordian style, making a fold every inch or so. After the folding is done, help the children punch holes on the tops of each and every section about ½ inch from the top. Finally, thread a long piece of yarn or string through the holes to form the ruffles. The string should be about 24 inches long to make sure there is enough to tie the ruffle loosely around the children's necks. *Note*: While the children are not wearing their clown outfits, they could be displayed by using balloons for clown heads. Have the children draw faces on the balloons with markers and set the balloon heads on top of the ruffles and top off with the hats.

Circus Class Project

Clown Parade

Many accessories for the clown parade can be found in the art section of this chapter. Dress up with the fancy hats, clown shoes, clown hats and ruffles, and even the lion mask and tail. Prepare greasepaint for use with other makeup to make your class into a group of clowns.

Greasepaint. For each child you will need 2 teaspoons of cornstarch, 1 teaspoon of water, 1 teaspoon of cold cream, and, if desired, a few drops of food coloring. Stir the cornstarch and water in a small dish until smooth. Stir in the cold cream, then add the food coloring. Apply a thick coat to the children's faces in the desired areas, but staying away from the eyes. The greasepaint washes off easily with soap and water.

When all are dressed in their best clown faces, have them look in the mirror. Do they recognize themselves? Parents might appreciate photos of their chidlren. When everyone is ready, have a parade. Line everyone up and walk through the school or outdoors along the sidewalk. Percussion instruments carried by some of the children add to the merriment.

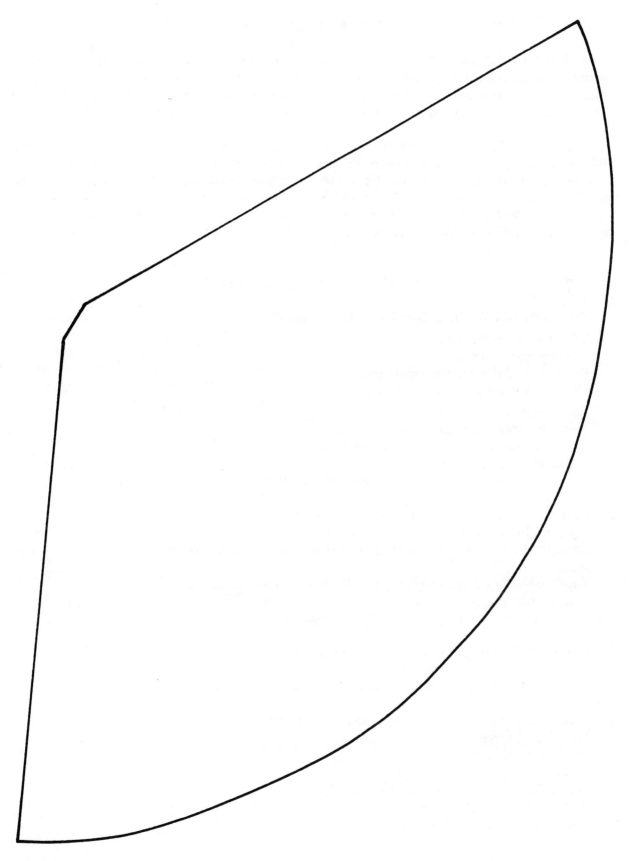

Fig. 8.9.

Circus Story Time

1. **CLOWN COSTUME.** To enhance story time for your listeners, try reading to them in a clown costume or other costume appropriate to the story. If you are reading a book about clowns, have the children put on clown makeup like yours. Start with the greasepaint, paint on the lips, cheeks, and eyes. Put on an imaginary wig and imaginary baggy pants and large shoes.

2. **PANTOMIMES.** If you are reading books that explain how the circus is set up, have the children act out putting up the big top. Perhaps the children would like to be circus performers walking the tightrope or juggling, just like in the stories you are reading. Take time out during such stories for the children to imitate the actions the characters are performing in the books. After the story has been read, ask the children what their favorite circus acts are. Let the children take turns pantomiming them while the rest of the audience guesses what the performers are doing.

Circus Poems, Songs, Fingerplays

1. Sing to the tune of "Take Me Out to the Ballgame":

   Take me out to the big top.
   Take me out to the fun.
   Buy me some peanuts and candy bars.
   How do they get all those clowns in one car?

   Look, look, look for the tigers,
   And hope they don't make a fuss.
   For there's one, two, three rings down front
   At the old circus!

   —Carol Holland

2. First the ringmaster came marching out, (*march*)
   Followed by two white horses prancing about. (*prance.*)
   Three large elephants were swinging their snouts, (*clasp hands together and swing arms to and fro.*)
   Then four clapping seals were begging for trouts. (*clap hands together.*)
   Last but not least as you can see,
   Were five funny clowns all waving to me. (*wave.*)

3. Here's the big top, (*entwine fingers, palms down.*)
   Here are the clowns. (*wiggle fingers.*)
   See them all dancing around! (*continue to wiggle fingers.*)

4. With a funny hat (*place hand on head and lift hand up toward the sky.*)
   And sparkling eyes (*blink several times.*)
   With a big red nose (*touch nose.*)
   And shoes this size (*spread arms wide.*)
   Comes the clown to make you giggle (*smile.*)
   His arms flap flap (*flap arms*).
   And his body wiggles. (*wiggle around.*)

5. A little balloon,
   A bigger balloon,
   A giant balloon I see.
   I'll count the balloons that I have made
   One, two, three.
   (*Make circles with hands, increasing in size, and then count on fingers.*)

6. The circus parade makes it way through town,
   The ringmaster marches in front of the clown.
   The clown tumbles ahead of the amazing fliers
   Who walk back and forth on thin little wires.
   The fliers precede a steady supply
   Of elephants slowly marching by.
   Finally comes the calliope
   Cranking out music for you and for me.

7. Hey diddle, diddle,
   The clown has a fiddle.
   Shall we ask him to play?
   The song we would like
   Should be pretty and bright.
   Do you think he'll oblige us today?

8. This little clown leads the way. (*thumb.*)
   This little clown laughs all day. (*index finger.*)
   This little clown looks tall on stilts, (*middle finger.*)
   And this little clown has a flower that wilts. (*ring finger.*)
   This little clown is by far the smallest, (*pinky.*)
   But wouldn't you know—he's by far the smartest!

9. The big blue balloon burst with a bang.

10. Eleven elegant elephants eventually entered the ring.

Circus Music List

Cassettes

"The Man on the Flying Trapeze." *Disney's Children's Favorites, Vol. 1.* Walt Disney Music Co. 606054, 1979.

Under the Big Top. Melody House Records MH91.
    This cassette includes a collection of circus songs and activities.

Circus Book List

Fiction

Austin, Margot. *Barney's Adventure*. E. P. Dutton, 1941.
    A little boy wins admission to the circus by helping the circus clown.

Birdwell, Norman. *Clifford at the Circus*. Scholastic, 1977.
    A large and shaggy dog finds adventure at the circus.

Freeman, Don. *Bearymore*. Viking, 1976.
    A circus bear must build a new act, but wishes to hibernate instead.

Giesel, Theodore (Dr. Seuss.) *If I Ran the Circus*. Random House, 1956.
    A young boy tells of the strange new acts he would use to entertain people.

Hill, Eric. *Spot Goes to the Circus*. Putnam, 1986.
    This peekaboo book engages the readers to find Spot's ball which he lost at the circus.

Petersham, Maud, and Miska Petersham. *The Circus Baby*. Macmillan, 1950.
    The circus elephant tries to teach her baby to eat at the table just like the clown family. A mess develops!

Wahl, Jan. *The Toy Circus*. Illustrated by Tim Bowers. Harcourt Brace Jovanovich, 1986.
    As a young boy dreams, his toy box explodes into a magical, melodious circus.

Walt Disney Productions. *Dumbo*. Golden Press, 1977. (Other printings also available.)
    This is the classic story of a baby elephant who learns to fly.

Wildsmith, Brian. *The Circus*. Oxford University Press, 1970.
    Wild art leaves us with impressions of the circus.

Nonfiction

Gaskin, Carol. *A Day in the Life of a Circus Clown*. Troll Associates, 1988.
    This book contains a factual account of a clown's busy day.

Harmer, Mabel. *The Circus*. Children's Press, 1981.
    Many color photographs highlight this simple account of life under the big top.

Special Help

Klayer, Connie, and Joanne Kuhn. *Circus Time: How to Put On Your Own Show*. Illustrated by Carol Nicklaus. Lothrop, 1979.
    This book contains fun ideas for many circus activities and entertaining magic tricks that the teacher may wish to perform for the children.

9
WAY BACK WHEN
(Old West)

Focus on the Old West

The inhabitants of the Old West were a diverse group of people. The activities in this chapter will introduce westerners of various cultures.

Consider discussing these subjects:
    The frontier
    Cowboys and their jobs
    Native American cultures
    Various gold rushes and mine workers
    Spanish settlers
    Sod busters
    Wagon trains
    Old versus modern
    Western garb
    Geography: desert, plains, mountains
    Rodeos

Old West Motor Skills

1. **LARIAT TOSS.** Tie a loop in one end of a 4-foot length of stiff rope. Pull the other end through until you have a large loop, about 18 inches in diameter. Show the children how to toss the lariat at a chair back or post and encircle it. Once the target has been "caught," tell the children to pull the rope tight. After the children have practiced, let them count how many tries it takes them to lasso the target. If some children have problems roping their target, suggest that they stand closer, until they can do it successfully.

2. **HAY RIDE.** Fill a children's standard metal red wagon with hay. Have the children take turns being the "old gray mare" that pulls other children around in the wagon.

3. **PANNING FOR GOLD.** Find some small pebbles and spray paint them yellow or gold. When the "gold nuggets" have dried, mix them with several scoops of sand from the sandbox. Put the whole mixture in the bottom of a large tub or bucket. (A metal washtub works well.) Put a few inches of water in the washtub to cover the sand. Provide a few pie tins for the children to "pan for gold" by scooping up a small amount of sand from the bottom of the tub and swishing the sand around with a little water. The water will rinse away some of the sand, enabling the children to pick out the yellow pebbles. If you wish, give the children some small cloth pouches to take their gold nuggets home.

4. **A "KNOTTY" PROBLEM.** Provide each child with an 18-inch length of thin rope or cord. Have the children tie as many knots as possible in their ropes. Once they have done that, have a race to see who can untie all their knots first.

5. **BEAT UP BALL.** In the old days, Indian children liked to play ball. Their balls were made of animal hide which they stuffed and sewed into the shape of a ball. The children can make and play with their own homemade balls. For each ball, use a brown paper bag stuffed with crumpled newspapers. Tie the top shut with some string. The children can throw, kick, or bat their balls.

6. **PINUP STEER**. Draw a large picture of a steer on butcher paper, omitting the horns and tail. Have the children help color or paint the steer brown. Pin the steer up on the wall where the children can reach it. Draw the tail and horns, paint them and cut them out. Also draw and cut out brand marks, if you wish. Put some double-stick tape on the back of the cutouts. Assemble the children in front of the steer. Hand one of the children a cutout and have the child look at the steer closely to determine where the cutout should be stuck. Blindfold and spin the child around a few times and point him or her toward the steer. The child's task is to stick the cutout to the appropriate place on the steer's body. Have the other children help by calling out instructions. The children can take turns until the steer is wearing its tail, horns, and a brand or two. After the children have seen the results, pull the cutouts off and start over.

7. **COWBOY BRANDS**. On index cards, make up and draw some cowboy brands. Put one complete brand on the left side of the card. Next to it, duplicate the brand, but leave a small part off. The child's job will be to use a marker or pencil to finish the brand.

8. **INDIAN TRAIL**. Place two long pieces of yarn or string parallel to each other on the floor. They should be about 12 inches apart. Ask the children to walk between the pieces of string, being careful to keep their balance. Have them walk forward and backward, on their toes, on their heels, etc. Move the strings closer and closer each time all of the children have had a turn to walk through them.

9. **STONE TOSS**. The first child tosses a stone on the ground in front of him or her. The other children take turns tossing their stones, trying to come as close as possible to the first one. The child who comes closest gets to start the game again. This game works best with groups of six or seven children.

10. **ROPE TWIRLING**. Give each child a length of rope, about 3 or 4 feet long. Show the children how to spin the rope so that the bottom end comes up off the floor, making a "c" shape. Keep spinning harder until the "c" is flattened, looking more like two parallel lines horizontal to the floor. Although it sounds complicated, this exercise is easy to do, and all of the children should master it in a few minutes. When the children have tired of rope twirling, group them into couples for a new game. Have one child hold the end of the rope low to the ground, and have him or her start turning around so that the rope turns with the child. As the rope passes by, the other child jumps over it. When the child misses and jumps on the rope instead of over it, the children change places.

11. **STICK PONY RACE**. Line the children up along one side of the playground. Using the stick ponies from Art Activity 1, show them how to gallop. Let the children race, galloping to the other side of the playground. Space permitting, relay races or steeple chases could also be arranged.

Old West Language Skills

1. **ECHO**. Beat a simple rhythm on a drum, and ask the children to imitate the rhythm. Or beat the drum and ask the children how many beats there were.

2. **BRANDS**. Show children some pictures of cattle brands and discuss their names. Make up some brands with the children, and invent names for them. See figure 9.1 for examples. On index cards, draw brands, making a second card with the same brands. When you have several pairs made up, let the children play a game of concentration, or with the cards faceup, they can simply find the matching brands.

HIGH 5

ROCKING A

TRIANGLE T

BAR-B-Q

Fig. 9.1.

3. **OLD MEETS NEW.** Collect pictures of old-time items and their modern counterparts. Some examples could include a modern range and a pot-bellied stove, a faucet and a well or water pump, a modern house and a log cabin, a modern tent and a teepee, a flashlight or lamp and an oil lantern or lamp, a cowboy hat and sunglasses, a supermarket and a general store, a chain saw and an ax, a car and a horse-drawn carriage, a pickup truck and a horse-drawn wagon, and modern clothing and old-fashioned clothing. First hold up a picture of an old-time item to see if the children can identify it. If they cannot, hold up the picture of the modern item to give them a hint, then tell the children the name of the old-time item. Discuss how the old-time items worked and how they are different from their modern counterparts.

4. **SQUARE DANCE.** Select some toe-tapping western music, and have the children pair up. Teach them simple commands such as "swing your partner," in which the children hook elbows and turn around each other. Other commands might be "skip" (skip around in a circle), "jumping bean" (jump up and down), "honor your partner" (bow or curtsey to your partner), "forward and back" (hold hands with your partner and walk forward three steps and back).

After the children have practiced your commands for a few minutes, start the music and begin the square dance. The traditional square has one couple standing on each side of an imaginary square. For the purpose of this listening exercise, however, keep the children standing far enough apart to prevent collisions.

5. **BEADS.** Using large wooden beads of different colors and shoelaces, assemble a necklace. Give the children verbal directions for making a copy of your necklace. For young children, this is a good exercise for helping them learn their colors. With older children, you may want to concentrate more on the shape of the bead when giving your directions.

6. **SHADOWS.** Glue or draw pictures with a western motif on index cards. Some ideas include boots, sheriff, stars, cacti, horses, spurs, cattle brands, cowboy hats, teepees, etc. Make a matching card with only the silhouette of the item on it. The children's task is to match the picture cards to the silhouette cards.

7. **GENERAL STORE.** Assemble several ½-pint milk cartons; cut off their tops and paint the outside of each carton. Cut posterboard into 1½"-by-6" strips, five or six for each milk carton. On each carton, draw a letter or shape such as silhouettes of items found in the general store like a sack

of flour, a coffee pot, etc. On the strips of posterboard, draw letters or shapes to correspond to the milk cartons. There should be five or six strips to correspond to each carton. Tell the children they work at the general store and their job is to sort the strips by putting them into the correct "bin."

8. **MARACAS.** In this exercise, the child will sort maracas according to the sounds they make when shaken. You will need to make identical-sounding pairs of maracas. Four or five sets do nicely for this activity.

For each set of two maracas you will need four sturdy paper plates, thick yarn or twine, something sharp to punch holes with, and two each of the following: sets of jingle bells, sets of pennies, ¼-cup of dried beans, ½-cup of rice, and "moo" toys. Punch toys at ¼-inch intervals around the perimeter of each paper plate. Bind two paper plates together by stringing the yarn or twine through the holes and around the outside edges of the plates. Before completely sewing the plates together, place a sound maker such as a set of jingle bells inside. Finish sewing the plates together. Decorate with a Mexican flair. Make another maraca as similar as possible to the first to keep the children from identifying the pairs by how they look rather than how they sound.

Old West Math Activities

In old western movies, cowboys with leisure time always seemed to be playing poker. Here are some fun math activities disguised as card games.

1. **MATCH THE SUIT.** Use a deck of standard playing cards. Place one card of each suit faceup on the table and place the rest of the deck facedown. Have two or three children take turns taking a card from the deck and placing it on the appropriate pile. The younger children can separate the cards by color. When the children have become proficient and quick, split the deck and let two children have a race doing this.

2. **ALL IN A ROW.** Divide a deck of playing cards into its four suits. Take out the face cards, leaving the cards numbered 1 to 10. Give the child one suit of cards and ask him or her to place the cards on the table in numerical order. If 10 cards are too many, try using only three or five and work your way up gradually.

3. **MISSING CARDS.** Place playing cards from 1 to 10 on a table in numerical order. Ask the children to close their eyes while you remove one of the cards; see if they can guess which one is missing. If all 10 cards are too much, use only one through five. Add the face cards or jokers for a little fun.

4. **ODDBALL.** Using a deck of cards, arrange three of a kind and add one that does not belong. Show the children your hand. Can they pick out the different card? Extend the activity by having the correct fourth card on the table with a few other cards. Can they find the card that will make your hand four of a kind?

5. **BOARD GAME.** On a piece of posterboard, make up a board game for the children. It could illustrate a miner trying to find gold, an Indian trying to find buffalo, or a cowboy trying to find lost cows. Instead of using a spinner or dice to determine the number of moves a player makes, have the children use a deck of cards. The cards should be placed facedown on the table. The child turns the card over and determines how many spaces to move. You might choose to use only cards numbered 1 to 5 for this unless the children are very good counters. For fun, throw in a face card that means "go to jail" or "get out of jail" or some other directive meaningful to the game.

6. **PEBBLE TOSS.** Prepare for this game by having the children collect at least 20 pebbles from outside. Connect cottage cheese containers or other types of plastic containers with tape or staples as shown in figure 9.2. Place the target you have just made on the floor. Draw a line several feet away for the children to stand behind while tossing pebbles at the target. Have the children toss all of the pebbles. When they have finished, have the children count how many pebbles went into each container and how many landed on the floor. Which was more? Which container contained the most pebbles? The fewest? Were any two equivalent? What other ways can the sets be compared?

Fig. 9.2.

7. **PATTERNS.** Make a pattern on a table using colored toothpicks. Repeat the pattern several times. Ask the children to continue the pattern. Make another design with the toothpicks. See if the children can duplicate this design.

8. **HORSESHOES.** Use corrugated cardboard to make 55 horseshoes (see figure 9.3 for a pattern). Set up 11 stakes. To make a simple stake, stick a craft stick or an unsharpened pencil upright in a lump of clay. Number the stakes 0 through 10. The children's task is to hook the appropriate number of horseshoes to each stake. Remember to point out that no horseshoes go on the stake marked with a zero. Another way to use a western motif for the same activity is to use painted pebbles ("gold nuggets") and numbered pie tins.

9. **TALL, TALL CACTI.** Draw and cut out several cacti, making each one taller than the previous one. Arrange the cacti on the table, and have the children put them in order from shortest to tallest. Start with three cacti for young children, gradually adding more.

10. **EAGLE FEATHERS.** Purchase 15 colored feathers from a craft store. Cut five bird shapes out of felt and number them 1 through 5. Place the naked birds up on a flannel board. Have each child dress the eagles with the correct number of feathers.

Old West Science Activities

The following three activities illustrate the importance of the sun to the people who lived in the Old West. Without today's modern conveniences, such as electricity, people made use of the sun often in their daily lives. Here are just three of the many ways pioneers used the sun.

1. **FOOD PROCESSING.** Long ago there were no refrigerators in which to keep food fresh for long periods of time. Farmers grew food, and would sell or eat it. They could not eat all of the food at once; they needed to save some for the months ahead. To keep food from spoiling, people often dried it. For centuries, Native Americans roasted or dried corn, or ground it into flour. Beef could also be dried by cutting it into thin strips and hanging it in the sun for several days. Many people today still enjoy dried beef, or beef jerky. Here are instructions for making a dried fruit snack.

Choose some fruit to dry, such as apples, apricots, peaches, and plums. Wash the fruit, then peel it and remove the pit or core. Slice the apples or peaches. Apricots or plums can be halved and pricked with a fork. Place the fruit on a cookie sheet that has been covered with aluminum foil. Place the pans of fruit in an area that receives sun for most of the day. With the children, check the fruit after one day, then two, then three. Explain to the children that the sun is dehydrating the fruit, that is, taking the moisture out of it. Do the children know that this is how raisins are made from grapes? If

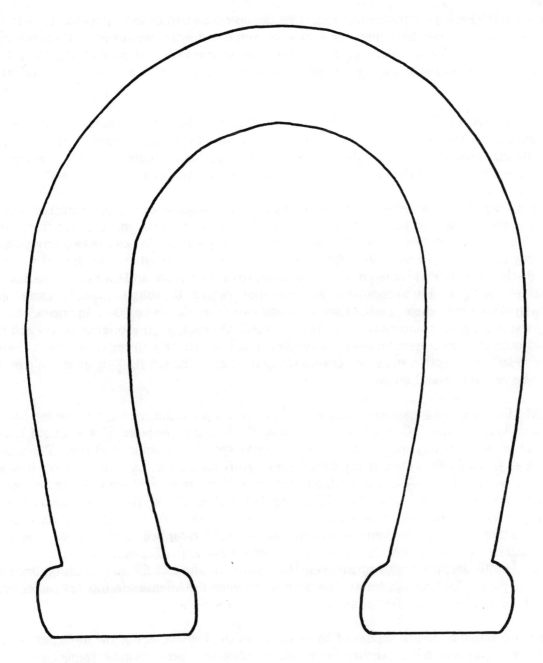

Fig. 9.3.

the fruit is receiving a good amount of sun, it should take only two or three days to dry. After it is dried, eat the fruit during snack time. How does the fruit taste? Are there any other fruits that might taste good dried? Soak a few pieces of the dried fruit in some water to rehydrate them. Does it taste like fresh fruit? Show some examples of packaged dehydrated foods that hikers and campers use today.

2. **COMMUNICATION.** Long ago, before the telegraph and the telephone, the only way to communicate was through the mail. It sometimes took weeks for letters to reach friends in other towns. In the Southwest, soldiers thought of a quick way to communicate using the sun. The children can communicate the same way the U.S. Cavalry did years ago.

On a sunny day, divide the children into two groups. Give an adult in each group a mirror. The two groups should split up and go as far away as possible from each other, making sure there are no obstructions standing between them that would obscure any signals. When the two groups are in place, they should take turns sending signals using the mirrors. The adults can show the children how to do this. The mirrors should be held at an angle to catch the sun, and then tilted to a different angle to end the signal. Try to coordinate long and short signals. Regroup to make up some signals and attach meanings to them. Perhaps one long and two short signals could mean "hello." Several quickly flashing signals could mean "I understand you." Go back to your original places and have the children take turns communicating. Remember, it is not necessary to see each other as long as there is no large obstruction standing between the two groups. The sun flashing on the mirrors can actually be seen for several miles.

3. **FIRE.** Before we had matches and lighters, there were more primitive ways of making fires for cooking or keeping warm. One way was to twirl a stick on another piece of wood until friction started a fire. Another way was to strike a flint to make sparks that could start fires. The sun can also be used to start a fire. On a sunny day, use a magnifying glass and a piece of paper to start a fire. If you wish, some kindling and small logs may be laid out in a barbeque to show the children how campfires are made. Hold the magnifying glass in the direct rays of the sun and focus it on the piece of paper. The paper will soon burn at the point of focus. First the paper will start to turn brown, and then it will start to flame. If showing the children a campfire, use the paper to ignite the fire. Explain to the children that the sun is our most important source of heat. The magnifying glass helped the sun to start the fire by intensifying the rays of the sun and focusing them on one small spot on the paper. Explain that forest fires often start when the intense sun hits dry tinder in the forest. This would be an excellent time to discuss fire safety.

The next two activities discuss modes of construction in the Old West. For the most part, people used what was available to build shelter. Some nomadic Native Americans made teepees out of long logs and animal skins. These structures were easy to put up and take down, making it easy to move from one location to another. Some pioneers on the Great Plains made their houses out of sod because that was the only building material they had. Sod houses were made by cutting actual dirt bricks from the ground and stacking them. Adobe is similar to sod. Adobe was used and is still used widely in the Southwest. Old forts and missions made of adobe in the 1800s are still standing today. Here is an adobe recipe for making your own adobe bricks. If you are ambitious, a whole adobe house can be built.

4. **ADOBE.** *Materials*: Empty milk cartons trimmed to only 1 inch high, dirt (clay-based, if possible), dried straw or grass clippings, water, and a large tub for making the mixture. *Directions*: Have the children help mix the soil and some water in the tub until it is of batter consistency. Add

the grass or straw; have the children mix it well. Explain to the children that the grass or straw is used to help the mud stick together. Can they tell that it helps by the way it feels during the mixing? After mixing, have the children help spoon the mud mixture into the prepared milk cartons. Tamp down the containers so that the mud settles and makes the surface of the brick flat for stacking. Place the bricks in the sun for several days to dry. The bricks will dry better if you take them out of the molds after they have set. Discuss evaporation and dehydration. After several days, when the bricks have dried, use the bricks to make a simple adobe structure. More mud is used as mortar to hold the bricks together. The adobe house may be plastered with additional mud to form smooth walls, if you wish. Let the house dry thoroughly before using it.

5. **NEWSPAPER LOGS.** Many pioneers had forests from which logs could be gathered for use in construction of houses, Army forts, fences and corrals, etc. In lieu of real logs, newspaper logs can be made to build child-size structures.

Make as many newspaper logs as possible for constructing log cabins, forts, corrals, etc. To make each log, place two sheets of newspaper together and roll them up as tightly as possible. Fasten with small pieces of masking tape. Some structures will support themselves, while others will need to be propped up or taped in place. Using the logs in this manner not only illustrates possible ways pioneers may have built log cabins, but also teaches the children cause and effect, structure strength and design, angles and shapes, and balance.

Old West Art Projects

1. **STICK PONIES.** *Materials*: For each pony you will need one broomstick or dowel with a 1-inch diameter, sandpaper, one large tube sock, yarn, paper or felt scraps, markers, glue, newspapers, and duct or electrical tape. *Directions*: Show the children how to sand their broomsticks or dowels to get rid of any roughness or splinters. Let each child wad up newspapers and stuff them into the tube socks until the tube socks are firm and full. Have the children make the horse's face using felt, paper scraps, and glue, or markers for the eyes, nose, and mouth. The mane can be made from yarn cut into 3- or 4-inch lengths and glued into place along the "neck." When the face and mane are completed and dried, attach the head to the end of the broomstick. Wrap the tape tightly around the base of the neck to hold it to the stick. The children can make reins using yarn or ribbon attached near the horse's mouth and looped around the back of the neck. Show the children how to hold their ponies and gallop, being careful that the stick does not hit other children.

2. **HEADGEAR.** Here are four different types of hats to make.

Headband. *Materials*: For each headband you will need a 2½-by-24-inch strip of felt, yarn, glue, scissors, and lots of tiny beads. *Directions*: It is simple for the children to make their own headbands. Have the children trim the felt strips to fit their heads, the ends overlapping by 1 inch on each end. Once the headband fits, the children can apply glue to the felt in a geometric design, such as squares or triangles. Have the children drop the beads onto the wet glue. Let dry. To attach the headband to the child's head, poke two holes in each end of the felt and overlap the ends. Thread a short piece of yarn through the holes, and tie in place.

Sun Bonnet. *Materials*: For each bonnet, you will need one sheet of 12-by-18-inch construction paper, glue, scissors, hole punch, hole reinforcers, yarn, and rickrack or lace. *Directions*: Make a template out of the bonnet pattern for the child to use (see figure 9.4). Have the children trace

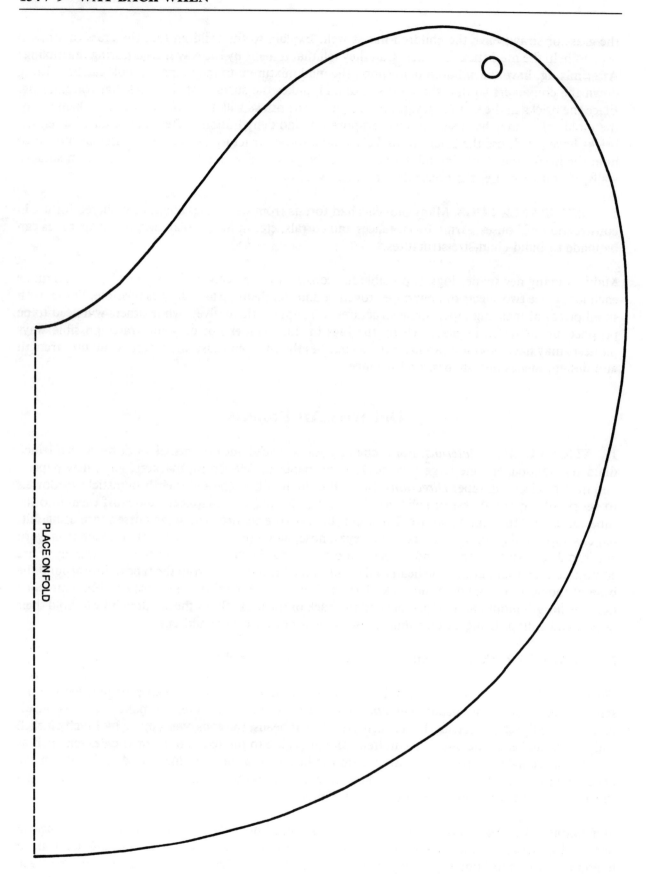

PLACE ON FOLD

Fig. 9.4.

around the template on a piece of construction paper, and then cut it out. Show the children where to punch the holes and place the reinforcing rings. Have them glue lace or rickrack around the edges of the bonnet. Cut two 12-inch pieces of yarn, and tie them through the two punched holes. When dry, place the bonnet on the child's head with the yarn ties going behind the ears and tying under the chin.

Cowboy Hat. *Materials*: For each hat you will need one 12-by-18-inch piece of sturdy construction paper or brown paper from a grocery sack, ribbon, felt scraps or markers, scissors, and glue. *Directions*: Cut the construction paper into a large oval shape. Using the illustration as a guide (see figure 9.5), draw a rectangle on top of the oval shape large enough to accommodate the child's head. Help the child cut three sides of the rectangle out. Have the child fold the flap up and then in half. The child may make a band for the hat using felt scraps, ribbon, or markers.

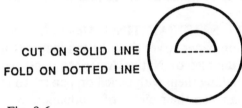

CUT ON SOLID LINES
FOLD ON DOTTED LINES

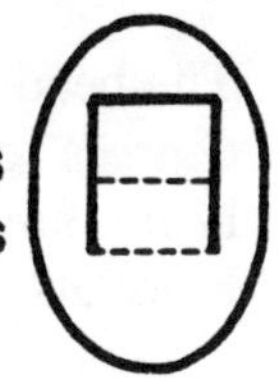

Fig. 9.5.

Sombrero. *Materials*: For each sombrero obtain a 12-by-18-inch piece of construction paper. If larger paper is available, use it. Glitter, glue, yarn, a hole punch, and hole reinforcing rings are also needed. *Directions*: On the construction paper, draw a large circle with a minimum diameter of 12 inches. (A larger circle is even better if you have paper large enough.) Cut the top of the hat out where indicated (see figure 9.6), and fold up. Show the child where to make the two holes with the paper punch, and how to attach the reinforcing rings. The child can decorate the hat band area using glue and glitter. Gently roll the outer edges of the hat up and have the child decorate under

CUT ON SOLID LINE
FOLD ON DOTTED LINE

Fig. 9.6.

the edges as well as on top. Cut two strands of yarn, each 12 inches long. Tie the yarn through the holes punched in the hat. After the glue has dried, place the hat on the child's head. The yarn goes behind the ears and ties under the chin.

3. **WESTERN BANDANA**. *Materials*: Muslin or a clean white sheet, pinking shears, and permanent markers. *Directions*: Cut the cloth into 18-inch squares using the pinking shears. Let the children decorate their scarves with the markers. When the scarves are dry, show the children how to tie the scarves loosely around their necks. Explain that they were left loose so that when dust was blowing, they could be brought up around the nose and mouth to help the cowboys breathe.

4. **DESERT IN A JAR**. *Materials*: Each child will need one small glass jar (such as a baby food jar), three or four different colors of sand (found in craft stores), and a large toothpick. *Directions*: Put each color of sand in a different bowl. Let the children spoon the sand into their jars, starting with one color and putting in enough sand to completely cover the bottom of the jar. Each additional layer the children put in should be at least ¼-inch deep. Caution the children to make sure they do not shake the jars and disturb the layers. After the jar is at least half filled with sand, give the children a toothpick. Show them how to poke the sand down on the edges to make designs in the sand.

5. **INDIAN BEADS**. *Materials*: To make approximately 50 beads of various sizes, you will need 1 cup of flour, ½-cup of salt, food coloring, water; large nails, unsharpened pencils, or screwdrivers to use as forms; aluminum foil; and a cookie sheet. *Directions*: Mix the salt and flour together. In a

cup, add a few drops of food coloring to some water. Add just enough water to the flour and salt to make a stiff dough. Give each child a small lump of dough, enough to make five or six beads. Show the children how to mold a small piece of dough into a ball, and have them pierce the ball with the nail. Place the beads on a foil-covered cookie sheet. To prevent the beads from flattening, place the holes perpendicular to the cookie sheet. Another way to make a bead is to roll a small piece of dough out into a snake shape, and then wind it around the nail. Beads can also be shaped into plump pancakes or small cubes.

The beads may be placed outside in the sun for two or three days to dry or baked in an oven at 250 degrees for two hours. Whichever method you use, be sure to turn the beads over once. When the beads are hard, have the children string them on yarn or leather thongs to make necklaces or bracelets.

6. **DESERT SCULPTURE.** *Materials*: Clay or Play-doh, dried flowers or other dried plants, sticks, rocks, wire, feathers , or other items reminiscent of the Old West. *Directions*: Provide each child with a large piece of clay. Let the children choose from the other items you have assembled. Have the children form balls with their clay, making sure they flatten it on one side so that it forms a sturdy base for the desert sculpture. Let the children stick the dried flowers and other items into the clay to make an interesting western arrangement.

7. **SANDPAINTING.** *Materials*: Each child will need a sheet of sandpaper, a sheet of construction paper larger than the sandpaper (for mounting), glue, and paint. *Directions*: Show the children examples of Native American sand painting, if possible. Discuss geometric shapes and practice making them with pencil on paper. To make their own version of sand painting, the children simply paint on their pieces of sandpaper. When dry, put glue on the back of the sand painting and help each child mount it in the center of a colorful piece of construction paper.

8. **SHERIFF'S STAR.** *Materials*: Star pattern, masking tape, cardboard, pencil, scissors, glue, and aluminum foil. *Directions*: Make templates of the star pattern for the children (see figure 9.7).

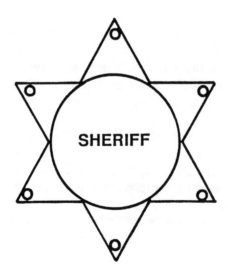

Fig. 9.7.

Have each child put the pattern on a piece of cardboard and trace around it. Assist the child in cutting out the star, if necessary. Give the child a square of aluminum foil, cut slightly larger than the star and place the foil, shiny side down, on the table, with the star centered on top of the foil. Glue into place. When dry, have the child cut slits midway between the points of the stars and fold the foil, molding it over the cardboard star. You may "engrave" the star by drawing directly on the star with a ball point pen. The last step is to make a small tube from a piece of masking tape and stick it to the back of the foil-covered star. Allow the child to become a deputy sheriff by sticking the star to the front of his or her shirt.

Old West Class Project

Pioneer Village

Designate a large area outside as a pioneer village. Discuss the possibility that American pioneers, Native Americans, Spanish, and even Chinese people (on the West coast) sometimes lived together in the same community. The village may include an adobe building, log buildings, and teepees, or you may decide on one theme, such as an Indian village, a mining camp, or a miniature ranch. Instructions for adobe are included in the science project section, activity 4. Newspaper log instructions are in science activity 5. Simple canvas tents can be used for teepees.

Teepee Directions: (See figure 9.8). Use a large piece of cardboard (in lieu of real buckskin) from a refrigerator or mattress box. The cardboard can usually be obtained from department or appliance

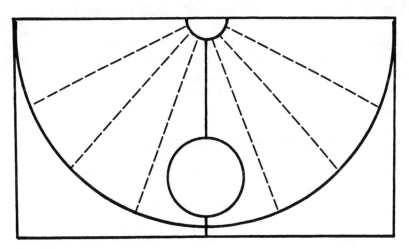

Fig. 9.8.

stores for free if you simply ask them. Lay the cardboard out flat and draw a line from one side to the other, straight down the middle. Cut a piece of string the same length as the line you just drew. Tack the piece of string on one end of the line. Using the string as a guide, draw a large half circle, using the string as the radius of the circle. At the top of the teepee shape, with the centerline in the middle, draw a half circle, about 6 to 7 inches wide, and cut it out. Near the bottom of the teepee shape, with the centerline in the middle, make an 18-inch circle for the door and cut it out. Divide the teepee into eight equal parts and draw lines as illustrated. Score and then fold along the lines. Tape some large sticks or cardboard cut to look like sticks to the inside of the teepee, so that they protrude out the top. Fold the whole teepee into a cone shape. Punch holes in the edges, overlap slightly, and fasten with twine. A circle of cardboard may be attached with twine over the circular opening; the whole teepee may be decorated with paint or markers.

Old West Story Time

1.   **CAMP FIRE TIME.** Children love novelty. During discussion time while studying the Old West, have the children sit around a pretend campfire you have made out of sticks, logs, paper, or even blocks. Read books, tell stories, and sing Western songs!

2.   **MUSICAL INSTRUMENTS.** Several of the books in this section are stories based on old folk songs: *Clementine* by Robert Quackenbush, *Ridin' That Strawberry Roan* by Marcia Sewell, and *Sweet Betsy from Pike* by Glen Rounds. Read the books to the children and teach them the song that the story comes from. Use homemade instruments to back up the singing.

Flute. Use a pencil to punch three or four holes into the side of a cardboard tube. Cover the end of the tube with a small square of waxed paper, holding it in place with a rubber band. Let the child decorate the flute with markers. Have the child hum into the uncovered end while moving his or her fingers on and off the holes.

Drum. Use a coffee can with its lid on to make a drum. The children can cover the sides of the can with construction paper. Use spoons or unsharpened pencils as drumsticks.

Shakers. Have the child decorate two paper plates or a cardboard tube. Place a handful of dried beans between the paper plates or into the tube. Tape around the edges of the paper plates to keep the beans in. Likewise, place aluminum foil over the ends of the cardboard tube and tape in place. Try using different fillings to achieve different sounds.

Old West Poems, Songs, Fingerplays

1.   The Indians are creeping, (*creep fingers along forearm*)
     Sh, Sh, Sh. (*raise finger to lips*)
     The Indians are creeping,
     Sh, Sh, Sh.
     They do not make a sound
     As their feet touch the ground (*tiptoe fingers on forearm*)
     The Indians are creeping,
     Sh, Sh, Sh.

2.   Trot, trot, trot, trot, trot, trot,
     Trot my little pony, trot.
     Lift your little legs so high,
     Toss your head as you walk by,
     Trot, trot, trot, trot, trot, trot,
     Stop my little pony, STOP!
     (*Give each child two wooden blocks to make trotting sounds with. Have them tap the wooden blocks together in rhythm to the rhyme, stopping abruptly on the last word, Stop.*)

3. Ten little Indians standing in a line,
    Nine little Indians strong, straight, and fine.
    Eight little Indians' tomahawks wave high,
    Seven little Indians yell a war cry. Wahoo!
    Six little Indians ride far out of sight, (*put fingers behind back*)
    Five little Indians come home safe at night, (*bring fingers back out*)
    Four little Indians to their wigwams creep,
    Three little Indians now are fast asleep.

    (*Hold up appropriate number of fingers and then act out the action of each line.*)

4. I ride and I whistle and I rope the steers.
    When chow time comes I grin ear to ear.
    My hair is short, my legs are long,
    And late at night I sing sad songs.
    If you see me in town you might think me strange!
    I'm just an old cowboy who rides the range.

5. To perform "She'll be Comin' Round the Mountain," assign actions to the action words at the end of each line. The words are cumulative at the end of each verse. After the first verse, you will say "Toot, toot!" At the end of the second verse, you will then say "Whoa, back! Toot, toot!" and so on. Of course, the younger children will be able to manage only a few verses at first. As they become more familiar with the song, however, more verses may be added.

    She'll be comin' round the mountain when she comes, toot, toot!
    She'll be comin' round the mountain when she comes, toot, toot!
    She'll be comin' round the mountain,
    She'll be comin' round the mountain,
    She'll be comin' round the mountain when she comes, toot, toot!

    Additional verses:

    She'll be drivin' six white horses when she comes, whoa, back!
    Oh, we'll all go out to meet her when she comes. Hi, Babe!
    Oh, we'll kill the old red rooster when she comes, cockadoodle-doo!
    And we'll all have chicken and dumplings when she comes, yum, yum!
    Oh, she'll have to sleep with Grandma when she comes, snore, snore!
    And she'll wear red flannel pajamas when she comes, whee-whoo!

6. Goodbye, old Paint,
    I'm leaving Cheyenne,
    Goodbye, old Paint,
    I'm leaving Cheyenne.
    I'm a-riding old Paint,
    I'm a-leading old Fan,
    Goodbye, little Annie,
    I'm off for Montan'.

    (*Ride stick ponies or pretend to gallop slowly around in a circle, waving good-bye at appropriate times.*)

7. Refrain:
   It's rain or shine, sleet or snow,
   Me and my Doney gal are on the go,
   Yes, rain or shine, sleet, or snow,
   Me and my Doney gal are bound to go.

   We'll ride the range from sun to sun,
   For a cowboy's work is never done,
   He's up and gone at the break of day,
   A-drivin' the dogies on their weary way.

   A cowboy's life is a dreary thing,
   For it's rope and brand and ride and sing,
   Yes, day or night in the rain or hail,
   He'll stay with his dogies out on the trail.

   We whoop at the sun and yell through the hail,
   But we drive the poor dogies down the trail,
   And we'll laugh at the storms, the sleet, and snow,
   When we reach the little town of San Antonio.

8. My pony, my pony,
   Come out of the barn. (*open arms*)
   The sky is bright blue and the sunshine is warm.

   My pony, my pony,
   Come home to the barn. (*close arms*.)
   The hay is so sweet, and your stall is so warm.

9. I had a little pony, his name was Jack.
   I put him in the stable and he jumped through a crack.

10. Hush-a-bye, don't you cry
    Oh, you pretty little baby.
    When you wake you'll have sweet cake
    And all the pretty little ponies.
    A brown and a gray,
    And a black and a bay,
    All the pretty little ponies.

Old West Music List

Cassettes

"Clementine." *Disney's Children's Favorites, Vol. 3*. Walt Disney Music Co. 606074, 1986.

"Down in the Valley." *Disney's Children's Favorites, Vol. 3*. Walt Disney Music Co. 606074, 1986.

"Get Along Little Dogies." *Disney's Children's Favorites, Vol. 4*. Walt Disney Music Co. 606084, 1990.

"Home on the Range." *Disney's Children's Favorites, Vol. 1.* Walt Disney Music Co. 606054, 1979.

"Oh, Susanna." *Disney's Children's Favorites, Vol. 1.* Walt Disney Music Co. 606054, 1979.

"On Top of Old Smokey." *Disney's Children's Favorites, Vol. 2.* Walt Disney Music Co. 606064, 1979.

"She'll Be Comin' Round the Mountain." *Disney's Children's Favorites, Vol. 1.* Walt Disney Music Co. 606054, 1979.

"Skip to My Lou." *Disney's Children's Favorites, Vol. 2.* Walt Disney Music Co. 606064, 1979.

"Sweet Betsy from Pike." *Disney's Children's Favorites, Vol. 3.* Walt Disney Music Co. 606074, 1986.

"Ten Little Indians." *Disney's Children's Favorites, Vol. 1.* Walt Disney Music Co. 606054, 1979.

Old West Book List

Fiction

Cox, David. *Bossyboots.* Crown Publishers, 1987.
    In the Australian outback, stagecoach robbers are no match for Bossyboots.

Quackenbush, Robert. *Clementine.* J. B. Lippincott, 1974.
    This is the story of love and loss at a mining camp, as based on the famous folk song.

Raphael, Elaine, and Don Bolognese. *Sam Baker, Gone West.* Viking, 1977.
    Greedy Sam Baker makes a deal with some Indians for more land than he needs, suffering the consequences. The story is suggested by Leo Tolstoy's "How Much Land Does a Man Need?"

Rounds, Glen. *Once We Had a Horse.* Holiday Press, 1971.
    Two very determined children teach themselves to ride a patient old horse.

Rounds, Glen. *Sweet Betsy from Pike.* Children's Press, 1973.
    Glen Rounds illustrates the classic folk song about the hardships endured en route to California in 1849.

Scott, Ann Herbert. *One Good Horse: A Cowpuncher's Counting Book.* Illustrated by Lynn Sweat. Greenwillow, 1990.
    This counting book designed for very young children follows a child and his father on a ride around the ranch.

Sewell, Marcia. *Ridin' That Strawberry Roan.* Viking Kestral, 1985.
    A bronco buster meets his match in this adaptation of an old folk song.

Turner, Ann. *Dakota Dugout.* Illustrated by Ronald Himler. Macmillan, 1985.
    An old woman tells her granddaughter what it was like to live in a sod house on the prairie long ago.

Nonfiction

Silcott, Philip B. *Cowboys.* Color photographs by Martin Rogers. National Geographic Society, 1975.
This excellent book explains the cowboy's job in simple terms.

Songs

Moon, Dolly M. *My Very First Book of Cowboy Songs.* Illustrated by Frederick Remington. Dover Publications, 1982.
Frederick Remington's captivating artwork highlights this collection of 21 easy musical arrangements.

10
LONG, LONG AGO
(Dinosaurs)

Focus on Dinosaurs

A unit on dinosaurs provides a good opportunity to discuss the difference between real and unreal. The learning experiences in this chapter will help the children learn about some real, yet extinct monsters that once roamed the earth.

Consider discussing these subjects:
Extinction
Reptiles
Fossils
Archaeology and paleontology
Carnivores
Herbivores
Real versus unreal
Dinosaur names
Dinosaur dimensions

Dinosaurs Motor Skills

1. **PREHISTORIC SNAKE WALK.** Ask the children to sit on the floor with their legs wrapped around the child in front of them. The children move forward by inching along on their bottoms. Try this exercise with small groups of four or five. Have races or play tag. Try to get the whole class into one large snake.

2. **DID YOU EVER SEE A DINOSAUR?** The children form a circle with one child in the center. As everyone sings "Did You Ever See a Dinosaur?" to the tune of "Did You Ever See a Lassie?", have the child in the center act out funny dinosaur movements for the other children to imitate. Repeat.

3. **PREHISTORIC SNAKE DANCE.** Position the children so that they are scattered around the play area. Take one child by the hand and lead him or her around while saying the following chant:

> I'm a snake, a snake.
> Rattle, rattle, slither, slither,
> Hissss!

Weave between all the children. When the chant ends, stop walking and have the child nearest you take the hand of the last child in line. Repeat until everyone is a part of the snake.

4. **DINOSAUR SHAPES PUZZLE.** Cut some dinosaur shapes out of cello sponges. Trace the shapes, leaving their outlines on a sturdy piece of poster board. Decorate around the outlines in a jungle motif to make the puzzle more attractive. The child can place the dinosaur sponges onto the appropriate outlines of the puzzle.

5. **BONE HUNT.** Cut some large bone shapes out of sturdy white paper. Have enough for each child to find at least one. Hide them around the classroom or play area for the children to find. Explain to the children that they are paleontologists searching for dinosaur remains. After the bones have all been found, take inventory. Are there enough to build a dinosaur?

6. **RUN AND STOP**. Tell the children to run and run and run and stop. Then have them fly, fly, fly, and stop. Have them jump, skip, slither, lumber, etc.

7. **BALANCING**. Give the children small items to balance on their heads, such as a small plastic dinosaur toy, a dinosaur bone cutout, a small rock, etc. The children must all march around the room with their hands at their sides or folded over their chests while you play some music. If a toy falls off, the child must sit down and cheer the remaining balancers. Keep going until nobody remains standing.

8. **DINOSAUR STRUT**. The children line up at one end of the room, facing a finish line about 10 yards away. Remind the children that there were small as well as very large dinosaurs. Can they walk to the finish line taking giant steps? Count how few steps it takes to get there. Next, try tiny, baby dinosaur steps. How many more steps does it take to arrive at the finish line? Experiment with all kinds of dinosaur struts.

9. **DINOSAUR TAG**. Provide the children with pictures of different dinosaurs to wear pinned or taped to their chests. They must travel around the room, doing their best dinosaur imitation of the picture taped to their chests. One child, who is "it," tries to tag the other children. When he or she catches one, they trade pictures and the new child chases the other dinosaurs.

10. **ANOTHER DINOSAUR TAG**. Give the children a 2-foot length of crepe paper streamer to tuck into their belts or tape to their dresses as a dinosaur tail. Play tag in the same manner as flag football. A child is tagged when somebody swipes his or her tail.

Dinosaurs Language Activities

1. **MATCHING VOCABULARY WORDS**. Cut construction paper into 2-by-7-inch strips. Print each vocabulary word on two separate strips of paper. Use words such as reptile, dinosaur, fossil, bone, paleontologist, tyrannosaur, etc. Have the child look at each card and try to match the first card with its twin.

2. **FELT SHAPES**. Cut out felt dinosaur shapes, and make a corresponding card for each shape. Put several felt shapes on the flannel board. The children can draw a card from the pile and then match it to one of the flannel pieces.

3. **WHO IS DIFFERENT?** On blank index cards, paste four dinosaur stickers. Three of the stickers should be the same or similar and one should be different. Perhaps you will have three green dinosaurs and one purple one, or three dinosaurs with wings and one that walks. The child's task is to pick the sticker that is different from the other three. If you wish, the cards can be covered in clear adhesive paper and a crayon used to circle the sticker that does not match.

4. **YES AND NO**. Ask questions of the children to which the answer would be either yes or no. Some sample questions include:

Are there any dinosaurs alive today?
Are there dinosaurs at the zoo?
Did dinosaurs eat plants?
Were all dinosaurs very large?
Would you like to have a dinosaur as a pet?

5. **CRASH, BOOM, BANG**. Use three words such as crash, boom, and bang. Assign an action to each word. For example, crash could be the clapping of hands, boom could be the stamping of feet, and bang could be knees knocking together. Start out by saying each word slowly while doing the corresponding gesture. Repeat several times until the words and actions flow smoothly. Say them faster and faster, until nobody can keep up. Now try again, switching the order of the words.

6. **SUPERLATIVES**. Cut out construction paper dinosaurs to illustrate the following:

tall, taller, tallest
small, smaller, smallest
fat, fatter, fattest
fierce, fiercer, fiercest
thin, thinner, thinnest

The children will order the shapes and describe them using superlatives.

7. **DINOSAUR CARDS**. Make or purchase cards with pictures and the names of dinosaurs on them. Show the children the card and pronounce the name. Ask the children what they would name the dinosaur. Share information on each dinosaur and ask the children questions about the dinosaur on the card. How many legs does it have? What color is it? Does it seem fierce or gentle? Allow time for the children to explore the cards on their own.

8. **DINOSAUR CHORUS**. Sit with the children in a large circle on the floor. Have one of the children make a sound like a dinosaur or other animal which the second child repeats, and so on around the circle. When all the children have had a turn, the second child gets a chance to make a new sound. Repeat until everyone has had a turn. Remember some of the better sounds and try to hum a song using that sound.

9. **LISTENING GAME**. Sit on the floor in a large circle. On a chair in the middle of the circle sits one child who has been chosen to be "the mean dinosaur." The child is blindfolded or hiding his or her eyes. Under the chair is a small snack, such as a cracker or cookie. The teacher points to one child in the circle. That child, who portrays a "cautious dinosaur," creeps towards the chair, occasionally making quiet dinosaur sounds. The child on the chair listens and tries to tag the creeping child without moving off the chair or opening his or her eyes. If tagged, the creeper becomes "it." If the creeper can grab the snack and go back to the original spot without being tagged, he or she gets to eat the snack and gets to appoint a new mean dinosaur.

Dinosaurs Math Activities

1. **MEASURE UP**. Use a 6-inch ruler and some plastic dinosaurs or other toys. Some items should be shorter than 6 inches, others should be longer. The child will measure and store the items in two separate baskets or boxes. One box is for dinosaurs less than 6 inches, one box is for dinosaurs larger than 6 inches. As the activity progresses, ask the children to estimate before they actually measure.

2. **ROCK SORTER**. Cut 3 to 5 holes in the lid of a shoe box. Make the holes different sizes, and place them from left to right in decreasing sizes. Provide the children with different-sized stones to sort in their rock sorter. Tell the children that they are paleontologists who have collected rocks

that might contain fossils. They must sort the rocks before taking them back to their laboratories by placing each rock in the hole closest to its size.

3. **SORTING DINOSAURS.** Prepare some different colored and shaped construction paper dinosaurs. Make several of each shape. The children will sort them by color, shape, and number of legs, and if they are walking or flying dinosaurs. They may also be ordered by size.

4. **DINOSAUR CAVES.** You will need 11 "caves" for this activity. Small boxes, berry baskets, or even deli containers will do. You will also need 55 small plastic dinosaurs. Label the containers 0 through 10. Have the children place the appropriate number of dinosaurs into each container or "cave." Stress that zero is the empty set and no dinosaurs should be placed in the cave labeled "zero."

5. **DINOSAUR TRACKS.** Make 10 dinosaur footprints by drawing large monster feet on cardboard and cutting them out. Number the footprints one through 10. Go higher if the children show interest in larger numbers. Ask the children to place the numbered tracks on the floor, helping them to arrange the prints in numerical order. Once this has been accomplished, have the children walk on the tracks in numerical order, saying the numbers out loud as they step on them.

6. **NUMBER PICTURE.** Draw a picture of a dinosaur in a jungle. Try to incorporate as many numbers into the picture as you can. Cover the picture with clear adhesive paper, and have the children circle all the numbers that they can find with a crayon.

7. **DINOSAUR WHEELS.** Obtain a cardboard pizza disc or use other sturdy cardboard cut into the shape of a circle. Using a marker, divide the circle into eight equal sections. On each section draw a dinosaur or simple geometric shape. Numerals can also be used. On eight clothespins, draw or glue pictures of the same shapes. The object of the game is for the child to clip each clothespin onto the wheel at the corresponding section.

8. **HIDING DINOSAURS.** Give a plastic dinosaur and some large blocks to the children. Their task is to construct caves large enough for their dinosaurs to fit inside, but small enough so that theirs is the only dinosaur that will fit. Have the children make caves for different numbers of dinosaurs, too.

9. **BONES.** Use number cards and construction paper "bones." (The pattern from art activity 1 may be used.) Your little paleontologist can pick a card with a number on it and take that many bones out of the pile to take back to his or her lab to study.

Dinosaurs Science Projects

1. **QUICKSAND.** In prehistoric times, the land was covered with many swampy areas. Many dinosaurs probably lost their lives when they became mired in mud or quicksand. This activity illustrates exactly how quicksand works. Simply fill a large clay pot (the kind with a drainage hole in the bottom) with fine sand. Turn on the nearest garden hose and place the nozzle in the hole on the bottom of the pot. This forces water through the sand from bottom to top. Now place a heavy object such as a rock on top of the sand and watch it sink.

2. **FOSSILS.** Explain to the children that we learn about dinosaurs by studying fossils, the remains of the dinosaurs that have been preserved in rock. Paleontologists dig the fossils out of the ground. Sometimes bones are fossilized, but sometimes scientists find an imprint of a fern or a footprint made in mud millions of years ago. Here are directions for making your own fossils. Flatten out a piece of clay or dough. Press a bone, a piece of a fern, or even the foot of a plastic dinosaur into the clay. See how it leaves an imprint. If using bakers clay, preserve the imprint by drying and shellacking it. If using plain Play-doh or modeling clay, have the children experiment with making all sorts of imprints in their soft clay.

3. **VOLCANOES.** When we think of prehistoric times, we often think of volcanoes. Here are instructions for making your own erupting volcano. Obtain a large peat pot from the local garden center. Place it upside down in a bowl of water until the top is softened. When it is soft, push the top down gently to form a crater. Set the peat pot on a cookie sheet. Next to the "volcano," place a jar of vinegar and a container of baking soda. Allow the children to take turns spooning small amounts of baking soda into the crater and then using an eye dropper to add drops of vinegar to the volcano to make it erupt.

4. **DARE TO COMPARE.** It is difficult for children to imagine the actual size of the dinosaurs. By comparing them to familiar objects, we can make it easier for them to understand. If possible, take a walking tour around the school to show the children the following examples of size:

Diplodocus, as long as three school buses

Apatosaurus, as long and twice as high as a semi-truck

Tyrannosaurus rex, tall enough to look into an upstairs window, longer than a semi-truck, eyes as large as soccer balls, 6-inch long teeth, 8-inch talons, 4-foot high head, 30-inch long arms

Pterodactyl, from the size of a sparrow to the size of the largest hawk

Brachiosaurus, 4-stories high, long enough to stretch across a baseball diamond, weighing as much as 12 elephants

Compsognathus, the smallest dinosaur, only the size of a rooster

Triceratops, heavier than an elephant, longer than a pickup truck, 3-foot long horns, 640 teeth

5. **OLD VERSUS NEW.** Compare prehistoric animals with those that are alive today. Show pictures of animals that have changed very little: mammoth versus elephant, testudo versus tortoise, phobosuchus versus crocodile, ichthyosaur versus dolphin, ornithomimus versus ostrich, meganeura versus giant dragon fly. Books about dinosaurs contain many additional types of birds, insects, and lizards that are similar to the ones alive today.

6. **STALACTITES AND STALAGMITES.** The class project activity involves making a toy cave with stalactites. Here are instructions for making "real" stone icicles. All you will need is some water, two glasses, a saucer, some string, and a box of Epsom salts. Dissolve as much of the Epsom salts as you can in hot water. When cool, pour it into the two glasses. Place the glasses on opposite sides of the saucer. It works best if the glasses are about 4 inches apart. Place a string with one end in the bottom of one glass and the other end in the bottom of the other glass. The string should drape across the area over the saucer, sagging in the middle. The string will soon start to absorb the water and start to drip at its lowest point. In a few days, stalactites and stalagmites will start to form. This is what happens in caverns containing these types of formations; the only difference being that limestone is dissolved in the water rather than Epsom salts.

Dinosaurs Art Projects

1. **SAMMY SNAKE.** Most dinosaurs were reptiles, and a snake is a reptile that lives today. Here are instructions for making a snake mobile.

Materials: Each child will need one standard white paper plate, approximately 12 inches of string or yarn, markers or paint, and scissors. *Directions*: Mark cutting lines on the paper plate according to the illustration (see figure 10.1). The child can decorate the paper plate with markers or paint. After the plate has dried, the child can cut along the cutting line marked previously. Discard the shaded section. Help the child use a paper punch to make a hole at the top of the snake's head. The child can then thread string through the hole and tie it in a knot to hang the mobile.

Fig. 10.1.

2. **DINOSAUR EGGS.** Dinosaurs were reptiles and they laid their eggs and hatched their babies on dry land. Here are instructions for making dinosaur eggs.

Materials: Each child will need a small round balloon only partially inflated, newspaper, craft glue, water, paint, small sponges to apply the paint, and small, flat containers to hold the paint. (Pie tins work well.) Four-inch Styrofoam eggs may replace the balloons, if preferred. *Directions*: Cut the newspaper into plenty of 6-by-3/8-inch strips. Mix the glue with the water (two parts glue to one part water). The children will dip the newspaper strips into the glue mixture and pull the strips between their fingers to squeeze off the excess. The children will then cover the small balloon or Styrofoam egg with the strips of paper, being careful to overlap them, smoothing out the wrinkles. After the egg has dried, it can be painted. Pour small amounts of paint into the pie tins. The children can dip the sponges into the paint and then apply it to the egg. Two or three coats may be applied to achieve a speckled effect. Let the eggs dry before allowing the children to take them home.

3. **DRIPPY DINOSAURS.** *Materials*: Each child will need a large piece of blank newsprint, a paintbrush, paint, and markers or crayons. *Directions*: Using a large paintbrush, let the children drip some paint onto half of their pieces of newsprint. Help them fold it over so that the paint is enclosed. Press, being careful not to let any stray paint squish out the sides. Open and allow to dry. The children will then add features to the paintings with markers or crayons, transforming them into dinosaurs or monsters.

4. **SHRINKIES.** *Materials*: Each child will need a Styrofoam tray from the deli or the butcher shop, permanent broad tip markers, and string or yarn. You will need something sharp to punch a hole in the Styrofoam, a nonstick baking pan, and an oven. *Directions*: Transfer the given patterns (see figure 10.2) or one of your own onto the children's Styrofoam trays. Help them cut out the patterns. Let the children paint the dinosaurs with marking pens. Punch a hole in the top, 3/4-inch from the top. Place the dinosaur painted side up on the cookie sheet and place in the oven. Bake at 250 degrees for 3 to 5 minutes. Watch constantly. If the foam starts to curl, flatten it with a spatula. At first the Styrofoam will not look like it is melting, then suddenly it shrinks to a tiny size. After removing the shrinkie from the oven, cool briefly. Help the children thread yarn through the hole to make a necklace.

5. **THREE-PART CREATURES.** *Materials*: One large sheet of drawing paper and an assortment of crayons are needed for each child. *Directions*: Fold each piece of paper into thirds (across the short way) before giving them to the children. Tell the children to keep the papers folded. Ask them to draw dinosaur or monster heads on the top section with their crayons. When they finish, turn

Fig. 10.2.

each child's paper so that the head is hidden and the next section of the paper is exposed. Have the children pass their papers to the child on the right. Everyone now draws a body on the middle section. When the bodies are finished, fold and pass along the papers again. The third child completes the creature by drawing legs and feet on the final section. After all the dinosaurs or monsters are finished, the children may open up the pictures. Let the children display their creatures and give them names or tell stories about them.

6. **LONG-NECK PUPPET.** *Materials*: A tube sock, felt pieces, yarn, and craft glue will be needed for each puppet. *Directions*: Cut felt pieces into eyes and mouths for each puppet. Have the children put the socks over their hands and arms. Help them glue on the eyes and mouths where they seem to fit. Let them take off the socks and glue on additional felt pieces or yarn scraps to further decorate their dinosaurs.

7. **DINOSAUR STENCILS.** *Materials*: Cardboard, tape, paint, construction paper, and cookie cutters or pictures of dinosaurs for patterns. *Directions*: Make stencils on the cardboard pieces by tracing around dinosaur cookie cutters or your own pictures. Cut the shapes out of the cardboard to form the stencils. Help the children tape the stencils to their pieces of construction paper. Let the children paint inside the stencils. After they have finished, help them remove the stencils. Dispose of any stencils with large amounts of paint on them. Allow the painting to dry. For extra fun, tape the stencils to the classroom windows and let the children paint them there.

8. **SWINGING DINOSAURS.** *Materials*: Each child will need one drinking straw, some string, glue, tape, markers, and a dinosaur pattern cut out of construction paper (see figure 10.3). *Directions*: Transfer the pattern of either dinosaur to construction paper and cut it out for the child. Let the child decorate it with the markers and glue on the legs or wings; help him or her poke a small hole in the head and tail of each dinosaur. Tie one end of the string through the hole in the dinosaur's head using tape to secure it, if needed. Repeat with another piece of string through the tail. Tie the other end of the strings to the straw and secure them with tape (see the illustration). The child can hold the straw at the bottom and gently swing it back and forth to make the dinosaur move.

9. **BONE COLLAGE.** *Materials*: Construction paper, glue, and markers. *Directions*: Cut out several bones (see figure 10.4) for each child. The child will then glue the "bones" to construction paper, trying to make a dinosaur. This will show the child just how difficult it is for scientists to reconstruct dinosaurs from the bones they find. Use markers to decorate the collage.

10. **DINO.** *Materials*: Construction paper, markers, scissors, a cardboard tissue paper roll, and three pipe cleaners are needed for each child. *Directions*: Transfer a Dino pattern onto a piece of construction paper for each child (see figure 10.5). Allow the child to decorate the dinosaur pattern with markers, and help the child cut it out. After Dino is cut out, slide its body into the tissue paper roll, then wind two of the pipe cleaners around the tube to form Dino's legs. Bend the ends of the pipe cleaners to form the feet. The third pipe cleaner is to be molded into the dinosaur's spine. Tuck the ends of the spine into the other pipe cleaners to hold it in place. Dino's neck may be "stretched" by sliding the construction paper body back and forth in the tube. See the illustration for help in assembling Dino.

(Text continues on page 175.)

Fig. 10.3.

Fig. 10.4.

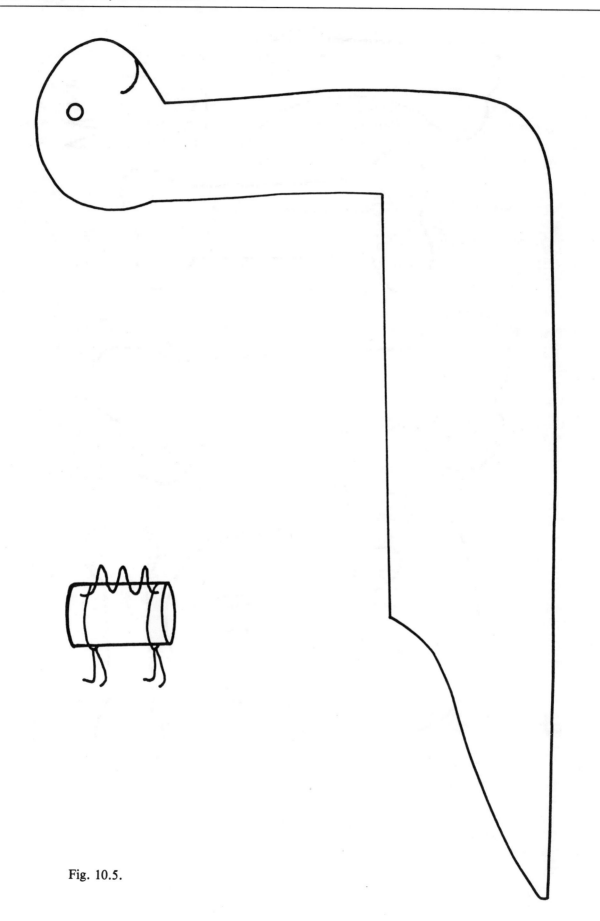

Fig. 10.5.

Dinosaurs Class Project

Caves

Cut round openings in large cardboard boxes from appliance or department stores. Several boxes can be connected to each other with duct tape. Children can paint the cave brown or gray. Hang paper stalactites from the ceiling and draw stalagmites coming up from the ground on the inside walls. When the paint dries, hop right in.

Dinosaurs Story Time

1. **DINOSAUR DISPLAY**. Ask the children to bring any dinosaur toys that they have to class to display along with all of the books you have gathered for dinosaur week. Stuffed toys, models, and small plastic dinosaur toys are all acceptable. It is up to you whether these priceless items should be played with in the library corner or whether they are to be a "dinosaur museum" for viewing only.

2. **TRACING DINOSAURS**. Most picture books about dinosaurs or reptiles will include large color illustrations. After reading some of these aloud to the children, let the children familiarize themselves with the books. Provide tracing paper and a pencil for the children to trace pictures of their favorite dinosaurs straight from the book. After they have traced a picture, let them cut out the picture and color it with crayons. Write the name of the dinosaur on the back. Give each child a drinking straw or craft stick to glue to the back of their dinosaur to make it into a puppet.

Dinosaurs Poems, Songs, Fingerplays

1. Two terrible lizards sat in the sun.
   (*Hold up index finger of each hand*.)
   One was eyeing the other one.
   (*Bend index fingers toward one another*.)
   They both were hungry and wanted to eat
   (*Rub stomach and smack lips*.)
   Each other's meal from its head to its feet.
   (*Point first to head, then feet*.)

2. (Sing this to the tune of "Frère Jacques.")
   Dinosaurs playing, dinosaurs playing,
   In the sun, in the sun,
   Tumbling, jumping, stomping,
   Running, flying, romping.
   Oh, what fun. Oh, what fun.

3. One brontosaurus standing before us is all we need for a brontosaurus chorus.

4. Reptiles, reptiles everywhere,
   With plenty of scales, they don't need hair.
   Some like water and some like land,
   They lay their eggs in the warm, dry sand.

5. (Sing this to the tune of "What Do You Do With a Drunken Sailor?")

    What do you do with a brontosaurus?
    What do you do with a brontosaurus?
    What do you do with a brontosaurus,
    Early in the morning?

    Ride on his back like a broncobuster,
    Ride on his back like a broncobuster,
    Ride on his back like a broncobuster,
    Early in the morning!

    What do you do with a pteradactyl?
    What do you do with a pteradactyl?
    What do you do with a pteradactyl,
    Early in the morning?

    Put him in a cage and feed him bird seed,
    Put him in a cage and feed him bird seed,
    Put him in a cage and feed him bird seed,
    Early in the morning!

    (*Can the children think of other things they might do with these creatures*?)

6. Dinosaurs lived so long ago.
    How long ago, I do not know.
    They lived in caves
    And wore no clothes.
    They got too cold
    So I am told
    And disappeared without a trace.
    In other words, they blew this place.

7. I'm a dinosaur and I'm okay. (*put thumb on chest*.)
    I sleep all night, (*lay head on folded hands*.)
    And I eat all day. (*gnash teeth*.)
    I love to chomp and I love to bite. (*chomp and bite*.)
    My body's big, (*extend arms*.)
    But my brain is slight. (*hold thumb and index finger an inch apart*.)

8. (Clasp hands together and then raise fingers. Then hook thumbs together to make a stegosaurus.)

    The stegosaurus was a dinosaur
    Who lived in days of yore.
    He had a back
    With racks of tacks,
    Now who could ask for more?

9. Four giant dinosaurs (*hold up four fingers*.)
    Walking out to eat. (*walk fingers*.)
    Three like plants (*hold up three fingers*.)
    But one craves meat. (*hold up one finger*.)

    —Carol Holland

Dinosaurs Music List

Cassettes

Polisar, Barry. "Brontosaurus with Bronchitis." *Naughty Songs for Boys and Girls.* Rainbow Morning Music ISBN 0-9615696-5-4, 1978.

Polisar, Barry. "Dinosaur Song." *Stanley Stole My Shoelace and Rubbed It in His Armpit.* Rainbow Morning Music ISBN 0-961-5695-7-0, 1980.

Polisar, Barry. "I'm a Three-Toed, Triple-Eyed, Double-Jointed Dinosaur." *Family Concert.* Rainbow Morning Music ISBN 0-938663-12-7, 1974.

Polisar, Barry. "Reptile World." *Stanley Stole My Shoelace and Rubbed It in His Armpit.* Rainbow Morning Music ISBN 0-961-5696-7-0, 1980.

Polisar, Barry. "Tryannosaurus Nix." *Naughty Songs for Boys and Girls.* Rainbow Morning Music ISBN 0-9615696-5-4, 1978.

Silber, Nancy, and Tony Soll. "Dinosaur Dreams." *Dinosaurs, Dolphins and Dreams.* CMS Records CS X4695, n.d.

Valeri, Michele, and Michael Stein. *Dinosaur Rock.* Dinorock Music CPN-1739, 1984.
This recording contains a story about dinosaurs, with music and songs throughout.

Dinosaurs Book List

Fiction

Brown, Marc, and Stephen Krensky. *Dinosaurs Beware! A Safety Guide.* Little, 1982.
Listen to these safety tips illustrated by drawings of silly dinosaurs.

Carrick, Carol. *Big Old Bones.* Illustrated by Donald Carrick. Clarion Books, 1989.
After digging up bones, a scientist is not sure how they fit together.

Carrick, Carol. *Patrick's Dinosaurs.* Illustrated by Donald Carrick. Clarion Books, 1983.
Patrick is frightened, imagining dinosaurs everywhere when his brother tells him about these extinct giants.

Hennesy, B. G. *The Dinosaur Who Lived in My Back Yard.* Illustrated by Susan Davis. Viking Kestral, 1988.
A child imagines what life was like for the dinosaur who must have roamed her neighborhood eons ago.

Hoff, Syd. *Danny and the Dinosaur.* Harper and Row, 1958.
Danny wanted to play and so did the dinosaur exhibit. What could be more natural than that they leave the museum together?

Most, Bernard. *If the Dinosaurs Came Back*. Harcourt Brace Jovanovich, 1978.
This picture book explores what might happen in the unlikely event that the dinosaurs return.

Most, Bernard. *Whatever Happened to the Dinosaurs?* Harcourt Brace Jovanovich, 1984.
This book contains fantastic and funny explanations about what might have become of the dinosaurs.

Murphy, Jim. *The Last Dinosaur*. Illustrated by Mark Alan Weatherby. Scholastic, 1988.
This gripping adventure depicts what life may have been like for the last triceratops roaming the earth. (This book may be a little intense for very young children.)

Nonfiction

Aliki. *Digging Up Dinosaurs*. Thomas Crowell, 1988.
In simple pictures and text, Aliki explains how dinosaur bones get to museums.

Aliki. *Fossils Tell of Long Ago*. Thomas Crowell, 1972.
This introduction to fossils explains where they come from and how they were formed.

Aliki. *My Visit to the Dinosaurs*. Thomas Crowell, 1985.
This beginning science book introduces the topic of dinosaurs.

Barton, Byron. *Dinosaurs, Dinosaurs*. Harper and Row, 1989.
Dinosaur characteristics are explained and illustrated in splashy colors.

Blumenthal, Nancy. *Count a Saurus*. Illustrated by Robert Jay Kaufman. Macmillan, 1989.
This very original book depicts groups of dinosaurs and other prehistoric creatures. Additional text is located in the back of the book for more interesting information.

Booth, Jerry. *Big Beast Book: Dinosaurs and How They Got That Way*. Illustrated by Martha Weston. Little, Brown, 1988.
Though designed for elementary age children, the teacher will find this book very useful. It contains an introduction to dinosaurs with instructions for related projects.

Kingdon, Jill. *The ABC Dinosaur Book*. Illustrated by Seymour Fleishman. Children's Press, 1982.
One dinosaur is highlighted for each letter of the alphabet.

Matthew, Rupert, and Tudor Humphries. *T. R. (Tyrannosaurus Rex) and Friends*. Discovery Toys, 1988.
Big dinosaur drawings make this book of dinosaur facts very entertaining.

Riddles and Poems

Keller, Charles. *Colossal Fossils.* Illustrated by Leonard Kessler. Prentice Hall Books for Young Readers, 1987.
 Keller compiles a large number of silly dinosaur riddles.

Polhamus, Jean. *Dinosaur Funny Bones.* Prentice Hall, 1974.
 This is a book of silly dinosaur poetry.

Sterne, Noelle. *Tyrannosaurus Wrecks—A Book of Dinosaur Riddles.* Illustrated by Victoria Chess. Thomas Crowell, 1979.
 Silly illustrations highlight this compilation of many dinosaur riddles.

11
INTO THE FUTURE
(Space)

Focus on Space

In addition to planets, our solar system contains many other interesting components. Activities in this chapter will help to introduce stars, asteroids, comets, meteoroids, and other features of our infinite galaxy.

Consider discussing these subjects:
    Solar system
    Stars
    Characteristics of the planets in our solar system
    Moons
    Gravity
    Space travel
    Infinite versus finite
    Constellations
    Planetariums
    NASA
    Day and night
    Moon myths
    Features of outer space: meteoroids, nebulae, comets

Space Motor Skills

1. **MOON-WINDER**. To make moon-winders for the children to wind and unwind you will need 4 feet of string and a wooden button cut from a dowel 1½ inches in diameter for each moon-winder. To make the button, saw off a ¼-inch slice of the dowel and sand it. Mark the center of the button and points ¼ inch on either side of the center (see figure 11.1). Drill holes at the two points with a 1/16-inch bit. Thread the string through one hole and then back through the other. Tie the ends of the string together. Have the children spread the string loop between their hands, letting the wooden button slide to the center. Ask them to wind up the string by swinging the button around about 30 times. To make the moon-winder work, the children should pull their hands apart and together, making the button spin.

Fig. 11.1.

2. **DOT-TO-DOT**. Draw dots or tiny stars on paper for the children to connect. Help them learn geometric shapes by placing three dots on the paper for a triangle, four for a square, etc. If you like, you may place dots in such a way as to form the Big Dipper and the Little Dipper. To challenge the children even further, make a small grid using either 9 or 16 dots. Connect some of the dots in a certain way, and see if the child can copy your pattern.

3. **PASS A PLANET**. Have the children sit in a circle on the floor. While playing music, have the children pass one or two balls around the circle. When the music stops, the child who holds a ball should stand up and spin around like a planet. When the child sits down again, he or she should sit facing the outside. Continue playing the game until all of the children face the outside of the circle.

4. **SUN IN THE CENTER**. Tie a beanbag to the end of a jump rope. Twirl the rope around you close to the ground. Three or four children should space themselves toward the end of the rope, jumping over it as it reaches them. If a child misses and stops the rope more than three times, he or she may become the "sun in the center" and twirl the rope.

5. **BUILDING CARDS**. Make as many cards as possible from sturdy cardboard. Make cuts in the cards as illustrated (see figure 11.2). The children may use the cards to build space stations or other structures.

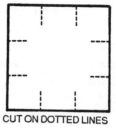

CUT ON DOTTED LINES

Fig. 11.2.

6. **FLYING SAUCERS**. Assist the children in tracing around plates or saucers onto cardboard or stiff paper. Help them cut out the circles, and then cut a narrow pie slice from the circle. The children can play flying saucers by tossing the discs through the air.

7. **DANCING COMETS**. Give each child a 3- to 4-foot long crepe paper streamer. Playing space music, allow the children to dance around the room, trailing their streamers as a comet would trail its flaming tail.

8. **BLAST OFF**. Ask the children to crouch down near the floor. Counting backward from 10, have them inch back up, bit by bit, until almost standing. When zero is reached cry, "Blast off!" signaling the children to jump up as high as they can.

9. **SHADOW TAG**. Take the children outside on a sunny day. Have them dodge, twist, and turn to avoid having their own shadows stepped on, while attempting to step on other children's shadows.

10. **MAGNETIC FOOL**. One child is the planet who has escaped orbit. The child moves around the room, becoming attached to other planets who get within the child's gravitational pull. The game continues until the whole group of planets is clustered together.

11. **MOON WALK**. Ask the children to imagine walking on the moon. Explain that there is less gravitational pull and that they would most likely float about in slow motion. Now, ask them how they would walk on a planet denser than earth, with a greater gravitational pull. In this case, the children would barely be able to lift their feet from the ground.

Space Language Activities

1. **GRAB BAG**. In a bag or box, place items that a child might wish to take along on a trip to the moon, such as a toothbrush and toothpaste, a teddy bear, a favorite book, small telescope, etc. Have one child choose something from the bag and describe it until the other children can guess what it is.

2. **ROBOT COMMANDS**. The teacher is the "commander" and the children are robots. The commander instructs the robots as to what actions to take, such as "raise your left arm" or "turn around twice and then sit down." Continue the game, allowing the children to each have a turn as the commander.

3. **BEEP, BEEP**. All of the children are robots and the teacher is the commander. The robots are programmed to behave in a certain way. When they hear one beep from the commander, they walk forward in a straight line. Two beeps mean stop and three beeps mean turn around.

4. **WISH UPON A STAR**. Make a wishing star by cutting a large star shape from cardboard and covering it with glitter or foil. (A fancy Christmas treetop ornament could also be used.) Recite the rhyme "Star Light, Star Bright." Pass the star from child to child, as each tells his or her favorite wish.

5. **DAY AND NIGHT.** Glue pictures onto index cards of things you see at night. Some examples include a house at night with the lights on, an owl, people wearing pajamas, the moon, stars, etc. Do the same with items that may be seen during the day, such as blooming flowers, the sun, children boarding a school bus, etc. Mix up the cards. Ask the children to sort them into a daytime pile and a nighttime pile.

6. **SAME AND DIFFERENT.** Cut oaktag into 24 playing cards, drawing a line dividing each card in half. Using a space motif, glue identical pairs of stickers on half the cards and different pairs of stickers on the other half of the deck. The children will sort the cards into "same" and "different" categories.

7. **LETTER ROCKETS.** Using the pattern given (see figure 11.3), cut 26 rockets and tails from construction paper. Print uppercase and lowercase letters on each rocket as shown. Cover the rockets and their tails with clear adhesive paper to preserve. Using double-stick tape on the backs of the playing pieces, ask the children to tape the rockets and their corresponding tails up on a bulletin board or wall.

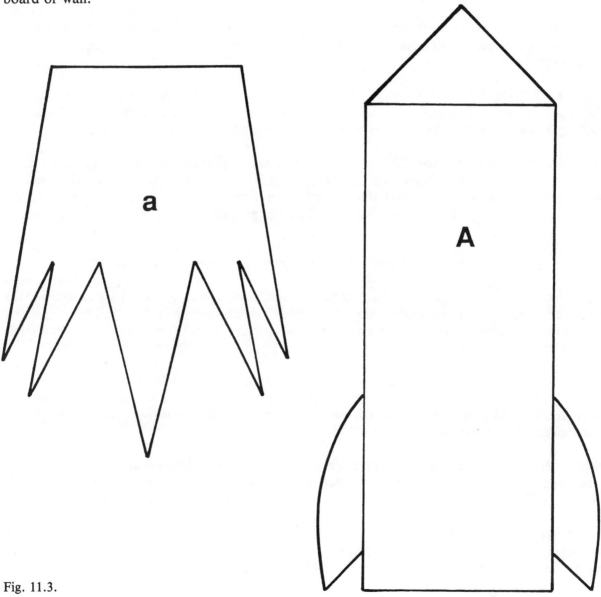

Fig. 11.3.

8. **I'M A STAR.** Using the pattern given in figure 11.4, cut one small star for each letter of the child's name. Use sturdy construction paper or lightweight cardboard. Print the child's name on the stars, one letter per star. Place the lettered stars in their correct order on the outside of an envelope. Trace around each star. Write the child's name on the envelope, one letter per traced star. Place the cutout stars in the envelope. The child can pour the stars out of the envelope and spell his or her name by placing the cutout stars on top of the corresponding ones on the envelope.

Fig. 11.4.

9. **TRIP TO THE MOON.** For your imaginary trip to the moon, use heavy paper and crayons to prepare posters of what you think you might see out the window of a rocket on its way to the moon. Possible ideas include a sequence of three posters showing the earth getting smaller as you get farther away, three posters showing the moon getting larger as you get nearer to it, a shooting star, a satellite, etc.

To start the activity, have the children get ready for the journey. Discuss the rocket, the items you need to take along, and what you would need to wear. Have the children act out packing their bags, putting on space suits, and climbing into the rocket. Ask the children to count down backward from 10, and then blast off. Show the posters of earth getting smaller, using words such as far, farther, and farthest. When showing the moon getting larger, use words such as close, closer, and closest. Continue with the other posters. Finally, make your landing. Act out putting on space helmets and walking on the moon. If time permits, make the return trip to earth.

Space Math Activities

1. **CALCULATORS.** Provide the children with calculators for number practice. Ask them to press certain numbers, or let them press the buttons of their choice and identify the number. Request number sequences from more advanced students.

2. **MAGNET PICKUPS.** Use a strong magnet to see how many of a certain item it will pick up. Try to pick up paper clips, pins, washers, etc. Provide some items such as coins that the magnet will not pick up.

3. **SORTING.** Make cards or cutouts of the sun, moon, stars, and various recognizable planets (a red Mars, a Saturn with rings, etc.). The children can sort and count how many are in each set.

4. **ORDERING PLANETS.** Using a textbook or poster of the planets as a guide, make a cutout of each planet to scale. The child's task will be to put them in order by size.

5. **COUNTDOWN.** With toy rocket in hand, assist each child in counting backward from 10. Younger children can count from five. After the countdown, the child may yell, "Blast off!" and fire the rocket into the sky.

6. **STAR DOMINOES.** Make a set of dominoes using 2-by-4-inch tagboard rectangles and gummed foil stars. Divide each domino into two halves and place a number of stars in each half. Refer to an actual set of dominoes with help in the placement of the stars, if necessary. To play, have 2 to 4 children divide the dominoes between themselves. The first child will place any domino in the center of the table, and the second player will try to match one of the halves. If a child cannot make a match, his or her turn goes to the next player. The children continue matching dominoes in turn, until a player wins by using all of his or her dominoes.

7. **BOARD GAME.** Make up a board game, drawing a pathway from earth to the moon. Along the pathway, alternate between 3 or 4 geometric shapes. Use a spinner or cards containing the same shapes. With tiny toy rockets or space creatures as markers, the children will move along the path by placing their markers on the appropriate space. Continue until each player reaches the moon.

8. **ORDERING BY WEIGHT.** Select 4 tin cans of the same size and cover with construction paper. Pour sand in the cans, filling one full, one ⅓ full, and one ⅔ full, and leaving one empty. Cover the tops of the cans with lids or place plastic wrap over the top and hold in place with a rubber band. Trim the excess plastic wrap. Use the example given (see figure 11.5) to make cones for the tops of the cans, transforming them into rockets. (You may need to adjust the size of the cone to fit your cans.) The child's task will be to order the rockets from light to heavy. Once this is done, explain that the heavier the rocket, the more fuel it will need to shoot into space. Once the child can feel the difference in the weight of the rockets, you may wish to add four more in equal amounts so that the child can match equal pairs.

9. **CRATERS AND CREATURES.** Use 11 paper plates, drawing one crater on the first, two on the second, three on the third, etc. Continue in this manner until the plates, or planets, all have craters. The eleventh planet should contain no craters. Draw 11 space people, each with a numeral from 0 to 10 on its chest. The child's job will be to match each space person to the planet with the corresponding number of craters.

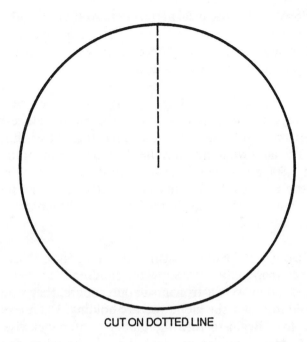

CUT ON DOTTED LINE

Fig.11.5.

Space Science Activities

1. **OATMEAL BOX PLANETARIUM**. To help the children begin to identify several well-known constellations, prepare a simple projector using an oatmeal box and flashlight. With a pencil, sketch a familiar group of stars on the box lid, such as the Big Dipper or Orion. (Find these in an encyclopedia or in *Glow in the Dark Constellations* by C. E. Thompson.) Using a pick or a large darning needle, make holes in the lid where the stars should be. To view, place a lighted flashlight upright in the box, put the lid on, and darken the room. Hold the box upright toward the ceiling so that the stars are projected there. Read or tell about the constellation and how it was named. If enough oatmeal boxes are available, make one constellation per box. If you have only one oatmeal box, other constellations can be poked out of pieces of cardboard cut to fit over the top of the one box and interchanged with the constellation cut from the lid. Show the constellations often, until the children can remember the name of them on first sight.

2. **TWINKLE, TWINKLE**. Why can stars be seen only at night? To show the children the answer to this question, perform the following experiment.

On a specified day, have each of the children bring a flashlight to school. Have half the children stand at one end of the darkened classroom, with their flashlights, or stars, turned on. The remaining children should notice how brightly the flashlights shine. Slowly lighten the room. Are the lights still easy to see? Ask the children watching to trade places with the children holding the flashlights. Darken the room and repeat the experiment.

3. **THE SUN**. Take the class outside on a sunny day. Have the children look around and notice that the sun shines down everywhere around them, warming the air and giving us light. Returning to the classroom, explain that the sun is really a star, a huge ball of fiery gas, and that there are many

stars in the sky. The sun looks so big because it is closer to us than the other stars. To illustrate this, cut a large yellow sun from a piece of construction paper. Bring it close to the children so that they can see it easily. Now back away, asking the children if they can see the paper sun as well. Does it look as large as it did when they were standing near it?

4.   **THE EARTH.** How is the earth like an egg? To find out, provide the children with a hard-boiled egg with which to experiment. Begin by cutting the egg in half, exposing the white and the yoke. Explain that the earth resembles an egg in that it has three layers just as the egg has the shell, the white, and the yoke. The land we stand on is the shell, 5 to 18 miles thick. Under the shell is the egg white, or a rock layer 1,800 miles thick. The yolk represents the molten inner core, which is 800 miles in diameter. Show the children the cracked shell, and explain that the earth's crust has cracks in it, too. Show the children a picture of the Grand Canyon of the Colorado River, or other pictures of canyons or faults in the earth. Like the egg, the shell can crack, leaving the egg white intact.

5.   **DAY AND NIGHT.** Bring a globe of the earth to the classroom. Discover together where North America is and identify the other continents. Show the children the oceans and the north and south poles. Tell the children that if they were astronauts in outer space, they would see far away stars and the moon. The earth would look like the globe you are holding. Place a piece of tape on the globe over the state where you live. Begin to turn the globe counterclockwise. Explain that the earth rotates on its axis like this, day in and day out. Ask the children where the sun goes at night. Most will say it goes behind the mountains or under the ocean. Tell the children that the sun always stays put and that we on earth are the ones to move. Have someone keep turning the globe slowly. Get a flashlight and pretend that the flashlight is the sun. Shine the light on the slowly rotating globe. Explain that where the sun is shining it is day and on the other side of the globe, where it is dark, it is night. Point out the piece of tape. Show how it goes from day to night. Explain that it takes a whole day and night, 24 hours, to make one revolution.

6.   **GRAVITY.** Do a flannel board story or use props to illustrate what would happen if there were no gravity. The story can go something like this:

> Once upon a time there was a little girl named Mary. She had a strange dream. In her dream she was floating in the sky above her house. She saw cars float by, then a dog, and then her friend, Sam. Mary and Sam decided to play catch with a ball, but the ball would not go where they threw it, so they decided to go home. Finally, Mary awoke from her dream. She was glad to discover things were normal.

Ask the children what they found strange about the dream. Ask them if they know what was missing in the dream, or why everything was floating. Explain that because the earth spins, there is gravity that is always pulling us down toward the middle of the earth. Fill a plastic bucket ¼ full of water. Ask the children what they think will happen if you swing the pail of water around in a circle. Most will predict a watery mess. Grasp the handle of the pail and swing your arm around in a quick circle, perpendicular to the floor. The water stays in the bucket. Explain that you were creating a force of gravity by twirling your arm quickly. If you were to spin your arm slowly, the water would spill. The earth rotates quickly enough to keep the oceans and everything else from flying off the planet. Explain that gravity is an invisible force. Use a magnet and paper clip to show the children another invisible force. Place the paper clip on the table and bring the magnet near the clip until it starts to pull the paper clip without touching it. Tell how the astronauts experienced the moon's lower gravity, having to wear special weights in their boots to keep them from flying off the moon. Show the children a picture of an astronaut on the moon. Have the children do the "moon walk," pretending there is little gravity holding them down. Finally, have the children try to jump up as hard as they can to break the pull of gravity. When they cannot succeed, tell them that "whatever goes up, must come down!"

7. **SOLAR SYSTEM.** Place a lamp in the middle of the classroom on a low table to represent the sun. Give each child a turn at pretending to be the earth. Have the child face the lamp (day), make a quarter turn to the left (sunset), turn completely away (night), and make one more quarter turn (sunrise). Repeat more quickly.

Next, show pictures of the planets and talk about their names and characteristics. Make paper cutouts of the planets and the moon. Assign each child a cutout, and let the children take turns being the planets. Start with the earth. Ask the earth to walk around the lamp in a circle. Explain that the sun, like the earth, has a gravitational pull. The sun's gravity keeps all the planets spinning in their own orbits around the sun. The earth takes about 365 days to go all the way around the sun. Add the other planets to their orbits one at a time. Place Pluto very far from the other planets and give it a skewed orbit, sometimes coming between Neptune and Uranus, other times letting it be the farthest from the sun. Explain that the farther a planet is from the sun, the longer it takes to make its orbit. Pluto, being the farthest, takes 248 years. To complete your model of the solar system, you may add the moons spinning around their own planets spinning around the sun.

8. **SHADOW GAMES.** Set a strong lamp (with no lamp shade) on a low table near a blank wall. Turn the lamp on and let the children use their hands to make funny shadows on the wall. Explain that the sun and clouds sometimes make shadows on the earth. The clouds come between the earth and the sun just like the children's hands come between the lamp and the wall. Sometimes the moon moves in front of the sun and hides it, making a shadow on the earth. This is called an eclipse. At least twice every year, and sometimes more often, the moon's shadow falls somewhere on earth. On August 21, 2017 and on April 8, 2024, the shadow will fall on parts of the United States.

9. **MOON PHASES.** It takes 29½ days for the moon to complete its orbit around the earth. During this time, the sunlit surface we see changes. Use the patterns given (see figure 11.6) to make cutouts of these moon phases. Have the children glue each moon phase to a craft stick. Use the moon puppets to help the children learn the names of the different moon phases. Once the children can name the different shapes, help them put their puppets in the correct order to learn the progression of the lunar month.

10. **SCALE IT DOWN.** Two of the most striking characteristics of our solar system are the huge differences in size between the planets and the vast distances between the planets. Here are the instructions for making a wall display of our solar system roughly to scale.

First choose your largest blank wall for the representation. If one wall is too short, continue the model through the corner onto the next wall. Since the sun is a million times larger than the earth, it would be impossible to make it to scale with the other planets of our model. Placing as large a sun as possible made from cutout paper on the far left side of the wall, however, will still give the children some idea of its immensity. Make paper cutouts of the planets using these diameters:

Mercury 7/16", place 2 inches from the sun
Venus 15/16", place 3 inches from the sun
Earth 1", place 4 inches from the sun
Mars 5/8", place 6 inches from the sun
Jupiter 11", place 21 inches from the sun

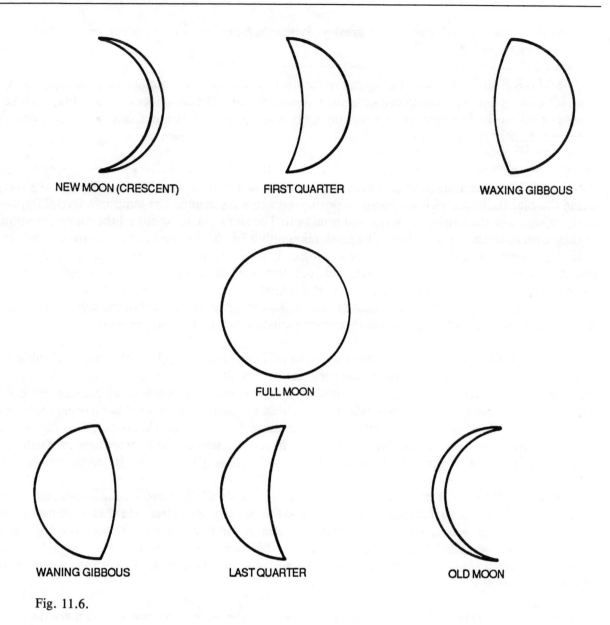

NEW MOON (CRESCENT)   FIRST QUARTER   WAXING GIBBOUS

FULL MOON

WANING GIBBOUS   LAST QUARTER   OLD MOON

Fig. 11.6.

Saturn 10", place 38 inches from the sun
Uranus 4 1/8", place 57 inches from the sun
Neptune 4", place 121 inches from the sun
Pluto 5/16", place 159 inches from the sun

Note that we always think of Pluto as being the planet farthest from the sun, but in 1979 Pluto moved closer to the sun than Neptune for the first time in hundreds of years. In 1999 Pluto will again be the farthest from the sun.

To complete the model, tape the paper planets to the wall the specified distances from the sun. Indicate each planet's name by printing it on a small sign and tacking it near the appropriate planet.

Space Art Projects

1. **STARRY SKY.** *Materials*: Each child will need one dark blue or black sheet of construction paper, gummed stars, two small scraps of white paper, glue, scissors, and crayons. *Directions*: Ask the children to cut two small circles from the white paper, one to represent the moon, one to represent the earth. The cutouts may be colored with crayons. Ask the children to glue the earth and moon to the dark piece of construction paper, and then stick on many gummed stars. The older children may wish to stick the gummed stars in the form of a constellation.

2. **CELLOPHANE GALAXY.** *Materials*: Each child will need a paper punch for making holes, a 4½-by-6-inch sheet of colored cellophane, a 9-by-12-inch piece of black or dark blue construction paper, and glue. *Directions*: Ask the children to fold their pieces of construction paper in half, so that they measure 4½ by 6 inches. Using the paper punch, punch as many holes as possible through both thicknesses of the papers. Then slip pieces of cellophane between the halves of the papers and glue into place. The cellophane will be sandwiched between the construction paper. When dry, hang the finished products in the window.

3. **STAR VIEWER.** *Materials*: Each child will require one 11-inch long cardboard tube, paint, and paintbrushes. *Directions*: Provide different colors of paint for the children to decorate their viewing tubes. When dry, children will look through one end at the stars. The tube really helps them when trying to focus on one small patch of sky!

To turn the star viewer into a taleidoscope, use a warm iron to melt crayon shavings between two pieces of waxed paper. When cool, trim the waxed paper to a 3-inch circle. Wrap the circle around the end of the cardboard tube and fasten it in place with a rubber band. To view, the child should put his or her eye up to the open side of the tube and look toward a source of light.

4. **TAIL OF THE COMET.** *Materials*: Each child will need 1 spool, 3 crepe paper or cloth streamers about 3 feet long, glitter, glue, string, and a stapler. *Directions*: If you wish, allow the children to decorate the streamers using glue and glitter. When dry, have them staple the three streamers together at one end and glue to the spools. The spools may also be decorated with glitter and glue. When dry, help the children to tie a 3-foot length of string to the spool using the spindle hole. The comet is ready to fly.

5. **ROCKET.** *Materials*: Each child will need 1 cardboard tube from a roll of tissue paper or paper towels, paint, paintbrush, 3 fins and 1 cone (see figure 11.7) cut from construction paper, and glue. *Directions*: Ask the children to paint their entire cardboard tubes. While they dry, assist them in cutting out the cone and 3 fins from construction paper. Show them where to apply glue to the cones and help them shape the cones into place. Let the cones dry. Assist the children in folding the fins along the dotted lines and gluing them into place on the tube. Have the children glue the cones into place on top of the tubes. After the rockets dry completely, they may be hung from the ceiling with pieces of string threaded through the tips of the cones down through the bodies of the rockets. Attach both ends of the strings to the ceiling, angling the rockets to give the appearance of flight.

6. **SPACE TOPS.** *Materials*: Each child will need a 3-inch circle cut from cardboard or heavy paper, a pencil or dowel of similar diameter for the top to spin on, and a set of 2 colored markers, either yellow and red, yellow and blue, or red and blue. *Directions*: On the cardboard circle, draw 6

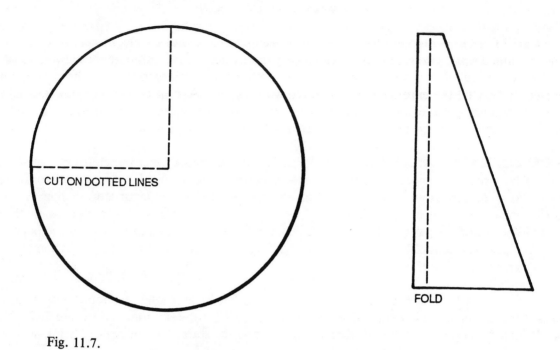

Fig. 11.7.

smaller circles as illustrated (see figure 11.8). Ask the children to fill in the smaller circles with marking pens. The colors should alternate as in the illustration, so that when the top spins the colors blur together to form a new color. Sharpen the pencil or dowel to be used in the top. With a small saw, trim it to about 2½ inches long. (The rest of it may be sharpened and used in other tops.)

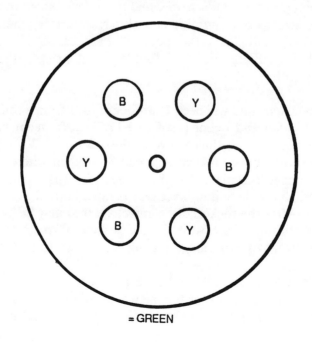

Fig. 11.8.

Push the sharpened pencil or dowel through the middle of the top. Show the children how to spin the top by twirling the pencil between their fingers and letting go of it on a table top or smooth floor. Can the children predict what color will show on the spinning top? Let them experiment with more color combinations by making several discs with their choice of color duos.

7. **TROPOSAUCER**. *Materials*: For each troposaucer you will need one reproduction of each pattern (see figure 11.9), markers, glue, scissors, and a pencil. *Directions*: Ask the child to color the

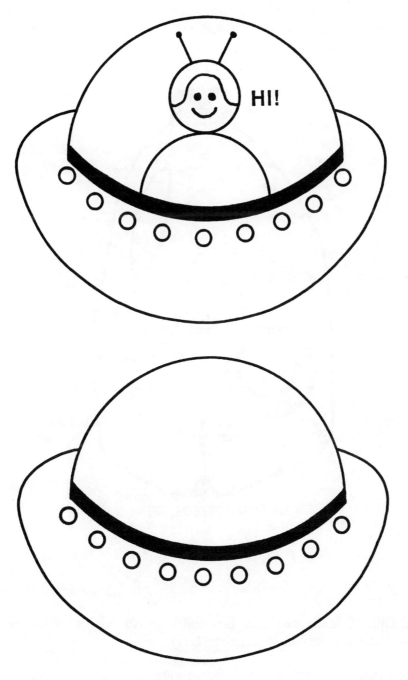

Fig. 11.9.

flying saucer and the martian with markers. Help the child cut around the edges, glue the two saucers together, and insert the pencil between the layers to act as the handle. When the troposaucer is dry, the child can twirl the pencil back and forth between the palms of his or her hands. The two pictures combine to make the martian look like it is riding in the flying saucer.

8. **SPACE HELMETS.** *Materials*: Each child will need a 1-gallon plastic milk container trimmed as illustrated by the teacher, glue, glitter, and markers. *Directions*: After cutting the milk container as illustrated (see figure 11.10), let the children decorate their helmets with markers or glitter and glue. Help the children write their names across the front of the helmets with a marker. Glue can be applied over the letters and then sprinkled with glitter. Once the helmets have dried, they can wear them on an imaginary trip to space, along with snow or "moon" boots to complete the costume.

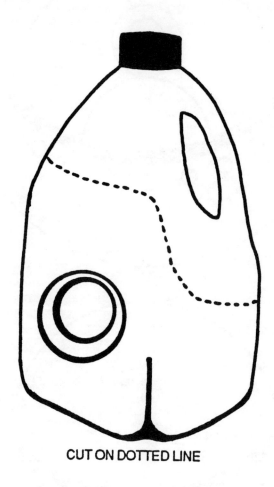

CUT ON DOTTED LINE

Fig. 11.10.

9. **FOLDED STARS.** Children love stars, but find it almost impossible to draw one. Here are instructions for a simple origami star (see figure 11.11).

Materials: A square sheet of paper, at least 8 inches wide.

Directions:
1. Fold the square sheet of paper in half, bringing the bottom edge up to meet the top.
2. Fold the lower right corner over until it reaches a point on the left edge a third of the way down from the top. Crease (A meets B).
3. Bring the triangle at the lower left-hand corner (C) to the right, creasing it along the edge made by the previous fold.
4. Bring the point on the right all the way over to the point on the left and crease (D meets A, B).
5. Draw a line across the folded paper from a point a third of the way up from the bottom point to the point that protrudes from the left edge. Cut or tear on this line.
6. Unfold.

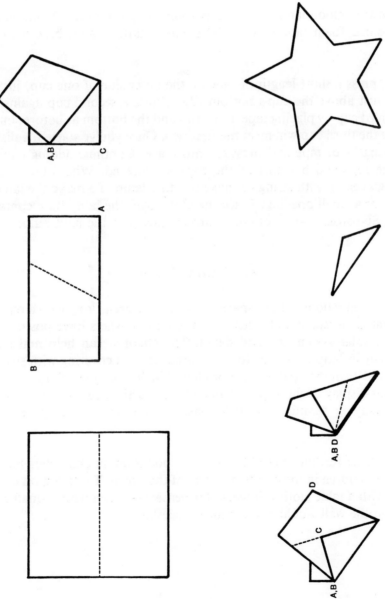

Fig. 11.11.

10.   **MAN IN THE MOON**. *Materials*: Each child will need a white paper plate, glue, silver glitter, and string. *Directions*: Show the children pictures of a full moon and discuss the belief that a man's face shows on the surface of the moon. Give the children paper plates to represent the moon. They may decorate the moon by making various circles on the surface with glue and then sprinkling on glitter to form sparkling craters, or to make a sparkly glitter face. When the glue has dried, have the children turn their plates on their sides onto an open newspaper to catch the excess glitter. Attach pieces of string to the tops of the moons and hang them as mobiles from the ceiling.

Space Class Project

Moon Lamp

To make a large, glowing moon lamp for the classroom, you will need 125 nine-ounce Styrofoam cups, white double-sided foam tape (about 500 inches total), a lamp base with a 25-watt bulb (optional).

Directions: To start, press a short length of tape on the outer side of one cup, just below the rim. Place another piece just above the cup's bottom edge. Press a second cup against the first at the taped spots. Add a third cup by placing tape at the rim and the bottom as before, but this time place it on two sides where the third cup will meet the first two. Once you've started, enlist the help of the children in cutting lengths of tape and pressing into place. Continue adding cups to the sphere, making sure that the tops and bottoms of the cups are aligned. When the sphere is complete, suspend it from a high ceiling with string or make it into a lamp. To make the lamp, leave out the last three cups to form a small opening. Place the globe over the lamp base containing a 25-watt bulb. Make sure the Styrofoam does not come into contact with the light bulb.

Space Story Time

1.   **BOOK DISPLAY**. Place books about space in the reading area along with a reproduction of the solar system. National Geographic and other educational publishers have posters and mobile kits available showing the solar system in vivid detail. The children can help make a papier-mâché mobile of the planets by inflating balloons to the desired size and covering with strips of newspaper dipped in wheat paste. When dry, paint appropriately. Hang from the ceiling with string or nylon thread. Other items for display might include a globe of the earth or earth's moon, a small telescope, a bulletin board displaying familiar constellations, or models of the space shuttle or other spacecraft.

2.   **ROCKET SHIP**. After reading several of the listed books about characters building imaginary spaceships, involve the children in the building of one of their own. Tables set on end, arranged in a square, and covered with a table cloth will work. Or perhaps a closet with 2 small chairs and glow-in-the-dark stickers on the wall would make a nice spaceship.

Space Poems, Songs, Fingerplays

1. I see the moon,
   And the moon sees me.
   God bless the moon,
   and God bless me.

2. Hickory, dickory dock,
   The sun is like a clock,
   In the sky from dawn 'til dusk,
   Hickory, dickory dock.

3. (Sing this to the tune of "Frère Jacques.")

   Stars are twinkling, stars are twinkling,
   Very bright, very bright,
   Shining down upon us, shining down upon us,
   Every night, every night.

4. The earth is a great big ball
   (*Draw a large circle with index finger.*)
   It isn't flat at all.
   (*Move hand horizontally.*)
   It spins around just like a top.
   (*Spin index fingers around each other.*)
   I'm sure that it will never stop.
   (*Fold hands together.*)

5. (Sing this to the tune of "Ring Around the Rosie.")

   Ring around Saturn
   Don't forget the lantern
   Moondust, moondust,
   All spin around.
   —Carol Holland

   To play as a game, join hands and circle left as you sing the song. On the last line, drop hands and spin around.

6. Mercury, Jupiter, Venus, Mars
   Nestled in among the stars.
   Saturn, Uranus, Neptune, too
   Hidden by our sky so blue.
   Pluto is so far to go,
   What other planet do you know?
   —Carol Holland

7. Star light, star bright,
   First star I see tonight,
   I wish I may, I wish I might,
   Have the wish I wish tonight.

8. There was an old woman tossed in a basket,
    Seventeen times as high as the moon;
    But where she was going no mortal could tell,
    For under her arm she carried a broom.

    "Old woman, old woman, old woman," said I.
    "Whither, oh whither, oh whither so high?
    To sweep the cobwebs from the sky;
    Then I'll be with you by-and-by."

9. The Man in the Moon came tumbling down,
    And asked the way to Norwich;
    He went by the south, and burned his mouth
    With eating cold pease porridge.

10. Higher than a house, higher than a tree.
    Oh! whatever can that be?

11. The Man in the Moon looked out of the moon,
    Looked out of the moon and said,
    " 'Tis time for all children on the Earth
    To think about getting to bed!"

Space Music List

Cassettes

Bartels, Joanie. "Swinging on a Star." *Sillytime Magic.* Discovery Music Co. ISBN 5-550-31594-7, 1989.

Newton-John, Olivia. "Twinkle, Twinkle Little Star." *Warm and Tender.* Geffen Records, n.d.

Newton-John, Olivia. "When You Wish Upon a Star." *Warm and Tender.* Geffen Records, n.d.

Stein, M. *Ride through the Solar System.* Caedmon Records CPN-1804, n.d..
    This recording contains eleven lively songs packed with facts about the planets.

"Twinkle, Twinkle, Little Star." *Disney's Children's Favorites, Vol. 1.* Walt Disney Records 606054, 1979.

LPs

Williams, John. *Star Wars.* London Symphony Orchestra. 20th Century Records 2T-541, 1977.
    Two records are contained in this album.

Space Book List

Fiction

Asch, Frank. *Moon Bear*. Scribner, 1978.
Worried that the moon is growing smaller each night, Bear decides to do something about it.

Asch, Frank. *Mooncake*. Prentice Hall, 1983.
Bear wonders what the moon tastes like, so builds a rocket to take him there.

Berenstain, Jan, and Stan Berenstain. *The Berenstain Bears on the Moon*. Beginner Books, 1985.
Two bears and their pup take a rocket ship to the moon.

Hillert, Margaret. *Up, Up, and Away*. Illustrated by Robert Maheris. Follett Publishing, 1982.
Two children travel to the moon in a spaceship.

Kandojan, Ellen. *Under the Sun*. Dodd, Mead, 1987.
Molly's mother explains where the sun goes each night. This book includes a science experiment for the readers to perform.

Keats, Ezra Jack. *Regards to the Man in the Moon*. Four Winds Press, 1981.
Louie and his friends travel through space with the help of their imaginations and a few scraps from the junk pile.

Kuskin, Carla. *A Space Story*. Illustrated by Marc Simont. Harper and Row, 1978.
This book contains a brief introduction to the sun and planets high in the sky beyond a boy's bedroom window.

Rey, H. A. *Curious George Gets a Medal*. Houghton Mifflin, 1957.
The monkey Curious George takes a trip on a rocket ship.

Sadler, Marilyn. *Alistair in Outer Space*. Illustrated by Roger Bollen. Prentice Hall, 1984.
Sensible Alistair is whisked off into outer space by silly creatures called Goots.

Salter, Mary Jo. *The Moon Comes Home*. Illustrated by Stacey Schuett. Random House, 1989.
On the trip home from his grandmother's house, a child observes the moon from the car window.

Scholberle, Ceile. *Beyond the Milky Way*. Crown Publishers, 1986.
Looking out his bedroom window and seeing the night sky, a child describes the awesome spectacle of outer space and imagines another child doing the same on a distant planet.

Willard, Nancy. *The Nightgown of the Sullen Moon*. Illustrated by David McPhail. Harcourt Brace Jovanovich, 1983.
This is an unusual story about the moon, who comes to earth to find a pretty nightgown to wear.

Nonfiction

Branley, Franklyn. *Eclipse.* Illustrated by Donald Crews. Thomas Crowell, 1988.
This book explains what happens during a solar eclipse in simple terms.

Branley, Franklyn. *Shooting Stars.* Illustrated by Holly Keller. Thomas Crowell, 1989.
This is an easy-to-understand introduction to shooting stars and meteorites, with illustrations suitable for young children.

Martin, Bill. *Moon Cycle.* Encyclopedia Britannica Press, 1975.
An accompanying recording is available with this lyrical book about moon phases.

Petty, Kate. *The Planets.* Illustrated by Mike Saunders. Franklin Watts, 1984.
Very simple text explains a little about each planet in our solar system.

Simon, Seymour. *Mars.* William Morrow, 1987.
This introduction to Mars contains many large color photographs of the red planet, taken by various space probes.

Thompson, C. E. *Glow in the Dark Constellations: A Field Guide for Young Stargazers.* Illustrated by Randy Chewning. Grosset & Dunlap, 1989.
This wonderful book gives a full-page glow-in-the-dark illustration of each constellation, tells where to find it in the night sky, the mythology behind the constellation, and more.

RESOURCE LIST

Birdwing Records
c/o Capitol Records, Inc.
1750 N. Vine St.
Hollywood, CA 90028-5274
(213) 462-6252

Caedmon Records
c/o Harper and Row Publishing Co.
Keystone Industrial Park
Scranton, PA 18512
(717) 343-4761

Capitol Records
1750 N. Vine St.
Hollywood, CA 90028-5274
(213) 462-6252

CMS Records
226 Washington St.
Mt. Vernon, NY 10553
(914) 667-6201

Dinorock Music
c/o Caedmon Records
Harper and Row Publishing Co.
Keystone Industrial Park
Scranton, PA 18512
(717) 343-4761

*Discovery Music Co.
5554 Calhoun
Van Nuys, CA 91401
(818) 782-7818

Geffen Records
9130 Sunset Blvd.
Los Angeles, CA 90069
(213) 278-9010

*Melody House Records
819 NW 92nd
Oklahoma City, OK 73114
(405) 840-3383

*Rainbow Morning Music
2121 Fairland Rd.
Silver Spring, MD 20904
(301) 384-9207

Random House Publishing
400 Hahn Rd.
Westminster, MD 21157
(800) 733-3000

---

*Most of the recordings listed in this book are available at retail stores. Those record companies marked with an asterisk will sell directly to the consumer.

ABOUT THE AUTHOR

Lucille Clayton has been researching and developing activities for young children since earning a degree in early childhood education and having her first baby. She has worked as a volunteer in the schools, offers workshops for teachers and parents on teaching preschool children, and plans a career in early childhood education. Lucille lives with her husband and her three preschoolers in Flagstaff, Arizona.